Benjamin
Graham's
NET-NET STOCK
STRATEGY

Every owner of a physical copy of this edition of

Benjamin Graham's
Net-Net Stock Strategy

can download the eBook for free direct from us at
Harriman House, in a DRM-free format that can be read on any
eReader, tablet or smartphone.

Simply head to:

ebooks.harriman-house.com/BenjaminGrahamNet-Net

to get your copy now.

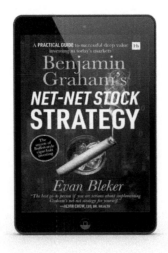

Benjamin Graham's
NET-NET STOCK
STRATEGY

A **PRACTICAL GUIDE** to
successful deep value
investing in today's markets

Evan Bleker

Hh

HARRIMAN HOUSE LTD

3 Viceroy Court

Bedford Road

Petersfield

Hampshire

GU32 3LJ

GREAT BRITAIN

Tel: +44 (0)1730 233870

Email: enquiries@harriman-house.com

Website: www.harriman-house.com

First published in 2020.

Paperback ISBN: 978-0-85719-707-8

eBook ISBN: 978-0-85719-708-5

British Library Cataloguing in Publication Data

A CIP catalogue record for this book can be obtained from the British Library.

For James

Contents

About the Author

Evan Bleker discovered investing during his senior year at high school when attending a consumer economics class, but he began intensive study in the early 2000s. Despite his focus on value investing, he only began to handily beat the market after discovering Graham's net-nets in 2010.

His ongoing success comes down to his ability to successfully apply Graham's net-net stock strategy and cultivate a strong emotional temperament. Evan spends much of his time reading about investing and business, including the early writing of great deep value investors who employed Graham's classic strategy. Since 2010, he has focused on finding enduring net-net investing principles that serve as best practices. This focus, along with developing a strong emotional temperament and sticking to his strategy through both good and bad periods have contributed to his great portfolio returns.

Evan graduated from Simon Fraser University during the Great Financial Crisis (GFC) with a degree in Analytic Philosophy. If there was ever a time for a philosophy major to look for a job, the GFC was not it. Evan joined thousands of other economic migrants and travelled East to teach English. He became totally consumed by net-net stocks, eventually launching www.NetNetHunter.com to help others find international net-nets and put together a high-quality net-net portfolio quickly and easily. The website is now a thriving little community of dedicated net-net stock investors.

While originally from Canada, Evan currently resides in Seoul, South Korea, and spends much of his time travelling around the Ring of Fire. When he's not investing in net-nets, or managing Net Net Hunter, he practises Brazilian jiu-jitsu, studies personal development, and helps friends start businesses.

Preface

This book is a modern take on Benjamin Graham's classic net-net stock strategy. It expands on teachings from the master himself and incorporates invaluable knowledge from other outstanding investors such as Warren Buffett, Peter Lynch, Joel Greenblatt, Peter Cundill, and David Dreman, to provide you with a practical investment guide.

The book also documents my own experience as a net-net stock investor, techniques I've used to grow my portfolio at roughly a 25% compound annual growth rate (CAGR) from 2010 to 2018, insights I've had, and idiotic blunders I've made (so you can avoid them).

This is not a book written for Wall Street pros. It's written exclusively for the little guy – the small private investor sitting at home in his den trying to figure out how to put his savings to work. Ultimately, the smaller your portfolio, the better the knowledge in these pages will work for you. If you're managing anywhere from $10,000 to $100,000, I hope you find this the most valuable investment book you've ever read. I would consider a $10 million portfolio to be the upper limit.

As you'll soon discover, an investor with a smaller portfolio holds a tremendous competitive advantage over Wall Street professionals. Ultimately, the size of the firms that trade as net-nets today exclude investors with larger portfolios from taking part in Ben Graham's classic strategy. With market capitalizations that typically range from only a couple of million to $150 million, and average daily dollar volumes often well below $50,000, the strategy remains viable only for those managing small investment portfolios. This is your competitive edge as a small private investor.

The book is split into five main parts. In the first section, I walk you through the basics of net-net investing: what net-net stocks are, who should buy them, why they work, my own performance, and why even value investors often hate these stocks.

In the second section, I introduce you to three tremendously successful investors who made good use of the strategy. One is now an investment giant managing billions of dollars, but they all earned their best returns by buying net-net stocks the rest of the world hated or ignored.

In the third section, I introduce you to the net-net investor's secret sauce: the Net Net Hunter Scorecard. This is the main tool I use to assess net-nets for my portfolio. I also walk you through a bit of the investment process itself, so you have a good understanding of exactly what I am doing when selecting net-nets.

In the fourth section, I present an in-depth discussion of the criteria on the Net Net Hunter Scorecard and why I've specifically selected each of them. These are what I consider to be the best criteria you can use when selecting net-nets.

Finally, I walk you through some real-world investing in the form of five net-net case studies, all stocks I've either purchased for my own portfolio or conducted research on. These examples will highlight just how important it is to have solid selection criteria.

In terms of your own understanding, I do presume that you know how to read company accounts and understand general principles of value investing. It's important that you understand the basics of accounting since the strategy relies heavily on balance sheet assessment. Accounting, after all, is the language of business. Also, while this book is written in an accessible way, those new to value investing may not understand some value investing terminology or principles, which will impede understanding.

If you're just getting started as an investor, I recommend Jason Kelly's *The Neatest Little Guide to Stock Market Investing*. It's a great overview of stock market investing. Those new to value investing specifically should consider picking up Christopher Browne's *The Little Book of Value Investing*, and David Dreman's *Contrarian Investment Strategies: The Next Generation*. These two lesser-read works provide a great, modern assessment of value investing's core principles and the mindset that you have to adopt to be successful. In terms of accounting, try to pick up the most recent college textbook you can find that introduces financial accounting.

Introduction

IN 2007 I nearly gave up investing for good. I had just spent six years pulling my portfolio out of a giant hole I'd accidentally kicked it into. My mistake was following a strategy whipped up by a pair of well-known faces who proved to be better marketers than investors. Among other things, they advocated only investing in companies with "funny advertising." I should have known better.

But that early devastation wasn't the problem. I was running a tiny portfolio and knew that my earning power would dwarf any early loss I suffered. What really got to me was the intense amount of work needed to find profitable investments. I spent hours each day scouring the markets for suitable candidates, and then countless more hours valuing a company, only to eventually reject it and start over. It was a tedious, mind-numbing, process – one you needed to make a career of to excel at.

Investing is impossible if you don't know what you're doing. I had some idea, but I didn't know enough to earn great returns while going to university full-time. I knew how the greats invested, but there was no way I could match their skill, experience, knowledge, or time commitment.

With such obvious hurdles, I resolved to liquidate my positions and dump the cash into an index fund, joining the masses as a passive investor. Then, surfing the net one day in 2009, I stumbled upon an article discussing an investment strategy I had heard about years earlier: *net-net stock investing*.

Like the rest of the value investing world, I had been told that the strategy was a relic of the ancient past, an approach employed during the 1930s, 1940s, and 1950s by a couple of Buffett's superinvestors and early capitalists. The mantra was that net-net stocks were dead, rendered extinct by rising market levels. Today, mainstream value investors still unthinkingly repeat the mantra. Others have a vested interest in peddling this popular delusion (to sell books or investment services, for example), and even the Columbia Business School is rumoured to be discouraging its students from looking for net-nets. Yet somehow, in 2009, I was staring at a post written by a real-life net-net stock investor still practising his craft.

I rushed upstairs to the stack of value investing books I'd collected. Dusting off Graham's *The Intelligent Investor*, I flipped through the pages to reread his comments.

> "It always seemed, and still seems, ridiculously simple to say that if one can acquire a diversified group of common stocks at a price less than the applicable net current assets alone – after deducting all prior claims, and counting as zero the fixed and other assets – the results should be quite satisfactory. They were so, in our experience, for more than 30 years."[1]

Digging further, the strategy seemed simple and lucrative. Graham wrote elsewhere that the strategy was good for a CAGR of around 20%. While I knew little of the strategy, I managed to stuff a small number of American net-nets into my portfolio. By luck, 12 months later, they'd risen sharply, so I dove head first into the literature, reading everything I could about the strategy.

I say "by luck" because, like most new net-net investors, I was making a risky mistake. Net-net investing is a statistical, rather than a one-shot-one-kill, strategy. Investors need to aim for a solid average group return rather than a big return on each stock bought. While net-nets perform well as a group and over time, each individual stock will vary quite a bit from the group average. An investor requires enough picks to leverage the average return associated with net-nets as a whole.

It's that average statistical return that determines a net-net investor's success or failure. While Graham used to hold over 100 positions to realise this statistical performance, I initially assumed that each net-net produced a near 20% return like clockwork. Starting with only two or three net-nets was like rolling dice.

Similarly, net-net investors need to focus on their strategy's performance over a number of years, at least five years, but ideally a decade. Like individual stocks, a net-net portfolio will produce yearly returns that stray quite far from the strategy's compound annual return. Employing the strategy over the course of one year to see how it would work was foolish. My returns could have ended up anywhere along the distribution of possible yearly returns for the strategy. If I had been unlucky enough to invest during a poor year for the strategy, I would have simply given up and opted for index funds the following year. I would have missed out on a decade of outstanding returns. Luckily, things worked out quite well over that first year, so I fully embraced the strategy. These obvious missteps seem crazy to me now, but they derail many would-be net-net investors.

---

1 Graham, *The Intelligent Investor*, 391.

By 2013, the markets had advanced, along with my understanding of the strategy. I had read nearly everything Graham had written on net-net investing, and commentary from other great deep value investors, and I dug up almost every single study assessing Graham's net-net approach. Better implementation meant better portfolio returns.

I should have been happy, but the market was beginning to make net-net investing difficult. Growing market valuations erode an investor's ability to identify exceptional deep value opportunities. As a bull market advances, fewer and fewer stocks trade below liquidation value and what's left is of questionable quality. While I had invested almost exclusively in American net-nets prior to 2013, it was clear that this chapter in my investment life was ending. Something had to give, or I'd have to abandon my approach entirely, due to a lack of investment opportunities.

Going international was an obvious choice, but the data on tiny international companies is often hard to come by. While there were free resources covering American net-nets, the only easy way to identify international net-net stocks was to subscribe to big data, and I wasn't about to pay $30,000 per year for access. I knew that the only option I had to continue using the strategy was to form a community of like-minded investors so we could hunt for these stocks together. That year, I decided to launch what has become one of my most valuable investment resources: Net Net Hunter.

Membership grew rapidly after the launch, quickly scaling into a tight-knit investment community. The flood of new members brought along a handful of seasoned net-net investors who had applied their craft throughout the 2000s. It's hard to overstate just how valuable intelligent feedback is to your growth in any area that requires skill. I'm indebted to those who've pushed, challenged, and expanded my own understanding of net-net investing.

Radically speeding up the investment process has also proven extremely valuable to me and most Net Net Hunter members. Small investors lack the time needed to sort through the approximately 1,000 statistical net-nets available globally. It's pretty simple to sort through the hundreds of low price-to-book stocks within a single country to arrive at a pool of net-nets to research, but the work really builds up when you start looking at additional countries. Still, the more rocks you turn over, the more gold nuggets you'll ultimately find. So, getting help to look through all of the net-net stocks globally pays large dividends. There's no way small investors could spend the 20 to 30 hours it takes each month to do the work themselves of searching globally for net-nets. Hiring someone to do the initial filtering has been a godsend. It's also proven a great source of strong investment candidates since the more members looking through these investment candidates, the more exceptional buys we end up finding.

Your approach to investing matters

Financial reporting is better today than it ever has been. All sorts of restrictions and regulations force companies to publish a mountain of information. Investment companies have to publicise sizeable holdings, and activist intentions, in publicly traded companies. In many respects, it's a much easier time to be an investor today than it has been over the last 50 years.

But despite the tsunami of information, the average investor ekes out a pathetic long-term return. According to *Forbes*, the average mixed equity and debt investor earned just 2.6% per year between 2004 and 2013.[2] By contrast, the S&P 500 returned 7.4% and fixed income 4.6%. Apparently, the flood of data and disclosure hasn't helped Joe Average earn better than average returns. Investors don't need more data; they need a better plan.

Fig. A: Ten-year annualised investment returns by category, 2004–2013[3]

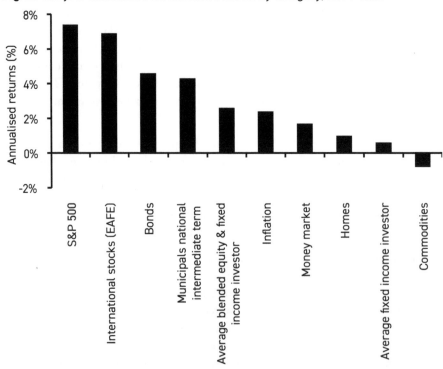

Source: Dalbar, Bloomberg, Morningstar, and Fast Track.

2 Hanlon, 'Why the Average Investor's Investment Return Is So Low', *Forbes* (24 April 2014).
3 Ibid.

Sure, math doesn't help. Investors as a whole can't beat the index because the index's performance represents the average performance of all investors. The trading or brokerage fees active investors are saddled with guarantee underperformance on average.

But math does not doom each and every investor to average returns or worse. And outpacing the market over the long term isn't just down to luck or god-like talent. As Sir John Templeton said, average tennis players win as many games as they lose, but that's no reason to give up playing tennis. Those players who practise hard and use good strategies are bound to do better than those who don't.

There's more to it than that. Being Canadian, I like to compare investing to hockey. If you practise skating, stick handling, shooting, positioning, and strategy, you're bound to play better than the other dads in your pickup hockey league. You're also bound to score more goals if you step onto the ice to face off against a team of six-year-olds.

Whom you play against has just as much impact on your win/lose record as how much you've practised. In the investing world, I see investors reading the same news, watching the same financial shows, hunting for the same sort of stocks as thousands of better informed, better skilled, and much better educated Wall Street professionals do. Is it any wonder the small investor's performance is so terrible?

It doesn't have to be this way. There are pockets of market inefficiency and successful strategies that small retail investors can hone to earn life-changing returns.

This book will introduce you to the best of those strategies – Graham's net-nets – and give you a thorough understanding of how it works, why it works, and some of the tricks that I've developed implementing the strategy since 2010. If you take the time to learn its nuances and implement Graham's strategy wisely, the approach should be just as valuable for you as it has been for me.

PART 1

WHAT IS NET–NET INVESTING?

1

Net–Net Investing Defined

By now you're well aware of just how tough I found investing before I realised that a net-net stock strategy was actually viable in this day and age. It's amazing that after all these years, this strategy still works so well.

It's also amazing that many investors haven't even heard of Graham's famous net-net stock strategy. Ben Graham isn't exactly a nobody in the world of investing and the strategy itself has been crushing the market since at least the 1930s. Since Graham is a legend in the investment world, and since his strategy has been around for so long, you'd expect that every small value investor would be using it to earn market-beating returns. Yet only a handful of thoughtful value investors actually are.

There are very important reasons for this odd state of affairs, but before we dive into that, we need to define exactly what net-net stocks are.

Let's get started.

A simple definition of net-net investing

Net-net investing is the process of buying a company's common shares below a conservative estimate of the firm's per-share liquidation value. Assessing a company's liquidation value in a conservative manner and then buying its common stock at or below that value is the essence of net-net investing.

Unlike other liquidation value approaches, such as low price to book[4] or net tangible asset value,[5] net-net investors completely disregard long-term assets during the valuation process. The result is a figure known as net current asset value (NCAV), a much more conservative estimate of liquidation value. It's helpful to think of NCAV as book value per common share, less the firm's long-term assets.[6]

These kinds of stocks have had a few different names over the years. While Ben Graham referred to them in *The Intelligent Investor* as working capital or net working capital stocks, contemporary investors prefer to call them net-net stocks, which is what I do throughout the rest of this book.

As you can see from the above definition, there are two crucial steps here:

1. Obtain the per-share NCAV of the company; and then
2. Check to see whether the company's shares are trading at a price below that figure.

1. Obtain the firm's per-share NCAV

Let's start with the first of these steps. In order to estimate a company's NCAV, the investor must turn to the firm's financial statements and pay specific attention to the balance sheet.

Company financial statements

A firm's financial statements are split into three main parts:

1. **Balance sheet**: A record of what the company owns, what it owes, the value of each, and what's left over for shareholders after liabilities are covered.
2. **Income statement**: A document that reports sales, expenses, and how the balance sheet has changed over a period of time.
3. **Cash flow statement**: A statement that shows the company's sources and uses of cash.

---

4 Book value is often used as a rough estimate of liquidation value by less discriminating value investors. There are obvious flaws to this approach, however. One such issue is the fact that balance sheets record the accounting value, not the market value, of assets.

5 Net tangible asset value is essentially book value less goodwill and other intangible assets. Excluding intangible assets from the valuation results in a more conservative assessment of liquidation value, but problems remain. One such problem is the uncertain market value of long-term assets. More on this in a later chapter.

6 The term *book value*, or *shareholder equity*, refers to the accounting value of the firm's net assets. One further difference between shareholder equity and NCAV is that net-net investors deduct the value of preferred shares in their NCAV calculation. More on that ahead.

Many investment strategies start by looking at a company's income statement or cash flow statement. From the data in these statements, the investor assesses a firm's profit potential and then assigns some multiple to the figure, or combines it with other information to predict future cash flows, which are then discounted back to the present, using an appropriate discount rate. These calculations help an investor value a company's current or future profits. But valuations based on earnings often prove evanescent as earnings fail to materialise, or the company's current profitability erodes.

Net-net stock investing is different. Rather than valuing a firm's current profits, or how much future profits are worth today, net-net stock investors focus on buying assets cheaply. Often, little if any thought is given to a firm's profitability, since net-net investors are not buying earnings; they're buying assets. And the only statement that a net-net stock investor can use to determine just how much the firm's assets may be worth, after factoring in the firm's financial obligations, is the balance sheet.

The balance sheet

The balance sheet is divided into three sections:

1. **Assets**: Things the company owns.
   - *Current assets:* Items the company expects to use up in less than 12 months, such as inventory the firm wants to sell, or receivables due from customers.
   - *Long-term assets*: Items the company won't use up within a year, such as property, vehicles, or a manufacturing plant.
2. **Liabilities**: What the company owes.
   - *Current liabilities:* Items due in less than 12 months, such as IOUs from vendors, debt due within a year, or taxes payable.
   - *Long-term liabilities*: Things like bank loans or capital leases that the company has committed to and that won't be paid back within a year.
3. **Shareholder equity**: Essentially, the value of assets left after the company covers all of its liabilities.[7] The most relevant items for the investor are:
   - *Preferred equity*: Capital raised through the sale of preferred shares.
   - *Shareholder equity*: The accounting value of a company's net assets, comprised of the firm's total assets less its total liabilities. This figure is often referred to as book value.

Of the assets listed, net-net investors are mostly interested in the firm's current assets, since these come into play when calculating NCAV. Again, while they may add value, long-term assets are completely ignored in the assessment. More on that ahead.

---

7 For now, we'll ignore off-balance-sheet assets and liabilities.

Calculating NCAV

Once investors note the company's current asset value, they subtract the firm's total liabilities to reach a rough, conservative estimate of the company's real-world liquidation value.

Graham referred to this value as net working capital. Working capital is the excess of current asset value over current liabilities. And net working capital is the excess of current assets over total liabilities and other senior claims, such as bonds, and preferred equity. This is shown in the formula:

Net Working Capital = Current Assets – Total Liabilities and Senior Claims[8]

Graham's original formula has been revised over the years, but modern net-net investors have arrived at the following:

> Current Assets
> Less Total Balance Sheet Liabilities
> Less Preferred Shares
> Less Off-Balance-Sheet Liabilities
> Equals NCAV

This formula is simple and runs a good balance between conservatism and statistical backing. In the 1950s and 1960s, some acclaimed investors preferred to further discount a firm's current asset account values to obtain a fire-sale[9] valuation for the firm. Contemporary investors have applied a standardised formula known as the net-net working capital (NNWC) formula to try to replicate this approach. While more conservative than the above formula, a NNWC approach to valuation requires expert knowledge and may provide little benefit when applied to today's balance sheets. More on this ahead.

Net-net investing is one of the few outstanding investment strategies that have the support of academic and industry studies. Graham tested his investment strategy as far back as the 1930s,[10] and many studies have been conducted since. This academic backing helps make Graham's net-net stock approach a very compelling strategy for small investors.

---

8 Graham, *The Intelligent Investor*, 391.

9 The term *fire sale* refers to a situation where business owners are motivated to liquidate its assets quickly, as in the case where a fire causes significant business disruption. If a business were to try to liquidate its assets in a hurry, prices obtained for the assets could be much lower than a more orderly liquidation that runs for a longer duration. Net-net investor Peter Cundill found that most liquidations followed an orderly process, rather than a fire sale.

10 Oppenheimer, 'Ben Graham's NCAVs', *Financial Analysts Journal* 42:6 (November–December 1986).

But academic studies do not usually include preferred shares and always ignore off-balance-sheet obligations when assessing how Graham's liquidation value approach performs. More often, studies reduce a firm's current assets by total liabilities alone in order to study net-net stock performance. This is a much less conservative assessment because, if present, off-balance-sheet items and preferred shares extract a cost during liquidation.

The approach described in this book doesn't rely on expert judgement to further discount current asset account values, but it does require that an investor account for preferred shares, including off-balance-sheet liabilities, when arriving at the final value. In this respect, the formula I use is more conservative than the one used by academics but not as conservative as the one used by famous practitioners, which is discussed later. In a liquidation scenario, a liquidator would have to reduce current assets by the value of the preferred shares and cover liabilities that the company may face but that are not listed on the balance sheet.

2. Check to see whether the company's shares are trading below NCAV

While we now have the company's NCAV, we still need to put that value on a per-share basis. Small investors usually buy shares, not entire companies, so it's useful to compare per-share values to the company's share price.

Luckily, this process is fairly straightforward. Investors should scan the firm's financial reports for the company's fully diluted shares outstanding figure. I use the company's diluted share count for conservatism, since it represents all of the company's outstanding shares plus any financial instruments that can be converted to common shares.

During a liquidation, an investor might face further claims on the company's assets, as holders of preferred shares, convertible debt, or stock options convert their instruments to common stock to cash in on the liquidation. Failing to take these instruments into account when valuing the firm means arriving at a less conservative liquidation value and possibly seeing that value eaten away by holders of convertible instruments. The price paid for the company, in that case, may have proven too high relative to its underlying value and may actually result in a loss.

To arrive at the firm's per-share NCAV, simply follow this formula:

NCAV / Diluted Shares Outstanding = Preliminary NCAV Per Share

Alert readers will immediately spot the fact that I skipped discussion of a firm's off-balance-sheet items. In order to tell whether a company is trading below its NCAV, investors need to factor in all obligations a liquidator would have to cover before realising any profit. This means assessing off-balance-sheet items, since an investor would have to cover these items as well.

But many net-net investors find it practical to arrive at a preliminary judgement about the investment's attractiveness by seeing if the stock is trading below its NCAV, as determined by balance sheet items alone. Off-balance-sheet items require some digging to uncover, and some judgement to determine their true cost. All net-nets, though, must at least trade at a price below the firm's NCAV, as determined by the balance sheet items alone. If a firm fails here, or the investor feels that the discount to fair value is not deep enough, the investor can stop the analysis and simply move on to the next firm. If a firm passes at this stage, however, it may warrant further assessment.

To tell whether a firm warrants further analysis, the investor now simply checks to see whether the share price is less than the firm's preliminary NCAV per share. If the company has a share price of $2, and a preliminary NCAV of $3, for example, its shares are trading below its preliminary NCAV and the company likely warrants further investigation.

If, on the other hand, the shares are trading for $4 against a preliminary NCAV of $3, the investor may want to pass on the firm in favour of other cheaper candidates. If shares are trading for $3, the price is equivalent to its preliminary NCAV per share. To justify a purchase in this case, the investor may require additional factors in the investment's favour. More on these ahead.

If an investor has uncovered a net-net bargain and wants to proceed with the analysis, he'll have to dig into the financial reports to uncover any off-balance-sheet liabilities in order to get a more accurate assessment of liquidation value. More on that, and a deeper look at the formula, in the next chapter.

As of now, you should have a solid understanding of the net-net investing formula and how we use it to calculate a firm's NCAV.

2

The Detail of the NCAV Formula

THE MODERN VERSION of Graham's net-net formula is simple and straightforward. Once an investor understands the principles behind this formula, applying it becomes much easier.

As I explained in chapter 1, the NCAV formula that I use includes four critically important elements:

1. Current Assets
2. Less Total Balance Sheet Liabilities
3. Less Preferred Shares
4. <u>Less Off-Balance-Sheet Liabilities</u>
   Equals NCAV

Deeper understanding of this formula allows investors to tweak the formula as they see fit, making adjustments to the formula to account for company-specific factors or special industry characteristics, based on significant reflection and study.

In this chapter, I will look at each of the four components in turn, explaining them in more detail. This is essential background information that an investor needs to understand in order to apply the formula successfully over time.

1. Current assets

As mentioned in the previous chapter, a company's current assets are items that the company owns and is likely to monetise within 12 months. They're typically designated in the assets section of a firm's balance sheet by the subheading "Current Assets" or "Short-Term Assets."

Current assets are also listed from most to least liquid, with cash and cash equivalents typically at the top of the list, followed by short-term investments, accounts receivable, inventories, and other current assets such as tax receivables. While financial accounting is beyond the scope of this book, investors have to understand basic accounting in order to be successful. Here is a quick explanation of the most common current-asset accounts found on corporate balance sheets.

Current assets breakdown

Cash and cash equivalents. Cash refers to currency held on site, in security boxes, or demand deposits at a bank, while cash equivalents typically refer to highly liquid securities that can be monetised quickly and have a certain value. US treasury bills or commercial paper are typical examples.

Cash and equivalents have the most certain value of any item on the balance sheet. Cash is cash, after all, and cash equivalents are so close to cash that they're listed in the same line item.

Short-term investments. Short-term investments typically refer to investments such as corporate bonds, stocks of other companies, and mutual funds that a company plans to sell within 12 months. While these investments can be liquidated in short order to provide cash for operations, they're more volatile and less liquid than cash and cash equivalents. This means that they also have a less certain realisable value, so their sale price may deviate somewhat from their balance sheet values.

Accounts receivable. Since companies compete for business, they sometimes allow customers to purchase on credit. Accounts receivable are essentially IOUs that the firm has extended to its customers in order to secure a sale. Receivables are typically collected within one to three months, after which the company is able to use the cash collected to fund operations.

Accounts receivable come with inherent risk. Sometimes customers simply don't pay what they owe, forcing the firm to write down the value of the receivable that is not likely to be collected. For this reason, almost all firms include an allowance for doubtful accounts and state the value of receivables after applying the allowance. Still, management may find that a greater amount of receivables is uncollectable than they first thought, resulting in further write-downs.

Inventory. Inventory refers to goods the company sells as part of normal business operations, or materials used to make those finished products. Toys sitting on the shelf at a toy store, for example, are inventory a firm aims to sell during the normal course of business. Manufacturing firms will also include raw materials used to manufacture goods and partially finished products in the value of their inventory.

The value of inventory is anything but certain. It may become obsolete with changing technology or consumer preferences, or may spoil, such as perishable goods. Management may also have to mark down the value of a firm's inventory if it becomes likely that the company will not be able to sell the products for the value listed on the balance sheet.

Net-net investors are more exposed to inventory risk than other investors. That's why more detail-orientated investors spend considerable time assessing a firm's inventory and the value it may fetch in a liquidation scenario. As mentioned, because this requires considerable skill and experience, many investors focus on applying a standardised formula. We discuss the approach in more detail ahead.

2. Total balance sheet liabilities

Total liabilities refers to all of the financial obligations the firm has taken on and has not yet settled. These items are listed on the firm's balance sheet, in both current liabilities and long-term liabilities. The two sections are sometimes summed up on the balance sheet under the line item "Total Liabilities".

While investors will find a number of different line items listed under either current or long-term liabilities depending on the country, accounting standard, and nature of the business, some entries are more standard than others. What follows is a discussion of the most common liabilities found on a balance sheet.

Current liabilities

Current liabilities refers to items a firm has to cover within 12 months. These typically refer to accounts payable, accrued salaries and other such expenses, financial or operating leases, deferred revenue, short-term debt, and the current portion of the firm's long-term debt. While a firm's current assets can vary in value, its current liabilities typically don't.

CURRENT LIABILITIES BREAKDOWN

Accounts payable. Accounts payable are IOUs the firm is obligated to pay to firms that have extended credit to the company. One company's accounts receivable is another company's (or customer's) accounts payable.

There is some flexibility as to when a firm has to pay these bills, but companies have to tread carefully. If a firm takes too long to pay its bills, the vendor might factor its receivables, selling the obligation for less than face value to a collection agency in exchange for cash. While the company faces a permanent loss on the value of the receivable, it can collect cash immediately to fund operations.

Accrued salaries. Accrued salaries and other expenses refer to payments the company has yet to make to employees for services rendered. Since employees are typically paid every two to four weeks, this value refers to the salaries incurred at the end of the reporting period that are not yet paid.

Lease payments (operating or financial). Financial or operating leases essentially refer to rental agreements, where the business obtains the use of premises in exchange for a rental fee. This line item denotes amounts that are required to be paid within 12 months.

Short-term debt. Short-term debt refers to a company's short-term borrowings. Sometimes a company will need short-term financing to purchase inventory, equipment, or to fund operations before acquiring longer-term financing. In these cases, a company can issue short-term corporate debt or seek loans from banks or private lenders. These obligations are often interest bearing.

Current portion of long-term debt. If the company has taken on debt with a longer-term maturity date, it may be required to retire a portion of that debt within 12 months. This amount is listed on the balance sheet as the current portion of long-term debt. The firm's long-term debt will have been reduced by this amount.

Long-term liabilities

A company's long-term liabilities refer to the financial obligations that the firm has taken on during its lifetime but has not yet paid and that are coming due at some point beyond 12 months. Some of the more common long-term liabilities are future lease obligations, capital lease obligations, bank debt, or bonds the firm has issued. The following discussion provides a brief overview of the most common long-term liabilities found on a balance sheet.

LONG-TERM LIABILITIES BREAKDOWN

Future lease obligations. This line item refers to the value of the payments the company has agreed to in order to gain the use of premises over a number of years. While financial leases typically used to be found on balance sheets, operating leases were often kept off of the balance sheet and buried in a company's financial reports. Accounting standards in the USA now require companies to record all future lease obligations on the balance sheet.

Debt. Debt refers to money borrowed, often from financial institutions but sometimes through private lenders. Debt agreements take many forms, and may be interest bearing, may lay claim to the company's assets, and may come with strict rules which restrict a firm's operating flexibility. A firm may be required to maintain minimum financial ratios, or keep a certain amount of cash on hand.

Notes payable (bonds). Sometimes a company will raise cash through the sale of bonds: debt agreements sold in small chunks to investors. Unlike bank debt or loans made by other financial institutions, bonds are bought and sold in debt markets in a similar way to stocks. This provides the company with a significant advantage since the firm can buy back its own bonds, when undervalued, to retire the debt at a discount.

3. Preferred shares

Preferred shares are a hybrid security, straddling the gap between common stock and bonds. While technically an equity interest in the company, they have a wide array of privileges and restrictions that distinguish them from common stock.

Their primary advantage is to grant first rights to paid dividends, but this comes at a cost. Preferred shareholders often miss out on the capital gains that common stock investors enjoy and an issuing firm can often buy back the stock at a specified price. If a preferred share rises to $120, for example, the security's contract may give the company the right to buy back the share at $110. There is a wide variety of rights and restrictions attached to preferred shares, which means that valuing the cost of these securities is no simple task.

In order to accurately assess the cost of retiring preferred shares, you need to read the security's prospectus to understand all of the rights and restrictions attached to an issue.

In some cases, redeeming the preferred shares will be as simple as buying them back for a prescribed amount. At other times, management won't have the ability to call the preferred shares at a fixed price and will have to buy the preferred shares back in the open market. If preferred shareholders do not want to sell their stake, management may have to make an above-market tender offer for the shares. The bottom line is that every preferred share issue is different, and you really must be well acquainted with the associated rights and restrictions to understand how much a liquidator would have to shell out during liquidation.

Because of the complications inherent in valuing preferred shares, many investors use a lazy shorthand: taking the face value of the preferred issue as stated on the balance sheet, or the entire issue's market value. While not nearly as accurate, it saves a great deal of time, and the difference in value may not make that much of a difference to the firm's actual liquidation value if the issue is small.

4. Off-balance-sheet liabilities

An off-balance-sheet liability is an obligation that isn't listed on a company's balance sheet. Unfortunately for investors, off-balance-sheet liabilities can pose nearly as large a challenge as valuing the cost of preferred shares. While theoretically there's an infinite number of off-balance-sheet liabilities, the three most common are:

1. unfunded pensions
2. uncertain legal payouts
3. operating leases

Pension plans are often introduced during profitable periods when the future looks great. But good times often don't last and a company can find itself saddled with large payments to former employees just when it can least afford additional costs. As a result, the company may skip contributing to the pension fund it set up, creating a shortfall. If this shortfall persists, workers expecting a company pension may find pension payments unavailable.

A shortfall in the company's pension plan means shareholders will have to fund this plan through future earnings, or by forking over some of the value obtained during liquidation. Luckily for net-net investors, the shortfall is often found in the notes to the firm's financial statements, making the liability easier to value.

Legal penalties are a bit trickier to assess. Unlike unfunded pension liabilities, the costs associated with a lawsuit are often uncertain. While lawsuits are listed in the notes to a company's financial statement, management must guess the size of possible legal penalties. Value investors looking for a simple and profitable way to assess true liquidation value by applying a simple valuation formula are out of luck. Even mechanical value investors face uncertainty when calculating intrinsic value, often having to substitute estimates for certainty. Generally, when taking into account legal penalties, I simply note the value of any potential payouts and include that in the off-balance-sheet liabilities.

Another source of pain for net-net investors is **operating leases**, a subcategory of leases, similar to renting. Again, accounting treatment will vary based on the accounting standards used within a country. (International financial reporting standards (IFRS) and the USA's generally accepted accounting standards (GAAP) are the most common.)

In the USA, accounting for leases has changed. Operating leases and their associated payments were formerly only listed in the notes to the firm's financial statements. But accounting standards change and operating leases have moved on to the balance sheet in many cases. When investing internationally, investors will happen upon various accounting treatments and may find off-balance-sheet leases which may need to be accounted for in a company's eventual liquidation value.

When operating leases are present, many net-net investors prefer to reduce current assets by a firm's total future operating lease payments to calculate liquidation value. They assume that these payments will have to be made regardless of whether the company uses the asset or not in the future. The proper treatment of operating lease payments is not that simple, however. In many cases, operating leases can be cancelled, which renders the future lease payments on a firm's financial reports irrelevant.[11] In cases where operating leases are cancelled, the company may have to pay a termination penalty, though one much smaller than the listed operating lease payments. In other cases, the company may be able to sub-let the space, again rendering the lease liability irrelevant.[12]

The best way to treat off-balance-sheet liabilities is to ask management whether these associated lease contracts can be cancelled during a liquidation and, if so, what the expected penalties would amount to. If they can't be cancelled, it's wise to check to see if the space can be re-leased to another party. Assuming you don't have the CEO's home number (or, as I awkwardly found out, they don't always appreciate 7am phone calls at home), it's reasonable to assume that operating leases can be terminated and the future payments ignored. In cases where a management team either state that operating leases can't be cancelled or can only be cancelled at a cost, your liquidation value will be more accurate if you include these values.

With all of that defined, let's now look at a practical application of the formula.

Practical application of the NCAV formula

The NCAV formula is pretty simple to apply after a bit of practice. Let's start off by applying the formula to a fictional company, Bert's Plumbing and Party Supplies, aka Bert's.

Bert's latest balance sheet statement works out as shown in table 1.

Table 1: Bert's balance sheet

	31 December 2018 ('000s)
Cash and equivalents	$150
Short-term investments	$50
Receivables	$200
Inventory	$300
Prepaid expenses	$40
Total current assets	$740
PP&E	$500
Goodwill	$160

---

11 Damodaran, 'Dealing with Operating Leases in Valuation', NYU Working Paper (1999).
12 'Greenblatt Columbia Lecture 2005 11 04 including Brian Gaines from Springhouse Capital', YouTube video, 2:33:42, posted by Net Net Hunter, 9 March 2020, youtu.be/xQYnK9b4gXw.

	31 December 2018 ('000s)
Total long-term assets	$660
Total assets	$1,400
Accounts payable	$80
Short-term debt	$20
Total current liabilities	$100
Long-term debt	$200
Total long-term liabilities	$200
Total liabilities	$300
Common stock (100,000)	$10
Preferred equity (500)	$50
Comprehensive income	$1,040
Total shareholder equity	$1,100

Looking at the very top section, Bert's has $740,000 in current assets. But we can't just take this value as liquidation value. We need to reduce this amount by anything a liquidator would have to pay before collecting profit on the liquidation (i.e., all obligations prior to the common).[13]

To start, we can simply plug the necessary values into the NCAV formula. As mentioned, current assets total $740,000. We must reduce this amount by total liabilities, which come in at $300,000. This is a pretty small amount relative to the firm's $740,000 in current assets, and the balance works out to $440,000.

Looking at the equity section of the balance sheet, the company lists preferred equity of $50,000, and states that there are 500 preferred shares outstanding. After some digging, it looks as if the company's preferred shares are callable at $105, which means that if we wanted to liquidate the company, we'd have to pay $52,500 (500 × $105) to retire the preferred equity. We'll include this value in the formula.

So far, we have:

---

13 'Prior to the common' is an archaic term that refers to claims over the company's assets that are legally required to be settled before common shareholders receive any value during a liquidation. For example, management may be legally required to pay bondholders an amount equal to the bond's face value and unpaid dividends before distributing any value obtained through the sale of the firm's assets to common shareholders.

Current assets	$740,000
Less total balance-sheet liabilities	$300,000
Less preferred shares	$52,500
Less off-balance-sheet liabilities	?
Equals NCAV	?

The firm's preliminary NCAV amounts to $387,500. Bert's lists 100,000 shares outstanding on its balance sheet, and the same figures as its diluted share count on its income statement. In essence, the company lacks stock options, or any other convertible financial instrument, that could be immediately converted into common stock. On a per-share basis, then, Bert's has a preliminary NCAV of $3.88.

Scanning the investor relations page on the firm's website, we find that its shares last traded for $1.50. Dividing $1.50 by $3.88 yields a ratio of 0.387, or 38.7%. The stock is trading for just 38.7% of the company's preliminary per-share NCAV. This amounts to a very large 61% discount to NCAV, so it's worth while proceeding with the analysis.

The initial valuation is a preliminary valuation, a rough assessment of the firm's NCAV per share based on balance sheet figures alone. A proper valuation requires us to include any off-balance-sheet liabilities that may exist. Since it can take much longer to dig up a firm's off-balance-sheet liabilities, we can compute a preliminary NCAV per-share value to quickly exclude firms that do not trade below NCAV. Since Bert's is trading well below its preliminary NCAV per share, it's worth spending more time combing through the firm's financial reports to fine-tune the NCAV per-share figure.

Digging into the notes to the firm's financial statements, we see that the company recently lost a court case involving a defective balloon. The company notes that the judgement against the firm may cost it $100,000, but the ruling is being appealed. To stay conservative, we'll include this penalty in the firm's off-balance-sheet liabilities.

The company does not have operating leases because it owns its five Bert's Plumbing and Party Supplies stores. The company does have a pension plan, though, and unfortunately it has not kept up with the payments it needs to make to cover future pension obligations. The shortfall is $10,000.

Balloon court judgement	$100,000
Unfunded pension	$10,000
Total off-balance-sheet liabilities	$110,000

We're now in a position to calculate the firm's actual NCAV. Values and resulting valuation work out to:

Current assets	$740,000
Less total balance sheet liabilities	$300,000
Less preferred shares	$52,500
Less off-balance-sheet liabilities	$110,000
Equals net current asset value	$277,500

If we were to liquidate Bert's today, it would be fair to expect roughly $277,500 in value to be passed on to the company's common stockholders. That works out to $2.78 per share.

With the company's common shares trading for $1.50, shares are selling for a price well below the firm's NCAV per share. This 46% discount makes the shares a possibly compelling opportunity.

Discount is not everything when it comes to net-net investing, though. And while Graham favoured a discount to intrinsic value of greater than 33%, I've found that buying net-nets that trade in line with their NCAV still provides outstanding returns when other favourable characteristics of the investment are present. More on that later.

For now, we have a stock that trades at a steep discount to its NCAV, suggesting good safety of principal and profit potential. Again, it's too soon to conclude that the stock is a buy. A smart analyst would want to examine further. I show how to do this later in the book.

3

A Closer Look at Graham's Net-Net Working Capital Formula

FAMED VALUE MANAGEMENT firm Tweedy, Browne once called net-net investing the oldest systematic approach to investing that they knew of. Net-net investing is indeed old, going back at least as far as Graham's early career. Graham first publicly discussed the practical utility of buying stocks below their liquidation value in the early 1930s. But it's unclear whether Graham was pointing out a new approach to investing or highlighting a much older tradition.

Net-nets first hit public awareness in a big way during one of America's darkest periods. The world had just suffered a terrifying stock market drop and was in the midst of the greatest economic depression of the previous 600 years.[14] Due to the massive market crash from 1929 to 1932, roughly one-third of all publicly traded companies were trading below a reasonable assessment of their liquidation value.[15] At the time, Graham referred to many of these as net quick companies, and included only cash, short-term investments, and receivables in his calculation.[16] Later in his career, when assessing liquidation value, he would come to include all of a company's current assets and recommend that enterprising investors focus on these working capital stocks for purchase.

---

14 Ross School of Business, 'A Conversation with Charlie Munger and Michigan Ross', youtu.be/S9HgIGzOENA.

15 Graham, 'Inflated Treasuries and Deflated Stockholders'.

16 Ibid.

Graham used a few different formulas as he developed the approach throughout his career, and his writings are littered with different terms for the strategy. Some of the most prevalent formulas and terms used throughout the past century include:

- **Net cash stocks:** Stocks that trade below their net cash value, cash and equivalents less all obligations prior to the common. Obligations prior to the common essentially includes anything that has to be paid by the owners of the business, such as loans, credit from suppliers, taxes, preferred dividends, or even the retirement of preferred shares.
- **Net quick stocks:** More conservative than today's approach, these only take into account a company's more liquid current assets. Here, cash and cash equivalents, short-term investments, and receivables are included while anything else (most notably inventory) is excluded from the calculation.
- **Net-net working capital stocks (NNWC stocks):** Less conservative than net quick stocks, these take into account all current assets but discount current assets (e.g., short-term investments, receivables, inventory, and prepaid items) for a more conservative valuation. Graham also included fixed assets, though at an extreme discount to their book values.
- **Working capital stocks/net working capital stocks/NCAV stocks:** Graham used these terms interchangeably but all refer to the same general approach, which takes into account all current assets.
- **Net-net stocks/net-nets:** A slang term derived from netting current assets against current liabilities, and netting this amount against long-term liabilities and obligations prior to the common.

In this chapter, I walk you through one of the most common alternative formulas: net-net working capital investing. In the process, I hope to help you build a deeper understanding of the main formula so you can apply it well in your own practice.

Net-net working capital revisited

In the 1934 edition of *Security Analysis*,[17] Graham wrote: "The first rule of calculating liquidation value is that the liabilities are real but the value of the assets must be questioned. This means that all true liabilities shown on the books must be deducted at their face amount. The value to be ascribed to the assets, however, will vary according to their character."

The NCAV formula is a very conservative way of calculating liquidation value because we exclude the uncertain value of long-term assets. But current asset values also vary somewhat from their stated balance sheet figures. As mentioned, the cash and equivalents figure is about as certain as balance sheet values get. While short-

---

17 Graham and Dodd, *Security Analysis*, 587.

term investments vary slightly in value, some receivables may remain uncollected, and inventory values can fluctuate much more due to breakage and obsolescence. Add to the mix prepaid expenses, some of which may not be refundable, and it seems you can't base a solid assessment of liquidation value on anything besides cash.

Because Graham realised this problem, he offered two solutions. He noted that while the value of receivables, inventory, and so on may shrink during liquidation, the value obtained through the sale of long-term assets would, on average, step in to take care of these shortfalls. While net-net investors purposefully exclude long-term assets during the valuation process, vehicles, office chairs, and warehouses still have value, albeit an uncertain amount.

Graham knew better than to assume that long-term assets would completely make up for shrinkage and therefore made it clear that this phenomenon would occur on balance. While, in some cases, the value of some companies' long-term assets would fail to make up for current asset deterioration, investors would find that other companies possessed long-term assets that were much more valuable than expected. In this way, over a large number of securities, shortfalls would be balanced by long-term asset value.

Graham's second solution gives the analyst a purpose for being. Rather than leaving it to the value of long-term assets to step in and fill in the gaps, an investor could simply discount the current asset accounts and estimate the amount of shrinkage that could take place. Discounting the accounts means an even larger margin of safety, by allowing for more shrinkage in value before liquidation value estimates are impaired. Graham went so far as to include long-term assets in his calculation for this approach, though he first heavily discounted their value.

Both Graham and Buffett used this approach when selecting net-nets for their own portfolios in the 1950s and 1960s. Both would also apply their business knowledge and experience to determine the best discount rate possible. Modern investors, on the other hand, don't worry too much about trying to estimate current asset impairment. Instead, they tend to take a standardised approach derived from Graham and Dodd's *Security Analysis* textbook.

In the book, Benjamin Graham suggested a range of values for various balance sheet accounts when calculating net-net working capital. The analyst needs to determine the exact discount applied to each balance sheet account based on his knowledge of the industry.[18] I've taken the following information from the sixth edition of *Security Analysis*, based on Graham's work in the 1930s.[19]

---

18 Assessing the true liquidation value of the firm, however, may yield values that fall outside of Graham's suggested range depending on the nature of the assets in question. For example, property may be listed on the balance sheet at cost but be assessed at a much higher value.

19 Graham and Dodd, *Security Analysis*, 560.

Table 2: Benjamin Graham's suggested range of discounts when assessing a firm's net-net working capital value

Type of asset		% of liquidating value to book value	
		Normal range	Rough average
Current assets	Cash assets (including securities at market)	100	100
	Receivables (less usual reserves)*	75–90	80
	Inventories (at lower of cost or market)	50–75	66 2/3
Fixed and miscellaneous assets	Real estate, buildings, machinery, equipment, nonmarketable investments, intangibles, etc.	1–50	15 (approx.)

Source: Graham and Dodd, *Security Analysis*, 6th ed.

In table 2, Graham specifies that receivables, for example, are to be discounted by between 10 and 25%, based on the nature of the business, customer, market conditions, and other relevant facts. Inventory, likewise, is to receive a 25 to 50% reduction, and long-term assets are to be marked down between 50 and 99%.

These multiples reflect the dependability of each asset class. The value of cash on the balance sheet is usually very accurate, while inventories can vary quite a bit. Rather than assess the relevant facts, investors today have simply opted to apply the average figures on the right side of the table, assuming that this additional conservatism would yield better returns. For example, when calculating NNWC, an analyst applies the following multiples to each relevant current asset account:

Cash × 1
Receivables × 0.8
Inventory × 0.67

This seems simple enough, but Graham misses a couple of accounting entries that the modern-day security analyst has to deal with: short-term investments, prepaid expenses, tax receivables, and current tax assets.

The real-world value of short-term investments can vary somewhat from their carrying value, depending on both the nature of the investments and current market conditions. Short-term government bonds usually only vary slightly in value compared to mutual funds or stocks. Here, analysts have to use their best judgement on probable changes to the values since the most recent balance sheet date. Even if there's been no change in asset values from the most recent reporting period, broker commissions have to be factored in when liquidating the account. Some investors have applied a blanket discount of 10%, or a × 0.9

multiple to the value of short-term investments on the balance sheet. This seems too aggressive when accounting for broker commissions today, but it does allow for some deterioration of the short-term investments account.

Short-term investments × 0.9

Many investors just mark prepaid expenses to zero, assuming that they're merely an accounting entry and carry no real value. This is a bold assumption. If you think about those times in your own life when you prepay for goods and services, you could probably get at least a partial refund most of the time if you request one. Again, industry or insider knowledge is crucial for assessing actual realisable values, but it seems reasonable to assume that a liquidator could retrieve 50% of the company's prepayments. While certainly not exact, it's at least more accurate than assuming prepayments are worth nothing or that the full value could be refunded.

Prepaid expenses × 0.5

Tax receivables are tax refunds: money owed to the company by some state tax authority. It's fair to say that other than in exceptional cases, the value of these assets is certain and investors do not have to discount the account in question.

Tax receivables × 1

Current tax assets are another matter entirely. Unlike tax receivables, current tax assets are an accounting entry and the value in question cannot be collected by the company. They usually stem from prepaying taxes owed by the firm.

Current tax assets × 0

Adding all of the above to Graham's original figures, the standardised NNWC formula becomes:

Cash and equivalents		× 100%
Plus	Short-term investments	× 90%
Plus	Receivables	× 80%
Plus	Inventory	× 67%
Plus	Prepaid expenses	× 50%
Plus	Tax receivables	× 100%
Plus	Fixed assets	× 15%
Less	Total balance-sheet liabilities	× 100%
Less	Preferred shares	× 100%
Less	Off-balance-sheet liabilities	× 100%
Equals	Net-net working capital value	

Applying net-net working capital to Bert's

Let's work through the above by revisiting our much-loved fictional company, Bert's Plumbing and Party Supplies. If you'll recall, Bert's had $740,000 in total current assets. Looking closer at the firm's current assets, we see that much of it is in inventory. What would happen if we wanted to find the firm's NNWC value? Let's plug the numbers into the most recent formula to find out.

Cash and equivalents	× 100%	$150,000
Plus short-term investments	× 90%	$45,000
Plus receivables	× 80%	$160,000
Plus inventory	× 67%	$201,000
Plus prepaid expenses	× 50%	$20,000
Plus tax receivables	× 100%	Not applicable
Plus long-term assets	× 15%	$99,000
Less total balance sheet liabilities	× 100%	$300,000
Less preferred shares	× 100%	$52,500
Less off-balance-sheet liabilities	× 100%	$110,000
Equals net-net working capital value		$212,500

Valued at $212,500 on a NNWC basis, the company doesn't appear to be as big a bargain as it once was. We initially estimated the company's liquidation value at $277,500. On a per-share basis, the firm's NNWC worked out to $2.13 rather than the previous $2.78 based on NCAV. The company is still a bargain basement stock.

Should net-net investors adopt NNWC?

At this point, you may be wondering whether you should abandon NCAV in favour of net-net working capital. In the above example, Bert's liquidation value was assessed to be much lower than it was when based on NCAV. This may suggest that NNWC is more conservative and therefore yields better returns.

While some value investors will adamantly defend NNWC, it doesn't make much of a difference when it comes to real-world investing.

First, while NNWC produced a much more conservative valuation in the case of Bert's, it won't always produce a more conservative result. When a firm has a significant amount of long-term assets, the liquidation valuation may be assessed higher than it would be in the case of a simple NCAV assessment. This may not be a rare occurrence. Many firms have significant long-term assets, which would come into play and produce higher valuations.

Second, applying standardised discounts to asset values seems somewhat arbitrary. To get the most out of the approach, an investor would need to apply acute business insight to determine the best treatment for each account. Applying a standardised approach could yield unrealistic values. For example, while the formula calls for discounting inventory by an average of 33%, inventory can actually be worth more than face value during periods of high inflation. Likewise, the company may have adequate reserves for losses on uncollectable receivables. Discounting them further in this case would produce much too conservative a valuation, perhaps causing the investor to miss out on a promising investment.

Third, while ample research has been published by academics and industry on the performance of NCAV stocks, no studies that I know of have been published on NNWC stock performance. While it's reasonable to assume that NNWC investments perform in line with NCAV stocks on average, there's a significant lack of data to back up that assumption. For this reason, investors set on using an empirically backed approach should opt for a NCAV investment approach.

Fourth, practical experience conveyed by one of the world's best investors, Peter Cundill, suggests that fire sale prices are not a foregone conclusion during liquidation. Instead, liquidations can take place in an orderly fashion allowing investors to obtain the full value of their assets during the liquidation process. In many cases, worry about fire sale prices may prove to be misguided.[20] This has been my experience, as well.

Fifth, if investors are really worried about shrinking valuations, there are better ways to deal with the issue. One would be to simply demand a larger margin of

20 Risso-Gill, *There's Always Something to Do*, 97.

safety, a greater discount to NCAV than Graham's minimum one-third. This would also allow investors to keep it simple, rather than having to compute a much larger number of figures to put together an adequately diversified portfolio.

Lastly, while net-net investing focuses on buying firms for less than their liquidation values, ironically few firms actually liquidate. Instead, net-net firms often recover at least enough to muddle along as marginally profitable businesses or are taken over by third parties. In these cases, NCAV often proves to be a highly practical estimate of minimum fair value. In other cases, as we'll see, the firms are very much alive and possess bright futures.

While I've been negative on net-net working capital in this section, the measure is not without its merits. Graham was absolutely correct in observing that some asset values were more reliable than others. Net-net working capital, then, can be used as a sort of acid test, a measure of how the firm's liquidation value may fair if stated asset values prove to be too lofty. In these situations, companies with a greater portion of their liquidation value in more liquid assets would possess more robust valuations.

Similarly, if there is a higher-than-average likelihood of liquidating, investors may opt to value a firm using the NNWC approach. In these situations, I would advise investors to opt for accuracy rather than simply applying a standardised assessment. Doing so will likely yield a more accurate assessment of liquidation value, providing a better estimate of whether the principal investment would be impaired or not. While it's difficult to know what price assets would likely fetch during liquidation, the closer the assessment is to the truth, the better.

Barring these two applications, most investors would be better served by sticking to the simpler NCAV approach and applying the scorecard I discuss later in this book. Not only is the valuation process simpler but applying the additional criteria when selecting stocks leads to better results.

A net-net stock's natural habitat

I know what you're thinking: "Who in their right mind would sell a business below liquidation value? I have never even seen a firm trading this cheaply before. Coke, Southwest Airlines, Sysco, they're all trading at multiples of their book value!"

Net-net stocks are indeed rare. In fact, the most net-nets in existence at one time, that I am aware of, occurred in the depths of the 1930s Great Depression, when just over one-third of all companies in the USA were trading below a conservative estimate of their liquidation values. The real number of net-net stocks may have been even higher, because the Graham account of the investment landscape mostly referred to net cash or net quick stocks. If one-third of American public companies had traded below net quick assets, given their more liberal valuation, many more firms would have traded below their NCAV.

Opportunities have dried up since the 1930s. Market valuations have much to do with it.[21] As market values rise, the price of most stocks rise, which means that fewer stocks are trading below their NCAV. During the 1950s and 1960s, a professional fund manager could make a very good living scouring the market's cheapest stocks for attractive net-net opportunities. By the late 1960s, net-nets had almost totally dried up,[22] but the 1970s market turmoil brought back a massive number of net-nets, allowing astute investors the chance to make large profits. Since that period, the markets have marched steadily higher, gradually lowering the number of American net-nets to a mere handful today.

Given the knowledge and skill of many professional money managers on Wall Street (don't laugh, I mean that seriously), and the number of fund managers who call themselves value investors, it's not surprising that net-nets are virtually impossible to find among companies with larger market caps. In fact, the higher up the market-cap ladder investors look, the fewer net-nets they're likely to find. Markets are more efficient among larger firms, so serious mispricings are far more likely to happen among the market's smallest stocks. Generally today, net-net investors rarely find NCAV stocks above a market cap of $200 million. During protracted bull markets opportunities are relegated to the tiniest firms – those with market capitalisations under $50 million.

The amazing shrinkage of the number of publicly traded American companies over the last two decades since 1996 complicates matters. Between 1996 and 2016, according to Credit Suisse, the number of public companies fell by half, from 7,322 to 3,671. Worse for net-net investors, the average market capitalisation of a publicly traded company has ballooned to $6.9 billion. These two facts mean that there are disproportionately fewer tiny firms, making it much harder to find net-nets in the USA today. Given that the American stock market constitutes roughly half of the world's publicly traded companies, this makes net-net investing tough for all but those managing the tiniest portfolios.

Today NCAV stock investors are forced to pick over the tiniest companies to find a handful of American net-nets.

Given the terrible reputation that micro- or nano-cap companies have, how are investors supposed to profit?

---

21 Graham, 'The Decade 1965–1974', www8.gsb.columbia.edu/sites/valueinvesting/files/files/DOC003.pdf.
22 Graham, *The Intelligent Investor*, 390.

4

Why Does Net-Net Investing Work?

IT SEEMS INCREDIBLE that net-net stocks work out so well. After all, they're the market's discarded trash – soggy cigar butts kicked into the ditch along the roadside. They're not great businesses with moats, brilliant management teams, or decades of growth ahead. Rather, they're marginally profitable firms at best, often facing massive business problems. Claiming that these stocks can produce such beautiful returns seems to bend reality. Yet, as many experienced deep value investors know, they do.

At first glance, the answer seems to be how cheap net-nets are relative to fair value, but that's only part of it. After all, investors who buy stocks based on low price to earnings multiples could buy their stocks at steeper discounts but still not perform as well. Alternatively, astute readers may assume that the greater risk these stocks face and market overreaction are responsible for the great returns. But these hypotheses have not proved to be feasible, according to academic studies.[23] Rather than just look at discount to fair value, the critical combination seems to be buying below a hyper conservative assessment of fair value. The method of valuation itself is in essence a margin of safety.

Graham's net-nets: the conservative value framework

It's not hard to buy the proverbial dollar for fifty cents. Today, there's a number of value strategies that would allow you to find stocks trading for half of what they're worth. Net-net investing, however, has the benefit of basing valuation on a far more conservative assessment of fair value: liquidation value.

---

23 Goebel and Athavale, 'The Persistence of NCAV Stock Selection Criterion', 77.

Liquidation value is the value an investor can receive after closing down a company, selling off its assets, and paying back its creditors. In these scenarios, a liquidator assumes that none of the firm's business divisions have much value as stand-alone operations; more money can be realised by simply closing up shop and then piecing out the firm's vehicles, machinery, inventory, and so on to whoever will buy them. If investors were to decide to unwind a company bought below its liquidation value, in theory they would be able to collect the company's net asset value in cash, which would provide a nice pre-tax profit.

I tend to look at valuations in a hierarchy, from most to least reliable. It's usually foolish to buy a firm based on the perceived value of its growth, for example, if the company doesn't have a moat. When growth inevitably collapses, investors scramble to find solid footing, often finding it much lower in the value hierarchy: in the company's earnings. But earnings valuations have their own problems, since earning power can collapse when competition heats up, or an economic trend turns sour. When earnings disappear, investors can at least find value in a firm's net assets.

A lot of investors emphasise book value or net tangible assets when calculating net asset value. The thought is that the firm should be worth as much as its net asset value, even if the business fails. That thinking is generally on point, but there's a complication for would-be Gordon Gekkos: balance sheets present accounting values rather than real-world values. (IFRS accounting has moved to right this wrong by having companies mark up or down the value of assets on the balance sheet, but the American GAAP has not made this change. Investors should be aware of the differences between IFRS and GAAP accounting if they intend to invest outside the USA.) The values found on a company's balance sheet are determined by accounting rules and can be sculpted by these rules to such an extent that they have little resemblance to real-world values that could be realised in private sales.[24]

Take real estate, for example. Accounting rules state that management must mark down the value of a building by a predetermined amount each year, even though property values tend to rise over time. Perhaps a company purchased an office building in Seattle in 1990 which now has an accounting value of $10 million. Recognising that Seattle real estate has risen in price significantly, management decide to sell the building and relocate to the suburbs. They quickly offer the building for sale and realise a $100 million sale price. In this case, the building's accounting value was one-tenth of its real-world value.

Values can be just as unrealistic on the upside as they are on the downside. Consider goodwill, which represents the amount paid above assessed fair value

24 Damodaran, 'Session 19: Asset Based Valuation', youtu.be/HmDQISjLxig; Graham, *The Interpretation of Financial Statements*, 48; Greenwald, *Value Investing*, 36.

when acquiring a firm. While some would argue that this amount correctly reflects the value of the acquired firm's ongoing business, or potential growth, what if the acquirer overpaid? In other cases, the equipment a firm uses could be worth less in a private sale than its carrying value as a long-term asset on the balance sheet. Basing value on a company's stated book value can lead to a grossly inaccurate valuation.

In contrast to long-term assets such as buildings, cars, or goodwill, current assets tend to have accounting values that are closer to their corresponding real-world values. In fact, assets are listed on the balance sheet according to the certainty of their corresponding values, from more certain at the top to far less certain at the bottom, so it's no wonder why we find cash and equivalents at the front of the list.[25] The value of cash is always certain since, while purchasing power may decline, a dollar is always worth a dollar. Cash equivalents are high-quality and highly liquid assets such as US T-bills or savings accounts, so they get lumped in with cash. Things get a little less reliable from this point on, but the accounting value of a company's short-term investments, accounts receivable, and inventory tends to reflect their corresponding real-world values more closely than long-term assets do.

Graham knew early in his career that a company's book value was often very different from its liquidation value, so he proposed a practical adjustment. Rather than looking at total assets, he only took into account a company's current assets before subtracting total liabilities to reach a value much closer to the firm's real-world liquidation value. Any shortfall in value when liquidating the company's current assets, Graham assumed, would be made up by value obtained for the firm's long-term assets.[26] In this way, the long-term assets ignored during the valuation process would step up to the plate to fill in any gaps left by customers who couldn't pay their bills, obsolete inventory, or prepayments that couldn't be refunded. Of course, this wouldn't happen in each and every case, but it would happen on balance when looking at a large number of companies.

While a rough estimate of a company's real-world liquidation value, Graham's formula was much more conservative than just looking at a firm's book value or its net tangible assets. This conservatism provides net-net investors with a powerful advantage: valuations are much less subject to downward revisions.

A good defence is a good offence

Focusing on NCAV when buying stocks has an interesting by-product. When investors buy at such a conservative assessment of value, thereby protecting their

---

25 Greenwald, *Value Investing*, 36.
26 Graham, 'Inflated Treasuries and Deflated Stockholders', *Forbes* (1932).

downside, they inevitably ignore many of the sources of value that other investors depend on for their valuations. But net-net investors can still realise these values in the market without assuming any of the associated downside risks. The market is often wrong to price a company below its net-net value, since doing so assumes that the company is only worth its liquidation value, or less. But the fact that many net-net stocks often rise well above their NCAV suggests that the market is making a systematic error. If some of these firms are ultimately worth much more than liquidation value, buying these firms below a conservative assessment of liquidation value means adopting another margin of safety, one grounded in the conservative nature of the valuation itself. Eventually, other investors step in to pay up for this ignored value, allowing net-net investors to reap abnormally large profits.

One way this plays out is grounded in mean reversion. When I was a kid, I went to school with a boy who was an absolute giant, the product of random biological chance. Despite attending three elementary schools, I had never seen a kid who was so much taller than me, not to mention the rest of my class. It looked as if he should have been a couple of grades ahead, but he was actually younger than me.

We lost sight of each other after elementary school but wound up on the same ice hockey team years later. He was still as enormous but despite his impressive stature, he was a shrimp compared to his dad. While the height difference between us remained the same, he'd never grow as large as his father.

Families' physical heights are interesting. As you would expect, enormously tall people tend to have tall children, but these children usually grow to heights closer to the population average.[27] Over generations, abnormally tall or short families tend to regain average stature, a phenomenon known as mean reversion: the phenomenon where extreme observations tend to be followed by less extreme observations over time.

My friend and his father are a clear example, but the phenomenon is found in many areas in life, from baseball to traffic, and even economics. In the world of business, all sorts of metrics mean-revert: net profit margins, return on capital, growth trends, and even stock prices. Firms with abnormally high margins, for example, attract competing firms which lower prices, elbow out incumbents to obtain supplies and, ultimately, lower the overall profitability within their industry.

When it comes to extreme observations, it's hard to picture anything more extreme than the performance of a company trading below NCAV. Firms trading as net-nets typically face large business problems. Their revenues have fallen off a cliff, profits have completely evaporated, and their return on capital has turned negative.

---

27 Mauboussin, 'Mauboussin on Strategy', Legg Mason Capital Management (14 December 2007).

Suffice it to say that near-term prospects, let alone long-term survival, seem bleak. This leaves investors scrambling for the exits, expecting the business to fail.

But remember that firms trading below NCAV have current assets that dwarf all liabilities. This gives management breathing room to focus on the problem at hand. The first step is usually to stop the bleeding by curtailing unprofitable operations, cutting down on staff, renegotiating purchase agreements, or shrinking the firm's store base. More stable operations allow a management team to identify profitable opportunities, which may include new products, new lines of business, or joint ventures. With enough hard work, both sales and profits can start to recover, attracting alert investors who gently push the stock price back up. If the firm continues its ascent to join the ranks of other profitable firms, investors can push the stock price well above liquidation value. This is mean reversion in action.

In terms of eventual outcome, those with the lowest acquisition cost often come out with the largest profits. In cases where a firm recovers, investors were wrong to think that it had no future, thereby pricing it below liquidation value. Net-net investors, in contrast, based their purchases on the firm's liquidation value rather than the value of the firm's ongoing operations, thereby capitalising on the value of the firm's future earnings and assuming little of the associated risk. Buying a stock trading below a hyper-conservative assessment of fair value allows investors to invest closer to the bottom, providing larger returns when a company recovers. In fact, while net-net investors celebrate a solid profit, those who bought the firm earlier, based on some other measure of value, are usually just happy to get their money back.

Coiled springs? Net-net stocks and the good news effect

But strong investment returns when a company defies death isn't the only evidence that an ultra-conservative assessment of fair value is responsible for the tremendous returns of net-net stocks. Equally as powerful is the coiled-spring phenomenon.

It's nearly impossible to find net-nets that aren't hated or feared. When an otherwise normal company experiences large business problems, investors can punish the stock, sending it down as much as –99% below its pre-crisis high. After all, as a minority investor, if you're sure that a company is going bankrupt, then its stock is not worth any price because buying would guarantee a total loss. Investors who bought when times were better, perhaps banking on future growth, become resentful towards the company and its management for the massive erosion in price. These investors exit the stock, post bitter comments on chat forums, and can stir up a drumbeat effect: angry investors chastising management for horrific performance and the free-falling stock.

Comments in response to an analysis I did on Emerson Radio in 2016 are instructive:

> "$39.5 million loss of revenue (over half the annual revenue) due to a major customer discontinuing the product is sufficient enough on its own not to invest in the company."

> "With as much competition in this space as there is, there is no demand for Emerson products."

> "This is more than a beaten up company. This is a company on the way out that needs to either replace its executive team, look for a buyer, or liquidate itself and shut the doors."

I sold the stock for a 115% gain two years later. Maybe the company didn't have much of a future and needed to shut its doors, but that didn't mean that the stock was still a dud. Trading 55% below net cash, other investors were essentially paying me to buy the stock.

There's a flip side to the intense negativity that pushes a firm below NCAV: it's akin to a thumb compressing a spring. Investors have a tendency to erroneously extrapolate trends into the future.[28] Most investors who expect net-net firms to slip into bankruptcy ignore strong balance sheets which give management time to take action. In the meantime, if a bit of good news comes out about the company, such as a big new contract, investors may realise their mistake and flood back into the stock, causing its price to spike well beyond liquidation value. It's as if that bit of good news gently slid the thumb off of the spring, launching the stock skyward.

InfoSonics is a great example. The company had made a decent living selling cell phones in South America during the 2000s. Somewhere along the way, it was hit with a large tariff and forced to watch a good chunk of its business dry up. While it had a solid balance sheet, the firm was not profitable and spent a number of years bouncing around at prices well below its former high. When I spotted the company in 2013, things had gone from bad to worse. Not only did the firm's near-term prospects seem bleak but it had also been hit with a patent infringement lawsuit. The stock had traded down from $1.60 the year prior to just $0.56 when I picked it up in November. While investors had no reason to expect operations to turn around over the near term, InfoSonics was then trading at a 51% discount to NCAV, with significant net cash and no debt.

It didn't take long for the investment to pay off. By mid-December investors had begun to nudge the stock a bit higher, perhaps spotting a bargain. But the real fireworks started on the nineteenth, when management issued a press release

---

28 Dreman, *Contrarian Investment Strategies*, 246.

announcing a major new distribution partnership with the American firm Ingam Micro. Now assured of a much brighter future, investors leapt back into the stock, sending its price past $1.40 per share. At that point I had more than doubled my money and I exited the position.

That proved to be an unfortunate mistake. To my horror, the NASDAQ issued InfoSonics a letter the following week, reinstating the firm's stock on the index. The shares surged another 100%, eventually peaking at roughly $4.50 before falling back down to $2.50. Even if investors had missed the peak and sold after the stock dropped, they'd still have been left with a 345% gain.

Price moves this large tend to only happen to terribly depressed firms, such as net-nets. Earlier investors who bought the stock for higher prices based on rosier valuation scenarios may have come out with a capital gain, but net-net investors did far better. By demanding an additional margin of safety in the form of an ultra-conservative approach to valuation, net-net investors got that additional upside for free. Of course, it was impossible to know what the company's prospects were worth or whether they'd be realised, but if you buy low enough, "something good may happen to you", as Walter Schloss was fond of saying.

Third-party takeovers support real-world valuation assessment

A third-party takeover is one of the rare occasions when value investing theory and pragmatic business decisions collide. In most other cases, value investors estimate the value of a firm's shares and then wait for other market participants to agree with them. But when interested component managers with a good understanding of the facts haggle over the selling price of a business, value investors get a peek at how accurate their estimated values really are.

Real-world business values are negotiated using many of the same factors that go into individual stock valuation: possible future growth, the current level of earnings, brand value, the price at which a similar competitor was acquired, and so on. While it's still difficult for a would-be acquirer to value an entire business, an acquirer and a firm's entrenched management team both benefit from superior knowledge of the firm's business and prospects. Management, intimately involved with the day-to-day operation and planning of the business, understand the firm better than anyone. Interested parties, on the other hand, can be granted a peek behind the curtain to help make a suitable offer. This allows both parties to arrive at a truer value than most outsiders can estimate.

The combination of limited information and the intangible nature of many of a firm's assets makes it easy for outsiders to incorrectly assess the value of a business.

If an investor overvalues the business, a third-party takeover at a more realistic value can mean losing money on the investment. At least in the case of takeovers, it's much better to err on the side of being too conservative than too aggressive, which is another area where net-net investing really pays off. Trading below a hyper-conservative estimate of fair value, net-net investors are not only excluding long-term assets from their valuation but are also excluding the firm's intangible assets and future prospects. Business relationships, the time involved in setting up a factory, synergistic opportunities, residual brand value, potential post-crisis earnings – all of these intangibles have real-world value for a would-be acquirer but are completely ignored by net-net investors. The result is that when takeovers do happen, they typically happen for a price at or above NCAV, making net-net investors more likely to come out with a profit.

It's not hard to see why a third-party would want to take over a failing firm. In some cases, it's simply the belief that the firm has a much brighter future than the market is giving it credit for. GTSI Corp is just one example. After some shady dealing, the government banned the company from selling to the government, its core business. With sales hit hard and a few top executives forced out, the firm's stock plummeted below NCAV. But the ban was quickly lifted, which meant that the company could bid on government contracts again, restoring revenue and profitability. I bought well after the crisis was underway at a 45% discount to NCAV. The shares started to rise soon after, but within a matter of months, the business was taken over by Unicom Systems, right at NCAV – a quick 85% return.

A company doesn't need an obviously bright future to become a takeover target. Some acquirers assume they would do a better job than the incumbent management team. Others want a quick and easy way to expand their geographic reach, either by acquiring retail locations or business relationships. An acquisition, in such cases, would allow acquirers to access sales channels they would otherwise have to spend time and effort setting up. In fact, the same goes for a wide range of assets: brands, factories, legal contracts, and even marketing teams.

Whatever the case, firms trading below NCAV make great takeover targets because their rock-solid balance sheets make financing an acquisition much easier. Some firms even have net cash or excess securities that can be quickly monetised to reduce the net acquisition cost. Net-net investors, who typically put a lot of stock into cash and only look at current assets, usually buy well below takeover prices. On the other hand, investors who purchased a firm at more generous valuations only to watch the company's performance slip may have their company sold out from under them for a deflated price. And prices this low stir up a lot of interest from third parties. Based on my observations, net-net firms tend to be taken over roughly 10 to 15% of the time. Takeovers are much more frequent for net-nets than they are for typical publicly traded companies, providing an additional way for net-net investors to profit.

Liquidations: profitable, but less important than you think

For a strategy based on liquidation value, it's surprising that so few net-nets actually liquidate. In fact, in my ten years as a net-net investor, I can't recall ever buying shares in a company that decided to close up shop and liquidate. But while liquidations are rare, they do provide a nice safety net for net-net investors.

Sometimes the problems a business is going through prove too large or complex to tackle. In these cases, shopping the business around to possible buyers is the obvious choice because a sale is the quickest way to realise fair value. Management may even be offered termination bonuses – golden parachutes – and look like heroes in their local community for saving jobs, all of which provide a powerful incentive to close a deal. But sometimes the business looks so ugly that nobody wants to touch it, so the only other option is to close it and sell off the firm's assets in bits and pieces.

It should come as no surprise that Graham's net-net valuation provides distressed investors with a powerful advantage. Since net-net investors base their valuation on, and ultimately buy below, liquidation value, they're likely to come out with a profit. Value investors who purchase stock based on some other source of value are almost guaranteed to lose money. Liquidation brings little comfort in these cases, as early investors are handed back just a small fraction of their principle.

Liquidations are fascinating to watch. Unlike the fire sales most value investors picture, assets are not always given away at ridiculous prices.[29] Rather, based on my experience, liquidations are often orderly and firms tend to liquidate for a value in line with NCAV. They usually start with management placing inventory and other perishable assets up for sale before moving to sell long-term assets. Wages and taxes are settled before paying debtors, and the remainder distributed to shareholders. Liquidations can be completed in less than 12 months or unfold over the course of a few years as management try to unload the firm's assets (and stretch out their salaries). In the latter case, the stock tracks closely to a well-assessed real-world liquidation value and management often make periodic capital redistributions which end up in investors' brokerage accounts.

Net-net investors typically buy a firm's stock in the hope that the business will pull through, thereby realising a good profit. A liquidation means falling short of this goal. Still, it's incredible that investors who don't see a better tomorrow can still come out ahead when the firm ultimately fails.

29 Risso-Gill, *There's Always Something to Do*, 97.

Graham's Achilles heel: perennial net-nets

Achilles is one of the great heroes in Homer's account of the Trojan War. Thetis, doing her best to ensure that her baby would acquire god-like invulnerability, dipped him into the river Styx. That holy water washed over Achilles' entire body, save for his heel, which Thetis grasped just above the waterline.

After a stunning victory over Hector at Troy, Achilles' weakness eventually caught up with him. Frothing with revenge, Hector's brother launched an arrow that, guided by Apollo's steady hand, drove deep into Achilles' heel. Even heroes have their weaknesses.

It's clear that buying below a hyper-conservative assessment of fair value provides Graham's net-net strategy with extraordinary returns. But despite the strategy's effectiveness, it does suffer from two major weaknesses. The first has become known as the perennial net-net. Sometimes a struggling firm just won't recover, won't see a third-party takeover, and won't be liquidated. In situations like this, investors remain incredibly pessimistic about the firm, as its stock trades below NCAV for years. Holding on to a perennial net-net may allow investors to preserve capital, but the opportunity cost of such an investment is very high.

Worse, sometimes investors unwittingly buy into a company that continues to unravel, losing money each year as the firm's asset base shrinks. At some point, liquidation value erodes below the investors' purchase price, seriously increasing the chance of suffering a permanent loss of capital. If the trend continues, the firm can even slip into bankruptcy, leaving the investors with a total loss.

Net-net investors are fortunate that these outcomes are rare. Well-selected net-net stocks have a much better chance of coming out as big winners than big losers. Still, ensuring the best outcome requires adopting sound selection criteria, a topic we'll explore in detail later.

5

Why People Avoid Buying Net-Net Stocks

WHEN NEW, DEEP value investors grasp the type of stocks I'm buying, they have a couple of questions. The first concerns the strategy's profitability. Studies show that investing in random baskets of net-nets and rebalancing yearly produce a compound annual growth rate of between 20 and 30%, depending on the study. This usually translates into a real-life 18 to 25% CAGR for investors running a plain-vanilla, mechanical, net-net stock portfolio. Returns are dampened somewhat by investor bias but can be improved a lot by adding some well-chosen criteria. More on this later. The second question concerns why so few people use the strategy if returns are this good. The answer is intimately tied to how firms slip below liquidation value in the first place.

When trouble surfaces, retail investors scatter

Few investors find bargain securities without a little hair on them; net-net stocks are no different. Most net-net firms begin their life as normal businesses with adequate profitability and reasonably competent management teams. Like most firms, they have the occasional business problem that management must address, but they overcome it without much trouble.

Every once in a while, though, a firm stumbles into a problem that calls the firm's future into question. Soured on the business, investors head for the exits, perhaps pushing the price to a low-multiple of earnings, sales, or cash flow before management can right the ship.

Firms trading below NCAV have suffered major business problems not adequately addressed by management. Perhaps government regulators ordered the business to stop selling its main product, a massive fire destroyed the firm's production capacity, or its industry suffered a major meltdown. Whatever the case, rather than taking a moderate hit to sales or profitability, the problems net-net firms face typically ravage operations, leading to enormous declines in revenue and ongoing losses. It's very common to see revenue decline by 50 to 80%, and stock decline by up to 99%. At this point, the company's shares generally trade for less than $5, and often less than $1, relegating them to penny stock status. If management prove unable to fix the firm's issues, the stock can trade at that low level for years.

The main reason individual investors don't buy these stocks is obvious: fear. When investors watch a business deteriorate, they naturally expect the business to keep eroding until there's nothing left or the company declares bankruptcy.[30] Nobody wants to buy into a situation where a company is likely to go bankrupt, and a quick look at the firm's recent stock chart and performance figures make bankruptcy look inevitable.

Bankruptcy, however, is usually not in the cards. In James Montier's fantastic paper, 'Graham's Net-Nets: Outdated or Outstanding?', Montier revealed that less than 5% of firms which trade below NCAV go on to produce a massive loss for investors, compared to 2% for stocks in general.[31] Part of the reason has to do with conservative balance sheets. Net-nets have more current assets than total liabilities, making them able, generally, to pay interest on debt, debt maturities, or other business expenses that crop up. Firms that can meet their obligations almost never slip into Chapter 11 bankruptcy protection.

Wall Street's wise men can't buy

Professional money managers should be much more willing to ignore recent price trends and turn to the company's balance sheet to tell if it's a bankruptcy candidate or a true bargain. Graham's net-net strategy is no secret; it has been used successfully by investors and tracked by academics for nearly 100 years. Many Wall Street pros have read classic investment literature, such as Graham and Dodd's *Security Analysis*, and have spent significant time reading research studies covering all sorts of investment strategies. Professionals are therefore much more likely to be aware of net-nets than average investors are.

Why then don't we see a great number of managers buying net-nets and producing great track records?

Knowledge of an outstanding investment strategy and the ability to make use of it are two different things. The hurdle for fund managers is size. In 2017, the

---

30 Montier, *The Little Book of Behavioral Investing*, 27.
31 Montier, 'Graham's Net-Nets'.

average actively managed American equity mutual fund had $1.8 billion in assets.[32] Investing this amount of money is a Herculean task. Management and research constraints make managing a large number of positions very difficult with the result that the average fund manager tends to own less than 100 stocks, for an average position size of $18 million. Unfortunately, fund rules typically restrict ownership to less than 10% of a firm's voting shares, so an $18 million position size means buying companies with market capitalisations of $180 million or larger.[33] Admittedly, this may be too optimistic. Jonathan Dudzinski and Robert Kunkel estimated the minimum market capitalisation at $695 billion (in 2014 dollars) in their paper 'Graham's NCAV Technique in the 21st Century'.

By contrast, firms with adequate discounts to NCAV are almost never found with market capitalisations above $180 million, except during periods of severe economic distress. Rather, they tend to have market caps of less than $100 million and can drop to an average of just $25 million when markets heat up. These market valuations are accompanied by thin, average, daily trading volumes, often dropping below $10,000 during bull markets – far too small for most professional managers.

At Berkshire Hathaway's 1995 annual meeting, Buffett explained:

> "We assume that there are a reasonable number of opportunities as you work with smaller amounts of capital because it's always been true. I mean it was – over the years, as I looked at things, clearly, you run into companies that are less followed as you get smaller. And there's more chances for inefficiency when you're dealing with something where you can buy $100,000 worth of it in a month, rather than 100 million."[34]

Follow the leader: the large firm bias

Small retail investors have a major competitive advantage when it comes to investing: their small portfolio size. Having a tiny amount of money to put to work means that small investors can capitalise on the market's best bargains, often found among the tiniest companies. But tragically, rather than leverage this advantage, small investors tend to follow the pros into larger companies.

Part of the reason comes back to fear. One bias that trips up retail investors is the belief that micro- and nano-cap investing is dangerous. Many investors believe that this space is dominated by scams and frauds which makes it very easy to lose

32 Investment Company Institute, '2019 Investment Company Fact Book', www.icifactbook.org/ch6/18_fb_ch6.
33 Dudzinski and Kunkel, 'Benjamin Graham's NCAV'.
34 Berkshire Hathaway, Annual Meetings, 'Afternoon Session – 1995 Meeting', buffett.cnbc.com.

the bulk of your principal investment. Add to this the fact that many net-nets are relegated to penny stock status and it's no wonder that so many small investors avoid this space.

These concerns are well founded. Many tiny companies have shady or inept management, excessive debt, or no viable business, making them incredibly speculative. But while investing in this area of the market is indeed fraught with risk, there are also exceptional bargains on offer if an investor treads carefully.

Another reason small investors opt for large companies rather than capitalising on their inherent advantage has to do with mindshare. Mindshare is the degree of primacy a thought or concept has over competing alternatives. Coca-Cola, for example, tends to have a lot of mindshare when it comes to soda drinkers. Ask soda drinkers to think of a canned beverage and most will automatically bring up Coke since the company has spent billions of dollars burning its corporate image into the minds of consumers. These soda drinkers can usually name competing alternatives but do so only after being asked to think of other options.

This sort of mindshare extends to the financial markets as well. Large companies don't usually advertise their stocks the same way that Coke advertises cola, but larger firms do get excessive coverage in the financial media which builds mindshare. This coverage makes it much more likely that investors in search of a new stock will turn to larger companies to begin their research. Mindshare makes it more likely that larger companies will be assessed first, and selected as investments more often than tiny companies. Add to that how business media covers rockstar investors who buy mega-cap companies almost exclusively and there's a very strong pull to invest in the largest publicly traded firms. When individuals hunt for large-cap stocks, they ultimately compete against skilled professionals with massive war chests, and earn far lower returns as a result.

Growth companies: if it looks good, it feels good; if it feels good, buy it

Even when small investors turn to smaller companies, they're unlikely to turn to net-nets. Many small investors approach investing with emotion, rather than reason. Decisions are often governed by what feels good rather than what the data suggests is the best course of action to take. This has become painfully clear to me working with small investors at Net Net Hunter since 2013. Many retail investors who show initial enthusiasm for net-nets are ultimately scared away by terrible past business performance. When questioned, value investors who abandon the strategy often admit they can't stomach buying these stocks, no matter how the strategy has performed in the past.

Ultimately, most retail investors want to feel good about the companies they own and therefore seek out good companies with rapid growth. It only takes a quick look at the late 1990s dotcom bubble, or the oil, housing, or bitcoin manias, to see this process in action. Hot sectors attract hot money, and as firms grow, investors feel better about buying their stocks. Today, FANG (Facebook, Amazon, Netflix, Google) firms have demonstrated massive recent growth and investors are extremely optimistic about their prospects. As a consequence, investors have flocked to the companies' shares, driving the price far ahead of the overall market.

Likewise, investors who dive into the micro- and nano-cap space also tend to look for tiny firms with explosive growth. Marijuana stocks or firms involved in emerging technology such as cryptocurrency are just a few examples. It's exciting to talk about the prospects for future technologies, impending sales contracts, and how large a company can grow once the stars align.

Net-nets are either scary or boring and certainly won't win you friends at cocktail parties. Instead, other investors who hear about your holdings are likely to be confused, and think you're a little weird. No firm facing such enormous business problems, with a stock that's declined to just 1% of its former high, could be a great buy. Party-goers may listen politely to your strategy and its historic returns but will think you're crazy. Even if they believe you about past returns, they're still likely to ignore your strategy in favour of bitcoin.

It takes a special sort of person to enjoy digging among the market's trash to find exceptional net-nets. It's a function of psychology more than brainpower. Investing in net-nets is simple blue-collar work that requires understanding the strategy and having a sound emotional temperament. Net-net investors tend to be strong contrarians who go against the grain in multiple areas of their life. They're not trend followers; they're loners. They're not convinced by the herd; they're repulsed by it. Turning their back on the pack is difficult for most people, but it can be enormously profitable.

Net-net stock myths: two misconceptions are costing investors money

Misconception 1: extinct net-nets

It wasn't long after I started investing that I read about Graham's net-nets. The strategy, so the author wrote, was a nearly foolproof way of earning large investment returns. Sadly, it continued, net-nets were a relic of the past – not a viable strategy for modern investors. It took me nearly a decade to realise this is a misperception.

Net-nets have been around since the 1930s. Depending on market conditions, though, they can become more or less prevalent. When the market's expensive, net-nets tend to dry up and those remaining have extraordinarily tiny market caps. More net-nets become available as the market drops. At market bottoms, net-nets are widespread and include many larger firms, and a significant amount of money can be employed using the net-net strategy. While net-nets are available during periods when the market is moderately valued, companies are still relatively tiny, preventing most fund managers from using the strategy.

The strategy is very much a relic of the past for Wall Street's big players, but not for small investors. During the depressed 1930s, 1940s, and 1970s, moderate-sized funds could put the strategy to work to earn great returns for their clients. During the late 1990s and 2000s, and through most of the 2010s, net-nets were out of reach for larger investors. Unfortunately, those with a large soapbox seem to have concluded that just because net-nets are tiny, they're uninvestable for everyone, ignoring the question of portfolio size. Others seem to be just repeating the mantra. Even Columbia Business School is rumoured to be teaching its students that net-nets are extinct.

Misconception 2: thin liquidity means tiny stocks are unbuyable

Another factor that dissuades many value investors is large bid-ask spreads.

All stocks have three basic prices:

1. **Bid price:** The amount of money that a stock broker offers to buy a stock for.
2. **Ask price:** The amount of money a stock broker demands for the stock.
3. **Market price:** The price that the trade is executed for.

When investors place a purchase order, their broker makes an offer to buy the stock on their behalf at a certain price, known as the bid price. A broker tasked with selling shares, on the other hand, offers those shares for sale at a higher price, known as the ask price. After some haggling, the sale is made at what becomes known as the market price. (Or at least this is how it happened in the past. Today, orders are executed by computer systems, but the principle is more or less the same.)

But investors do not typically receive the market price for their shares; they usually have to pay a price over, or receive a price under, the quoted market price. This difference goes to brokers as a fee for handling the trade. When investors buy or sell highly liquid shares, such as Facebook stock, the bid-ask spread is very thin, and brokers get a much smaller fee in percentage terms. Thin liquidity complicates net-net investing, however. When buying a thinly traded stock, as is the case with most net-nets, the bid-ask spread can be enormous – as much as 50% of the quoted market price. With such large bid-ask spreads, many investors assume that net-nets are essentially unbuyable. To make any profit at all, the stock would have to advance enough to cover transaction fees before providing any capital gains.

Investors with a bit of trading knowledge understand just how easy it is to circumvent this concern. We'll cover the simple trick I use to get around this issue later in the book. Despite the concern, large bid-ask spreads do not mean that Graham's net-net strategy is unusable today.

Okay, what's next? Following the bouncing ball

It's ironic that even when net-net investors find the strategy and start using it, they're unlikely to stick with it. The biggest reason has to do with the timing of returns. Net-net portfolios do not beat the market each and every year. Instead, they tend to produce different returns from year to year, and even lose money on occasion. It is performance in a small percentage of years that is responsible for the strategy's tremendous outperformance, while a portfolio may see scant outperformance in other years. Still, this record is good enough to produce an outstanding long-term compound annual growth rate.

Investors who start with a solid net-net portfolio in their first year often expect large market-beating returns over the short term. When these returns do not materialise, investors feel alienated and can ditch the strategy. Incredibly, this seems to be the case even if investors have read through academic research into net-nets and are aware of the variation in portfolio returns from year to year. Perhaps it comes down to patience. It's not easy to stick to a strategy when your first two years showed disappointing performance.

The same goes for individual stocks. It's very common for new investors to start by buying one or two stocks to test the waters, assuming that all net-nets work out fabulously. The reality is quite different, however. Just as portfolio returns differ from year to year, net-net stock returns vary considerably within a portfolio. It's very common for 60% of net-nets to produce positive returns, and 40% to lose money after 12 months, for example. And as in the case of portfolio returns, a few exceptional winners tend to produce the bulk of a net-net stock portfolio's outperformance.

With this in mind, it's easy to see where new net-net investors go wrong by picking only one or two stocks, initially. Those first picks could produce any sort of return, from a total loss to a return of 5,000 or 10,000%. Instead of testing the waters, overly cautious investors are simply rolling the dice with their financial futures at stake.

Solid net-net returns are no guarantee that an investor will stick to the strategy, either. And this is the strangest retail investor trait of all: Just as small investors tend to gravitate towards hot stocks, some private investors also seem to move towards hot new strategies rather than stick to what's working. Why is anyone's guess. Perhaps it's curiosity or intellectual boredom. Net-net investing is a lot like carpentry. Solid investing involves showing up day after day, crunching numbers, and making solid but routine decisions. While each day can present a new challenge, all carpentry problems are carpentry problems. If investors have overly enquiring minds, they can easily ditch an approach that works in favour of another promising path.

6

How the Penny Stock Prince Could Butcher Your Portfolio

IN THE SUMMER of 2012, John Babikian, aka the Penny Stock Prince, disappeared.

The 26-year-old had just spent the previous five years turning a small start-up e-business housed in his mother's den into a widely recognised Internet titan.

Awesome Penny Stocks wasn't just big; it was monolithic. In just a handful of years, the initially irrelevant website had grown to have over 700,000 email subscribers who eagerly lapped up the tiny stocks that Babikian recommended each month.

The arrangement was enormously profitable. Babikian would start by buying up blocks of stock and then begin hyping the firm through his email list. In two months, a prescription drug company he recommended soared to over $700 million, and that was just one of hundreds of trades.

Flush with cash, he soon began throwing the proceeds into shell businesses to use as investment vehicles, as well as expensive Los Angeles real estate, private airplanes, and even a million-dollar Bugatti Veyron. When allegations of tax evasion began to surface, however, Babikian dropped everything and fled his home province of Quebec not to be seen again.

SEC officials estimate that Babikian was able to boost the value of his holdings by as much as $3 billion when all was said and done, nearly all of that money taken from his mailing list subscribers.

Could the Penny Stock Prince butcher your portfolio?

Movies such as *Boiler Room* or *The Wolf of Wall Street* have shone a light on the investment industry's dark underbelly.

Years ago, teams of sales people gathered in smoke-stained offices to push shares in tiny unknown companies via evening cold calls. Brokers would identify a stock, scoop up shares, and then begin working their way down pages of leads hoping to convince ordinary people to purchase the stock. Those purchases pushed the price well above the brokers' initial cost basis, at which point they would begin quietly selling their stakes, earning massive profits.

Boiler rooms are much less relevant for pump and dump operations today. Now, kids just out of high school can start websites, put email lists together, and start hyping stocks in the hope of passing them along at inflated prices to unsuspecting retail investors. In the end, those same retail investors end up holding expensive shares in worthless companies.

Thanks to fraudsters, the term *penny stock* has become a derogatory name for any stock trading below $1. Rather than combing through cheap shares to find bargains, retail investors clutch their wallets whenever they see a stock trading for less than a buck. A case could be made for avoiding these stocks altogether, though avoidance would be less than optimal.

Some investors are attracted to penny stocks because they seem to be a quick way to make a lot of money. The idea is that if you buy really tiny companies with extremely low-priced shares and one of these businesses takes off, the inevitable returns would be astronomical.

This is indeed the case. If an investor selects the right tiny company, and if that company falls into an incredibly fortunate set of business circumstances, the shares are likely to soar and the investor likely to become very wealthy. But a critical problem is the lack of information regarding these companies and their actual business prospects, which opens the way to significant market manipulation.

You don't have to follow scammy websites to fall victim. Stock tips and anonymous sources have a very powerful impact on penny stock speculation. Many buyers look for tips on message boards from people who are, allegedly, close to the company, and then they buy, based on these perceived insights. As speculators pile in, the price balloons, allowing those who bought before the euphoria to exit with sizeable gains. At some point, however, the speculative enthusiasm gives way to scepticism and then fear as the stock turns the corner and begins to drop. As investors rush for the exits, the share price falls precipitously and those who bought much later often lose most of their principal.

Investors can avoid these devastating losses by staying away from penny stocks all together. That's the knee-jerk reaction many investors take, citing obscure prospects, and frequent scams. These concerns miss the real issue, however. The problem isn't actually with penny stocks, the lack of information on tiny companies, or the crooks who hype them. The real problem is the attitude some investors take toward their own investments.

It's not the fraudsters or the hype – it's you

It's possible to earn a lot of money investing in tiny companies with shares selling for less than a dollar, but only if you're one of Graham's intelligent investors. Speculators, on the other hand, are not likely to come out ahead.

According to Graham, "[a]n investment operation is one which, upon thorough analysis promises safety of principle and an adequate return. Operations not meeting these requirements are speculative."[35] In these two sentences, Graham lays out three requirements for intelligent investing:

1. thorough analysis
2. safety of principle
3. an adequate return

Graham's definition is general enough to apply to an investment enterprise as a whole, as in the case of mechanical value investing, or to individual investments for those managing concentrated portfolios. Despite its application, intelligent investment was the cornerstone of Graham's philosophy and would keep many penny stock speculators out of trouble.

Within the world of ultra-low-priced stocks is a real diversity of opportunity. Many investors are ignorant of that fact due to the terrible reputation that penny stocks have acquired. These days, many investors who consider themselves sophisticated completely avoid the space.

It's easy to understand the pain of loss that comes with being scammed, but the problem isn't the hype or the promoters; it's the failure to invest intelligently. Rather than buying based on rumour, investors must conduct adequate analysis to pick up real opportunities and protect their downside. It's the minimum requirement for intelligent investing and failing to do so means suffering financial agony.

There's nothing wrong with sourcing investment ideas from stock forums or investment newsletters. But you owe it to yourself to conduct proper research before investing, or to really understand the approach used before letting an advisor touch your savings. Failing here means walking into manipulation and

35 Graham, *The Intelligent Investor*, 18.

experiencing painful losses. You never want to blindly invest based on someone else's advice.

How to guard your principal and earn great returns in ultra-cheap stocks

Stocks are no more risky or less promising because they're priced at less than a dollar. If that were true, a reverse stock split could suddenly morph your 'risky' penny stock into a solid low-risk investment opportunity. Similarly, Microsoft's $110 stock would become a risky penny stock if the company conducted a 150:1 stock split. There's more to it than price. Key considerations include the stock's discount to underlying value, how stable that value is, and the firm's future prospects.

Serious bargains exist in the world of ultra-low-priced stocks. Sure, there are a lot of worthless companies trading below $1, but there are also incredibly undervalued firms with great business prospects. Why would it be any other way? Far more tiny businesses are traded on public markets while most investors stick to larger firms. This is an especially fertile hunting ground for deep value investors, since many stocks priced at less than a dollar are attached to larger organisations that have experienced large business problems. Their stocks are often crushed by intense negative sentiment about the company.

Should you consider net-net stocks among these outstanding bargains?

Maybe.

A net-net stock may or may not be a penny stock. It really comes down to the price the stock is trading at. Many net-net stocks trade below a dollar, technically qualifying as penny stocks, while many trade above $1 and avoid that label. In other words, while there can be overlap, penny stocks and net-net stocks are really two distinct classifications.

Whether a stock trades above or below a dollar is irrelevant to your ultimate success or failure as an investor. What matters is the situation you're walking into: whether you're buying shares that are backed by solid value and whether there is a high probability of seeing that value realised. This is the type of situation that Net Net Hunter's Investment Scorecard is designed to identify.

This scorecard has helped me to achieve very large returns since adopting Graham's strategy in 2010. Most of the companies that I've bought have had long histories of profitable operations, have been backed by solid value, and have been conservatively financed. Many have bought back stock, have had activist involvement, or have even been priced under net cash.[36] You can't find this type of bargain when investing in large caps.

It's also helped that I've ignored most of the noise on stock forums, keeping a stubbornly independent mindset. To paraphrase Sir John Templeton's mantra: to do better than the crowd you have to invest differently from the crowd.

My small portfolio size has also helped. As I'll later show you, small investors have a distinct advantage that allows them to beat even gifted professionals, such as Buffett. As a small investor, you can achieve the highest possible returns by seeking out great opportunities in areas of the market that just aren't open to larger investors. Luckily for us, large investors simply can't purchase many of these stocks. That's why this investment niche is still open to you today.

---

36 Net cash refers to cash and cash equivalents less all liabilities, off-balance-sheet liabilities, and preferred equity. Buying a company for less than net cash essentially means being paid to take stock in the company.

PART 2

THE EVIDENCE THAT NET–NET INVESTING WORKS

7

Eight Lessons from Exceptional Net–Net Stock Studies

Selecting a strategy is one of the most important investment decisions an investor has to make. It's a key component of investing rationally because it determines the types of decisions an investor should make, from where to hunt for stocks to how to assess them once found.

The first step in rational strategy selection is referring to academic, scholarly, or industry research to determine which approaches have shown good results in the past. Relying on data rather than subjective experience or investor opinions is akin to laying a firm foundation under a house. Strong empirical evidence that your chosen strategy actually works provides a solid basis on which to make smart investment decisions. Investors who ignore this firm foundation often end up relying on luck or hearsay or attempting to replicate the behaviour of those who have exceptionally rare talent.

Only a few investment strategies have a strong history of serious outperformance, according to academic studies, making them unusually solid candidates. Investors should be on the lookout for a long record of outperformance that stretches back over many decades and returns large enough to make pursuing the strategy worth their time. If a strategy barely edges out the market, on average, investment mistakes when employing such a strategy will likely erode returns, possibly wiping out any excess performance.

Once investors are convinced that a strategy shows great past performance, it's vital that they find evidence of successful practical application. It's one thing for academic studies to show that an approach produces returns far ahead of the market, but quite another to show that the strategy can be used successfully by investors. Both are vitally important. Some strategies with solid showings in academic papers may ultimately prove too difficult to employ in real life, making them worthless. More on this in the following chapters.

The empirical case for adopting Graham's net-nets

I have spent a few years collecting academic and industry studies assessing net-net stocks. Incredibly, while I have specifically sought disconfirming studies, I've only found one that fails to find significant outperformance. Every other study, 14 in total, has shown that Graham's strategy significantly outperforms major market indices.

As a reader, you should be immediately sceptical. Given the thousands of papers published each year, Graham's notoriety in the investment world, and how seemingly difficult it is to beat the market, there should be a number of research papers showing that the strategy doesn't work. Researcher bias can't explain the phenomenon either. Academia is notoriously harsh towards claims that any particular strategy can outperform the indices over the long term. Each year, thousands of college professors in badly fitting dress shirts lecture their students on market efficiency. A good number of these professors write papers, many critical of the ability of stock pickers to add value. If the strategy doesn't work, researchers should have produced a body of disconfirming evidence.

Given this solid backing, what exactly do the studies reveal?

Note: All the studies present returns to equally weighted portfolios net of fees and taxes unless otherwise specified. While investors' tax treatment varies depending on their jurisdiction, trading fees have become extremely low, making them a trivial concern. Today, it's even possible to buy thousands of dollars' worth of illiquid foreign stock for just a few dollars in fees.

While Graham tested the strategy through the 1930s, the bulk of the academic and industry research covers the most recent 40 years, from 1970 to 2010. The studies I've collected have been written by 26 researchers from seven different countries located on four separate continents. The 15 papers run the gauntlet in terms of market or economic conditions, from extremely troubled periods such as the 1970s to the strong bull markets experienced in the mid 2000s. This body of work provides a solid understanding of how the strategy performs over the long term versus various benchmark indices.

Large outperformance versus American markets

In this section, we'll take a look at a handful of studies examining the returns of American net-nets purchased below NCAV and provide clear, yearly, return figures. Some studies test portfolios of stocks bought above NCAV. While these contain important information, the immediate focus is on the performance of net-nets trading below NCAV. I further cover variant studies below. While all net-net studies include performance figures, some only report monthly returns. They are therefore not as suitable for highlighting how an investor would fare by running the strategy over the long term. But because they still provide valuable insights, we'll take a look at them shortly.

Ten years after Graham's death, a young associate professor of finance asked how investors would have fared investing in net-nets through the 1970s and early 1980s. Henry Oppenheimer's 1986 study pitted a basket of US net-nets trading at two-thirds of NCAV, or less, against stocks on the Security Owners Guide, AMEX, and NYSE, and traded over the counter.[37] He modelled his study on the behaviour of a hypothetical investor who accessed the securities guide on 10 December each year before forming his portfolios on the thirty-first. The study stretched over 13 years, from 1970 to 1983, and included the 1973 oil shock, the 1974 to 1981 recovery, and the 1981 to 1982 US recession. Far from a rosy period for investors, stocks spent most of their time trading well below their early 1970 high. Incredibly, net-nets returned a compound annual growth rate of 28.2% in contrast to the Small Firm Index's[38] 19.6%, excluding dividends.[39] (Oppenheimer's study accounted for look-ahead bias but not slippage.)

Joseph Vu confirmed the exceptional record of net-net stocks in his 1988 study.[40] Vu shifted methodology to include all net-nets trading from 1977 to 1984, a total of 107 NYSE or AMEX stocks taken from *The Value Line Investment Survey*. He formed portfolios at the end of the month in which a stock dipped below NCAV and then held those stocks for 24 months. As with Oppenheimer's original study, results were fantastic. Vu's net-nets returned 38.5% at the end of 12 months versus 15.4% for NYSE and Amex firms in general.

But Vu sensed that something was a bit off about his study's performance. He suspected that the returns he demonstrated were due to the greater returns attributable to investing in small firms, known as the small firm effect. In a follow-up study, he split the control group into smaller firms for a more direct comparison

---

37 Oppenheimer, 'Ben Graham's NCAVs'.
38 The full name of the index mentioned in the paper is the Ibbotson and Sinquefield Small-Firm Index.
39 Oppenheimer, 'Ben Graham's NCAVs'.
40 Vu, 'An Empirical Analysis of Ben Graham's NCAV Rule'.

and failed to find any upside for investing in net-nets.[41] Vu's size-controlled study remains the one black spot on the otherwise exemplary record of net-net stocks. I would advise new net-net investors against ditching Graham's strategy to simply buy tiny firms instead. Later studies found that Oppenheimer's results couldn't be explained by firm size alone.

One such study took place in 2010. Jeffrey Oxman, Sunil Mohanty, and Tobias Carlisle adopted Oppenheimer's methodology to extend his study from 1983 to 2008, a period of 25 years.[42] The team tracked performance against NYSE-Amex firms and The Small Firms Index. In his excellent book *Deep Value,* Carlisle reports that net-nets provided an average yearly return of 35.3% against The Small Firm Index's 18.4% average.[43] Investors should note that Oxman et al.'s study calculated average yearly returns rather than compound annual returns, which would have been somewhat lower. This outstanding performance is, however, consistent with Oppenheimer's original study and much better than those achieved by using Carlisle's The Acquirer's Multiple strategy. Oxman et al. later used the Fama-French three-factor model to compare net-nets against like-sized firms and found that the small firm effect did explain some, but not all, of the excess returns associated with net-net stocks. According to the team, net-nets still produced a compound annual return of 21.99% after controlling for the small firm effect, among other variables.

Oppenheimer and Oxman et al.'s studies provide a very solid overview of net-net performance over 38 years. Another look at net-net stocks was published by James Montier at The Société Générale Group. Montier, the only financial professional to ever wear a Hawaiian T-shirt in a professional business photo, tested baskets of global net-nets trading at two-thirds of NCAV or less.[44] His study ran from 1985 to 2007, and while he's kept mum on its structure, he found that net-nets located globally produced an average yearly return of 35% over the 22-year period versus 17% for global stocks. American net-nets had the highest outperformance, with a market-adjusted return of roughly 18.5%.[45] Again, Montier provides readers with an average yearly return rather than a compound annual growth rate. Despite the 35% returns cited in both Oxman et al.'s and Montier's studies, net-net investors should expect a somewhat lower compound annual growth rate.

---

41 Ibid.

42 Oxman, Mohanty and Carlisle, 'Deep Value Investing', Midwest Finance Association 2012 Annual Meetings Paper.

43 Carlisle, *Deep Value,* 26.

44 Montier, 'Graham's Net-Nets'.

45 Readers should view a market-adjusted return as the amount of excess return stock on top of the market. When the market returns 10%, for example, a 4% market-adjusted return means the test portfolio returned 14%. In this case, that 14% is subtracted (adjusted) by the market return to arrive at the excess performance.

Lesson 1: American net-nets beat the market by a wide margin over the long-term. Investors can reasonably expect a 15% yearly market-adjusted return on average when investing over a large number of years.

Despite the single blemish, all four of these studies provide a solid overview of American net-nets. As Graham taught, years ago, simply buying baskets of net-net stocks and holding them can produce excellent market-beating returns. But as we've seen, there's a catch.

Net-net stock availability: from year to year and country to country

Near the end of section two, we discussed why so many people avoid buying net-net stocks when they've proven so powerful as investments. Probably the single biggest reason comes down to the mistaken belief that net-nets no longer exist. While obviously false, the misperception touches on a bit of reality.

In *The Intelligent Investor*, Graham mentions that net-net stocks were plentiful in the first half of his career but became scarce in the late 1950s and 1960s.[46] Research since his death has provided clear insight into the availability of net-net stocks during various periods in the market cycle. What these studies find echoes Graham's observation years ago:

> "True, bargain issues have repeatedly become scarce in bull markets, but that was not because all the analysts became value-conscious, but because of the general upswing in prices. (Perhaps one could even have determined whether the market level was getting too high or too low by counting the number of issues selling below working capital value.)"[47]

The best of the recent studies comes back to James Montier. In 'Graham's Net-Nets: Outdated or Outstanding?', Montier presents the number of stocks trading below NCAV globally.[48] As we can see in figure 1, the number of firms trading as net-nets globally from 1986 to mid-2008 varied considerably. An investor would have struggled to find any in 1986, but was offered a very large group between 2001 and 2005, but they then dropped significantly in number until the 2008

---

46 Graham, *The Intelligent Investor*, 390.
47 Graham, 'The Decade'.
48 Montier, 'Graham's Net-Nets'.

NASDAQ meltdown caused their numbers to again surge.[49] The year 2003 saw the greatest number of net-nets since 1986, with just over 600 opportunities available internationally.

Fig. 1: Number of stocks trading as net-nets globally, 1986–2008

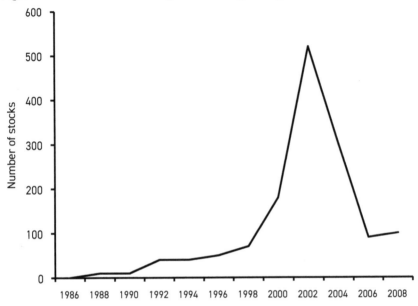

Source: SG Equity Research.

Taking a step back to look at the chart in its entirety, it's clear that Graham's earlier observations were correct. Net-nets all but disappeared during good economic periods but came back with a vengeance during market turmoil. Looking at the graph again, we see clear upticks during the 1991, 2002–2003, and 2008–2009 recessions. Similarly, Oppenheimer found the greatest number of net-nets between 1973 and 1979, a period of economic distress for Western countries,[50] while, Oxman et al., report US net-net availability closely aligned to Montier's chart.[51] Ultimately,

---

49 At the time of writing in 2019, we count roughly 600 statistical net-nets listed on www. netnethunter.com. It's incredible that even today, some 90 years after Graham first wrote about the strategy in the popular press, so many net-nets are available if an investor just looks for them. The catch, as mentioned elsewhere in this book, is that net-net firms today are tiny in terms of market capitalization and fairly illiquid, so out of reach for most larger investors. The fact that so few small investors know of the strategy, and that large investors can't buy these stocks, keeps the strategy available for Graham's enterprising investors.

50 Oppenheimer, 'Ben Graham's NCAVs'.

51 Oxman, Mohanty and Carlisle, 'Deep Value Investing'.

lower market valuations mean cheaper stocks and therefore a greater number of net-nets.

Given the extremely conservative valuation, it shouldn't be surprising that net-nets are only available among the lowest rungs of the market-cap ladder when they can be found at all. Montier reports that the median market capitalisation in 2008 was $21 million ($24.62 million in 2018 dollars) and the average market capitalisation, $124 million ($145.39 million in 2018).[52] With such a gulf between the average and median figures, it's clear that most net-nets are tiny and a limited number of giants really pull up the average. Most studies that report market capitalisation fall in line with these figures, with Vu reporting an average market cap of $51.3 million in 1988 ($109.47 in 2018),[53] and Dudzinski and Kunkel highlighting an average market cap of $174 million in 2014 after screening out firms smaller than $20 million.[54] With firm size this small, it's clear that net-net investing is only for tiny investors.

Fig. 2: Geographical source of net-nets in 2008 according to James Montier

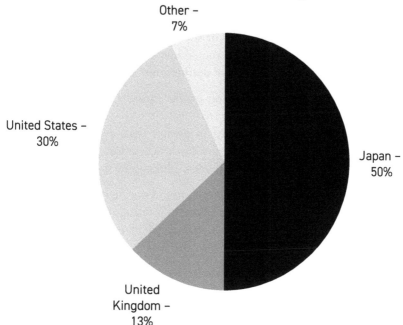

Source: SG Equity research.

52 Montier, 'Graham's Net-Nets'.
53 Vu, 'An Empirical Analysis'.
54 Dudzinski and Kunkel, 'Benjamin Graham's NCAV'.

While net-nets are tiny firms, they're mostly found in larger markets. In 2008, Montier found that most net-nets were concentrated in Japan, with the USA being a close second. This makes intuitive sense. Larger populations generally produce more instances of extreme outcomes, no matter what's being measured. Larger stock markets, then, are likely to produce both a greater number of extremely expensive and extremely cheap securities. Since net-nets are outliers, dirt-cheap firms priced below liquidation value, they're more likely to be found in larger markets. What's interesting was the prevalence Montier found when comparing the USA and Japan. While the overall US market is much larger, the overall Japanese market is much cheaper on a book value basis. According to *Forbes*, the Japanese market hit a fire sale valuation in 2011, at 1.1× book value. The ratio was even lower at the end of 2008, dropping to 0.9×. At that price, most of Japan's companies were trading below net asset value.[55]

Lesson 2: Net-nets are more available during periods of cheaper market valuation than when the market is on a tear; and more available in larger markets than in smaller markets.

Should investors invest internationally or stick with domestic stocks? Given the enormous number of Japanese net-nets, should investors dip their toes into Eastern markets? How about other international destinations? Did Ben Graham travel?

Value investing's core philosophy is built on the idea that investors should buy businesses for less than they're worth, that over time the excess value captured through bargain prices will be realised in greater-than-average profits. What matters is business value, not market moves or price action. So long as intrinsic business values differ from their quoted market values, value should work its magic.

Given the small number of American net-nets found during red hot market cycles, this question is critically important for anybody wanting to employ the strategy long-term. Over time, investors are likely to find opportunities dry up in any one market.

Is it possible to shift focus to overseas companies to continue the strategy?

Yes. A growing number of researchers have turned to assessing Graham's net-nets on their home turf, with great results. Not only do net-net stocks beat the market internationally but their returns closely mirror those experienced in the USA.

Japan is an odd place to start. It's incredibly rich society is thousands of years old, and very different from that of the USA. Despite being highly modern, both the business culture and the Japanese language are completely alien to many Westerners. Most outsiders don't even realise that Japan has its own calendar and

---

55 Harner, 'Whither Japan Stocks', *Forbes* (20 June 2011).

accounting systems, which makes it abnormally difficult to navigate the corporate world, let alone communicate. But like the rest of the developed world, Japan has well-functioning capital markets with a strong rule of law and minority shareholder rights. This makes it at least a viable place to invest. Does net-net investing work here as well?

Apparently so. In 1993, John Buildersee, John Cheh, and Ajay Zutshi published a study looking at the performance of Japanese net-nets from April 1975 to March 1988, a period of 12 years. Since they found comparatively few net-nets at the time, they tested firms with positive NCAV – that is, they didn't require a discount-to-liquidation value. Amazingly, even without a discount, firms with positive NCAV still beat the market each and every year. Positive risk-adjusted returns ranged from 0.5% to 1% per month. The team did find, however, that the greater the discount to NCAV, the better the stocks tended to perform. Apparently, Graham's net-net stock strategy is a viable way for Japanese investors to beat the market over the long term.

Montier thinks so, as well. In his 2010 study, Montier included both Japanese and European net-net returns alongside the performance of American net-net stocks.[56] While the average yearly performance of Japanese net-nets didn't keep up with those in the USA, they did outperform the Japanese index to nearly the same degree as net-nets do in the USA. Montier reported US net-net outperformance of 18% versus 15% for net-nets in Japan. (In other words, if each respective market had returned 10%, American net-nets would have returned 28% while Japanese net-nets would have returned 25%.)

According to Montier, European net-net stocks had the lowest outperformance of the three overall markets, outperforming the index by just 6% per year. While net-nets still beat the market in Europe, investors would have been better off sticking to the US or Japanese markets.

The story doesn't end there. In 2010, Philip Vanstraceele and Luc Allaeys published an industry white paper that looked at net-net stocks in the Eurozone from 1999 to 2009, excluding financial and insurance companies.[57] The team put net-nets trading at a minimum one-third discount to NCAV into equally weighted portfolios and then ran the simulation against the Dow Jones Euro Stoxx index. They repeated this process, varying the market-cap cut-off to see the impact on returns. While returns for the index were a negative –3.13% over the period, the team's net-nets returned a compound, average, annual-growth rate of between –1.55 and +13.44%, depending on the market-cap restriction. Assuming investors stuck to companies

---

56 Montier, 'Graham's Net-Nets'.

57 Vanstraceele and Allaeys, 'Studying Different Systematic Value Investing Strategies', valueinvesting.eu (May 2010).

with market caps of less than $100 million, investors would have seen a 10.48% to 13.44% CAGR while the market slid. More on the effects of market caps below.

The UK is a close cousin of the USA in terms of culture and business practice. Like the USA, it has well-functioning (and generally, free) markets, a strong rule of law, low levels of corruption, and a Protestant work ethic. Given the cultural similarities between the UK and many former British colonies, it should be no surprise that net-nets work as well in London as they do in New York.

In 2008, Ying Xiao and Glen Arnold published a study analysing the performance of Graham's net-nets on the London Stock Exchange.[58] The study covered 25 years, from 1980 to 2005, and included net-nets with a proper minimum one-third discount. The team also rejected regulated firms, financial firms, and firms with multi-share structures. They were left with 90% of the database intact, of which 2% of companies qualified as net-nets, which they fitted into equally weighted stock portfolios. The results were impressive: net-nets achieved a compound annual return of 31.19% versus the index's 20.51% return. The pair had even biased the sample towards lower returns, since they elected to wait six months after financials were published before fitting them into a portfolio.

So far, we've only discussed returns for modern first-world countries. Investors generally feel it's safer to invest in these locations because developed nations have a stronger rule of law and history of sound capitalist institutions. To put it more bluntly, investors often consider first-world markets more trustworthy. But it seldom pays to stick with the crowd when it comes to investing.

What happens when net-net investors venture further afield?

Two emerging market studies may have the answer. The first looks at the performance of Saudi Arabian net-nets from 2000 up to and including 2011. In the study, Nadisah Zakaria and Fariza Hashim found between 23 and 24 companies trading below NCAV in any given year, admittedly a small sample size.[59] Despite the study's handicap, the pair reported market outperformance of around 20%. That is, Arabian net-net investors would have seen roughly a 20% market-adjusted return.

This performance was dwarfed by Indian investors from 1996 to 2010. In their study of the Indian stock market,[60] Jaspal Singh and Kiranpreet Kaur found that buying properly discounted net-nets and fitting them into an equally weighted portfolio would have produced an average yearly 59.54% return! This equates to a 37.87% CAGR. While the study suffered from the same small-sample-size problem

58 Xiao and Arnold, 'Testing Ben Graham's NCAV Strategy'.
59 Zakaria and Hashim, 'Emerging Markets: Evaluating Graham's Stock Selection Criteria'.
60 Singh and Kaur, 'Testing the Performance of Graham's NCAV Strategy in Indian Stock Market'.

as the Saudi Arabian study, the best performance was seen in years that included the greatest number of stocks.

Lesson 3: Yes, international net-net investing works, and works well. Returns are comparable with returns in the USA, if not better.

Looking at this body of evidence, it's clear that Graham's net-net stock strategy works very well for international investors. This performance record means that investors should be more willing to look abroad if they can't find any cheap net-nets in their own backyard.

Net-net stock performance varies from year to year

Another often overlooked piece of the big picture puzzle has to do with yearly performance. As discussed previously, many new net-net stock investors assume that a net-net stock portfolio produces great returns year-in, year-out, like clockwork. Unfortunately, that's just not true. A net-net portfolio can produce a range of returns in any given year, and no study shows this better than Oppenheimer's 1986 study 'Ben Graham's NCAVs: A Performance Update'.

Fig. 3: Oppenheimer: American NCAV stocks vs the Small Firm Index year by year, 1970–1982

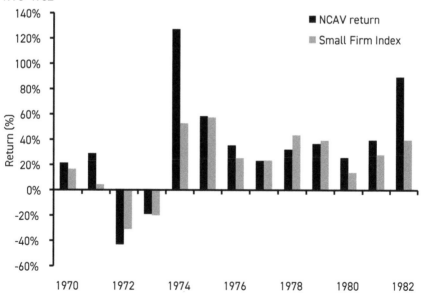

Source: Henry Oppenheimer, 'Ben Graham's NCAVs: A Performance Update', *Financial Analysts Journal* 42:6 (November–December 1986): 40–47.

Oppenheimer's study spanned 13 years, from 1970 to 1983. At the end of the period, Oppenheimer listed the yearly performance that net-net investors would have experienced if they had been along for the financial ride. Rather than a smooth sequence of great returns over that period, performance tended to bounce around. Investors would have experienced positive returns in the majority of years invested but would have only beaten the market in nine of those 13 years – 69% of the time. And in two years, the investors of Oppenheimer's study would have actually lost money. Still, this performance was enough to achieve a 28.45% compound annual growth rate. Much of the portfolio's great market-beating returns over the period came in just two years, 1974 and 1982, highlighting the need for a long-term commitment to the strategy.

Looking closer at the track record, it's clear that the small number of years studied were responsible for the portfolio's outperformance. Investors who missed just two of these years, 1974 and 1982, would have seen their compound return drop from 28.2% to 14.8%, underperforming the Small Cap Index. Since it's very difficult to know when these extraordinary returns will surface, Oppenheimer's findings are a good argument for remaining fully invested at all times.

Oppenheimer was far from the only researcher to stumble onto this rocky performance. In their 2008 study,[61] Ying Xiao and Glen Arnold looked at net-net returns from 1980 to 2005 and found that these bargain stocks underperformed the market 20 to 25% of the time when held for a five-year period. A shorter holding period seems to have improved performance for Oxman et al. in their 2011 study.[62] According to that team, net-nets held for 2.5 years beat NYSE-Amex firms 88% of the time from 1984 to 2008. While they had an excellent showing, net-nets still fell short of a perfect score.

Similarly, Joseph Goebel and Manoj Athavale found that a net-net portfolio saw a greater number of money-losing years, with positive returns in 25 of 37 years versus 31 of 37 years for non-net-nets.[63] While this 67.5% win rate is lower than in Oppenheimer's study, Goebel and Athavale's net-nets also had a greater number of outstanding years: 14 years of 30% or greater returns versus just six years for non-net-nets.

Lesson 4: Net-net stocks beat the market by a wider margin over time, not each year. Investors should expect moderate performance most years, with a few years of outstanding returns. Investors should also expect to underperform the market on occasion but rarely see negative portfolio returns. Because of this variance in yearly returns, investors have to be fully invested at all times for the best returns.

61 Xiao and Arnold, 'Testing Ben Graham's NCAV Strategy in London'.
62 Oxman, Mohanty, and Carlisle, 'Deep Value Investing'.
63 Goebel and Athavale, 'The Persistence of NCAV Stock Selection Criterion'.

Even a passive skimming of the literature makes something very clear: anybody who decides to adopt a net-net stock strategy has to be in it for the long haul to be assured of excellent performance.

Holding period has a large impact on returns

One of the least considered pieces of portfolio policy is the length of the holding period. Value investors typically assume that prices will revert to fair value quickly, or they become fed up and dump their holdings. Others are prepared to wait indefinitely for their stock to rise back to fair value. While either of these approaches may be appropriate in the right circumstance, academic studies provide clear guidance for net-net stock investors.

For investors managing a mechanical net-net stock portfolio, a strategy that applies predetermined buy and sell rules, investors will perform much better if they keep their holding periods as close to 12 months as possible. This does not mean replacing all of the stocks in the portfolio at the one-year mark, but combing through the list every 12 months to make sure picks still meet selection criteria and replace them if necessary. The longer you wait past 12 months to assess your past picks, the lower the compound annual rate of growth when running a mechanical portfolio.[64]

Part of this is probably due to shifting financials. All companies go through changes throughout the course of a year. Over those months, it's possible for a company to take on more debt or spend its cash on foolish acquisitions, destroying NCAV. In other cases, working capital can simply be used up, impairing liquidation value from a net-net perspective. Another reason may be that stock price appreciation slows after a stock rises back to NCAV per share. Whatever the reason, the data shows that investors have to shift to thinking more about their portfolios.

The drop in performance seen for longer holding periods can be pronounced. Joseph Goebel and Manoj Athavale varied holding period length by 12, 24, 36, 48,

---

64 Note that while mechanical investors will want to stick to a holding period close to 12 months, investors who focus on more qualitative measures, such as the growth of a new business division or upcoming catalyst, will often want to hold their net-net stocks long enough to see these factors play out. Net-nets typically only show promise as quantitative bargains, but in the rare case where an investor finds that the company has strong business prospects, holding on to the stock in order to realize those business improvements can lead to tremendous returns. Identifying net-nets that are likely to see significant business improvement requires significant business skill and experience (or what Charlie Munger refers to as "worldly wisdom") so it's much easier to stick to a quantitative framework. It's important to know the net-net investing approach you want to take before you start buying net-nets because it will inform your sell strategy.

and 60 months.[65] The pair found that returns dropped steadily with each year that passed, with portfolios reporting a 32.8% return after 12 months, to a compound annual growth rate of just 20.64% after 60 months. Holding on to a basket of net-nets from 12 to 60 months dropped the compound rate of return by –37%! Goebel reports that about 22% of firms were delisted before hitting the 60-month mark, and many of these suffered a –55% loss. In comparison, only between 2 and 3% of firms were delisted during the first 12 months. These delistings would have pushed down returns for longer holding periods.

Goebel and Athavale state that other research indicates the average loss of delisted stocks is –55%. If the pair couldn't find the delisting return reported by the University of Chicago's Center for Research in Security Prices (CRSP), they would apply a blanket –55% drop in price. While some firms were taken over through mergers, most were dropped from an index. Investors should keep in mind that losses due to firms being dropped from an index has not been my experience. In fact, firms trading over the counter still provide good net-net stock returns.

Xiao and Arnold also found lower returns for longer holding periods. In their study, net-nets returned 31.19% versus the market's 20.51% during the first year, and 254.02% versus 137.18% after 60 months.[66] The longer holding period works out to a CAGR of 20.49% for net-nets – again, quite a drop! Similarly, the pair experienced a large number of delistings throughout the longer hold periods. Unlike Goebel and Athavale, however, Xiao and Arnold saw many delisted net-nets with a –100% return. While this sounds ominous, keep in mind that the general market saw more delistings than did net-net portfolios during the period: 31.57% to the net-net's 26.82% drop rate.

These findings are consistent with Tweedy, Browne's study.[67] They report holding period returns of 28.8%, 53.5%, and 87.6% for periods of 12, 24 and 36 months. An 87.6% return is equivalent to a CAGR of 23.33%. While they're thin on details, one thing is clear: holding a portfolio of net-net stocks for a longer period of time is generally poor investment practice.

How about shorter periods?

Tweedy, Browne also reports six-month returns for a basket of net-net stocks.[68] According to the firm, a six-month holding period is associated with a tiny 3.4% return. This mirrors my own experience in investing at Net Net Hunter. My stock selections often drop after initial purchase, before rising back to produce good returns.

---

65 Ibid.
66 Xiao and Arnold, 'Testing Ben Graham's NCAV in London'.
67 Tweedy, Browne, 'What Has Worked In Investing', tweedy.com (2009).
68 Ibid.

Lesson 5: Shorter holding periods are associated with higher compound annual returns. Holding on to net-nets for too long can completely eliminate excess return. If you're aiming for the highest-returning mechanical net-net stock strategy, keeping a 12-month holding period in mind is vital.[69]

A team effort or a couple of star players?

New investors often mistakenly think that employing a high performance strategy means that every single stock they pick using that strategy will be a winner. This is dangerous thinking because investors who hold misguided expectations run the risk of becoming disillusioned and then abandoning the strategy, forfeiting decades of outstanding returns.

There is not as much data covering net-net stock performance within portfolios as there is for the performance of entire portfolios generally. But what is available is instructive. Net Net Hunter members generally refer to the percentage of winning stocks within a portfolio as the portfolio's or investor's win rate, and express this rate as a percentage. Dudzinski and Kunkel do a decent job of breaking down win rates for each year studied.[70] According to the researchers, roughly 67% of all net-nets identified over the period provided a positive return for investors. The best performance, of course, was seen during years with positive market returns, with 77.7% of net-nets providing positive returns. During 2008 and 2009, a period dominated by the Great Financial Crisis, only 33.5% of net-nets produced gains.

Montier provides further insight in his study.[71] While Montier doesn't discuss win rate, he does mention that roughly 5% of net-nets suffer a loss of –90% or greater during his study period, versus 2% of stocks in general. Investors running mechanical net-net stock strategies have to expect some big losers and should prepare accordingly, but not many more than the overall market.

---

69 While a 12 month holding period is beneficial for maximizing returns for a quantitative strategy, don't make the mistake in assuming that each and every 12 month period will produce good results. Just as the net-net stocks within your portfolio will vary in their return, yearly performance will also vary. Most of the performance benefits derived from the net-net approach are achieved in a small handful of years. Miss those years and you'll miss the bulk of the strategy's outperformance. While initially an investor may want to "just invest in net-nets during the good years", this strategy is highly impractical because it's next to impossible to identify those great years in advance. Therefore, an investor needs diversification in terms of both the number of stocks in his or her portfolio, and the number of years employing the strategy. I recommend sticking with the strategy for at least ten years to ensure you receive the performance benefits the strategy provides.

70 Dudzinski and Kunkel, 'Benjamin Graham's NCAV'.

71 Montier, 'Graham's Net-Nets'.

Lesson 6: Investors should expect to have a mix of winners and losers in their portfolio each and every year. The number of stocks that provide a positive return is largest during bull markets, while the number of net-nets suffering losses is largest when the market drops.

It is possible to increase the number of winners in your portfolio, as you'll see later. But for now, it's important to recognise just how important diversification is. Both studies highlighted here show how misguided it is to buy and hold only a couple net-nets to test out the strategy. Even during a good year, it's possible for any net-net you pick to perform badly, possibly destroying all of your invested capital. Diversification is a must.

Do deeper discounts mean better returns?

Value investors naturally assume a deeper discount will lead to a better return, which is why so many people are focused on trying to buy a dollar for fifty cents. When it comes to net-nets, the relationship between the size of the discount and the expected return is a little more complicated.

Early studies show that deeper discounts have a fairly pronounced impact on stock returns. In 1981, Greenblatt, Pzena, and Newberg looked at net-net returns from 1972 to 1978.[72] The group split stocks into four portfolios based on strict or loose price-to-earnings (PE) requirements, and stocks trading below 100% or 85% of NCAV. When controlling for PE ratios, stocks with the deeper discounts produced higher returns. The study seems to be flawed methodologically, however, as explained ahead.

Table 3: The performance of Greenblatt and Pzena's net-net stock performance grouped by varying NCAV and PE discounts, early to mid-1970s

	Portfolio 1	Portfolio 2	Portfolio 3	Portfolio 4
PE Ratio	>2× AAA Yield	>2× AAA Yield	<5×	<5×
P/NCAV	<0.85	<1	<1	<0.85
Return	20%	27.1%	32.2%	42.2%

Source: Greenblatt, Pzena and Newberg, 'How the Small Investor Can Beat the Market'.

This relationship was backed up in 1986 by Henry Oppenheimer. He wrote, "The conclusion is clear-cut. Returns and excess returns can be rank-ordered, with securities having the smallest purchase price as a percentage of net asset value having the largest returns. It appears that degree of undervaluation is important: The difference in both mean return and risk-adjusted return between quintiles 1

72 Greenblatt, Pzena and Newberg, 'How the Small Investor Can Beat the Market', *The Journal of Portfolio Management* 7:4 (1981), 48–52.

and 5 is over 10 per cent per year."[73] Oppenheimer's quintiles show that firms with the deepest discounts to NCAV had average monthly returns of 2.95% versus the market's 0.96%, while those with the shallowest discounts had returns of just 1.88%.

More recent studies, however, have found a much weaker correlation between deeper discounts and better portfolio returns. Oxman and his team found that deeper discounts were loosely correlated with higher returns, but the excess returns could not be rank ordered.[74] After splitting net-nets into five groups, they found that quintiles 2 and 3 tended to produce the highest returns, the cheapest net-nets in quintile 1 produced the worst returns of the group. This finding is unsettling for value investors who believe in buying stocks at a larger discount to some measure of value.

Complicating matters further are studies that purport to show great returns even if a net-net isn't trading at a minimum one-third discount. Beni Lauterbach's and Joseph Vu's study is just one example.[75] In 1993, they found that stocks trading for less than 100% of NCAV from 1977 to 1983 produced a 14% market-adjusted return. Likewise, Xiao and Arnold's British net-nets, which had an average price to NCAV of 145%, beat the index over all holding periods.[76] Most notable were the team's 12-month holdings, which saw a 31.19% return against their benchmark's 20.51% return. And further afoot, Zakaria and Hashim's Arabian study shows excess returns of 20.17%. Clearly, just being close to NCAV is enough to drive large excess portfolio returns.

To further complicate an already complicated matter, net-net studies are not directly comparable, since each is conducted over a different period of time, often in different markets, using slightly different criteria, and employing somewhat different test procedures. The best we can gather from the data here is that – yes – just being close to NCAV is enough for great returns, while better performance may be achieved by demanding deeper discounts.

Lesson 7: Just having positive NCAV is a benefit. But larger discounts to NCAV are still associated with larger returns.

If deeper discounts aren't strongly correlated with higher returns, are there any factors that really boost performance?

Apparently so.

---

73 Oppenheimer,'Ben Graham's NCAVs'.
74 Oxman, Mohanty, and Carlisle, 'Deep Value Investing'.
75 Vu, 'An Empirical Analysis of Ben Graham's NCAV Rule'.
76 Xiao and Arnold, 'Testing Ben Graham's NCAV in London'.

Alternative characteristics associated with higher performance as a group

To start off, we have to go all the way back to Oppenheimer's fantastic study of net-nets in the 1970s and 1980s. Oppenheimer's study is a great resource partly because of his inquisitive nature. Rather than just test a plain-vanilla basket of net-nets and then report his findings, he split his stocks into multiple sub-groups to see if he could find interesting correlations.

Oppenheimer tested the effect that dividends and profitability have on net-net stock returns.[77] Most investors would expect net-nets with positive earnings that are paying a healthy dividend to provide the best stock returns. Incredibly, however, these stocks produced an average monthly return of 2.01%, the worst in Oppenheimer's study. Avoiding dividend payments boosted monthly returns by 44%, to an average monthly return of 2.88%. Money-losing firms trailed behind with an average monthly return of 2.61%.

Far from just a one-off, the negative effect of dividend payments has been reported by a few net-net studies. Oxman et al. found that dividend-paying firms with positive earnings provided even lower returns, at a monthly average of 1.48%. Skipping dividend payments allowed money-making firms to achieve an average monthly return of 2.42%, but the best-returning stocks were actually those of money-losing corporations, which returned 3.38%. Based on these two studies, the data is clear: investors who avoid dividend-paying net-nets should have the best returns.

The mixed results for profitable firms trading below NCAV confuses many investors; we all intuitively feel that better companies provide better returns. One issue with the above studies are their failure to split profitable companies with significant earnings from those with token profitability. It's more likely that firms trading below NCAV with significant earnings are better businesses and significantly mispriced, while those with thin earnings are likely poorer-quality businesses or firms suffering larger business problems. It seems intuitively plausible, but by no means certain, that picking those few gems would boost returns.

As we saw in the discussion on varying discounts, modern superinvestor Joel Greenblatt was researching a far more powerful magic formula long before *The Little Book that Beats the Market* – namely, Graham's net-nets. Greenblatt's approach was to form a set of four portfolios grouped according to PE ratio and discount to NCAV. Greenblatt split stocks into those trading at a PE equivalent of two times the AAA bond yield or lower and stocks that met an even stricter 5× cut

---

77 Oppenheimer, 'Ben Graham's NCAVs'.

off.[78] When controlling for discount to NCAV, the portfolio with more strict PE requirements strongly outperformed the portfolio with more lax PE requirements: 20% to 32.2% for firms without a discount, and 27.1% to 42.2% for firms with a moderate discount.[79]

That final number is a staggering average return. But investors should resist over-optimism based on a single dataset. Greenblatt et al. compared portfolio returns without having each portfolio fully invested at the same point in time. Some portfolios sat in cash as the market dropped, and then began adding stocks as they became available during the market trough. Portfolios invested earlier would have seen a period of poor performance as those invested later would have bypassed this poor performance, yet benefited from the market rebound along with all other strategies. This is enough to call Greenblatt's reported relative performance into question. We simply can't conclude that the Greenblatt's criteria showed outperformance relative to all other net-nets due to this discrepancy. Later studies found that money-losing companies trading below NCAV provided investors with superior performance.

While an investor may sit in cash and then get lucky, entering the market at the bottom, staying fully invested seems to be best practice when investing in net-nets. At best, we can say that Greenblatt et al. provide us with an interesting study that needs a lot more examination.

While neither Oppenheimer nor Greenblatt et al. split firms into different-sized cohorts, other studies have found a strong relationship between firm size and portfolio return. While a small handful of massive companies trade below NCAV on occasion, these firms seem to offer no advantage to net-net investors.

One of the most clear-cut cases is presented in Vanstraceele and Allaeys's 2010 study of European net-nets, with portfolio performance dropping massively as average firm size increased.[80] While the smallest market caps – €25 million or smaller – produced market-adjusted 16.57% CAGR, increasing the market-cap limit to €5 billion destroyed returns, producing a market-adjusted CAGR of just 1.58%. Given how few large companies trade as net-nets, those in the study must have produced horrific returns to drag down returns by such an extent. Firms with market capitalisations below €100 still showed a healthy 13.61% return.

---

78 PEs can be flipped around to form earnings yields which can then be compared to the yields of other financial assets. To find the earnings yield, an investor simply divides 1 by the PE ratio. Here, Greenblatt et al. require an earnings yield that is at least twice as large as the AAA bond yield. For example, if the AAA bond yield is 7%, the team requires an earnings yield of 14% or higher, equating to a PE of less than 7.14×.

79 Greenblatt et al., 'How the Small Investor Can Beat the Market'.

80 Vanstraceele and Allaeys, 'Studying Different Systematic Value Investing Strategies'.

Table 4: Vanstraceele and Allaeys's net-net 20-stock portfolio market-adjusted returns ordered by market capitalisation limit, 1999–2009

Market Cap	25	50	100	250	500	1000	2000	5000
20 stock portfolio market adjusted CAGR	16.57%	15.37%	13.61%	14.19%	10.36%	10.27%	9.3%	1.58%

Source: 'Studying Different Systematic Value Investing Strategies'[81]

These findings echoed results found in Xiao and Arnold's 2008 study[82] which split UK stocks trading below NCAV from 1980 to 2005 into deciles based on size. Again, there was a strong relationship between firm size and average return, with the smallest decile returning an average 30.6% per year and the largest decile returning a much lower 17.17% average return. This relationship held for all holding-period returns studied, from 12 to 60 months. At least in Europe, the smaller the firm, the better the return.

But this begs the question: Aren't most small companies traded over the counter (OTC)? Wouldn't it be wiser to stick to the main markets, such as the NYSE?

Conventional wisdom rarely pays when it comes to deep value investing. Here again, investor intuition proves faulty. One of the most common themes running through the literature is the strong underperformance of net-nets listed on the NYSE. The issue doesn't simply come down to size, either. Again, Oppenheimer reported that their NYSE-listed net-nets were roughly the same size as net-nets traded over the counter, yet actually underperformed the NYSE-Amex index 0.56%–0.69% to the index's 0.96% average monthly return. OTC net-nets, on the other hand, returned an average monthly return of 2.66% to 2.87%.[83] Similarly, Goebel and Athavale found that NYSE-listed net-nets performed the worst of all net-nets in their study.[84] And not to be left out, Oxman et al. reported that NYSE-listed net-nets significantly underperformed their peers, providing a 1.47% to 1.67% monthly return versus 2.55% for all net-nets. For whatever reason, sub-liquidation value stocks trading on the NYSE provide the worst returns.

There is no clear reason for this. The NYSE is one of the oldest exchanges in the USA, and includes some of the most well-known business names in America. It's possible that a greater proportion of NYSE-listed net-nets are suffering significant business problems that can't be easily overcome. Another hypothesis is that there may be less negative sentiment attached to NYSE-listed net-nets, given their

81 Ibid.
82 Xiao and Arnold, 'Testing Ben Graham's NCAV Strategy'.
83 Oppenheimer, 'Ben Graham's NCAVs'.
84 Goebel and Athavale, 'The Persistence of NCAV Stock Selection Criterion'.

inclusion on the exchange. More research is needed to get to the bottom of this mystery.

One last word on increasing performance: despite the strong balance sheet of all firms trading below NCAV, it's still advisable to steer clear of debt. Tweedy, Browne, in its report *What Has Worked in Investing*, states that net-nets with a 20% debt to equity ratio or lower produced a 34.9% return, versus 28.8% for net-net stocks in general between 1970 and 1981.[85] The result is likely due to the fact that while a firm trading below NCAV may be solvent, it can still suffer a liquidity crisis and bankruptcy if it has trouble converting current assets into cash.

Lesson 8: Selecting for small size and low debt while avoiding dividends and the NYSE can significantly boost returns.

Key takeaways from the academics

Academic studies are solid proof that Graham's net-net stocks provide highly lucrative returns for investors who aren't afraid to sift through the market's junkyard. Strong evidence suggests that net-net stock investing is highly profitable, has worked over many decades, and is still viable today.

Better yet, the studies we've discussed provide a solid basis from which to develop a sound mechanical approach to net-net stock selection. Investors are fortunate to have a somewhat diverse body of studies that provide insight into factors which boost or drag down returns. Rather than formulating investment policy on hunches, mechanical investors aiming for the best returns are well advised to stick close to the actual data. Investors who lean more to qualitative analysis should at the very least stick close to the data when identifying warm leads, before diving into the company's story.

Based on what we've discussed in this chapter, a few simple rules are in order if you want to make the most of your time as an investor. When selecting net-nets:

1. Stick to the strategy over a large number of years. A decade seems like a reasonable minimum commitment if you want a reasonable assurance of good results.
2. Search international stock markets to uncover more, and better, opportunities than you could if you only invested in your own backyard.
3. Stay fully invested to take advantage of those few exceptional years that really drive long-term portfolio returns. You can't win if you're uninvested.

---

85 Tweedy, Browne, *What Has Worked in Investing*.

4. Aim for a discount to NCAV. While discounts are the essence of value investing, there is also some empirical evidence to suggest that deeper discounts provide better returns.

5. Unless you're an income investor, avoid dividends. Dividends are associated with lower net-net stock returns.

6. Buy the smallest firms you can. When it comes to net-net investing, small is beautiful. An investor has to keep liquidity in mind, however, and plan accordingly.

7. Avoid the NYSE, since NYSE-listed net-net firms have underperformed historically.

8. Look for net-nets that are free of debt. While a firm has to have a strong balance sheet to be called a net-net, illiquidity issues can still push a firm into bankruptcy. More on this later.

This is far from the last word on net-net stock investing. While data provides a solid foundation for making investment decisions, numbers only reveal so much. In the next chapter we'll take a look at how three exceptional practitioners earned their best track records through net-net investing.

8

Three Net–Net Stock Gurus to Model

RATIONAL STRATEGY SELECTION usually demands that an investor focus on approaches with solid performance in academic studies or industry white papers. Critically important considerations include the number of studies assessing a strategy, the date range those studies cover, and the overall performance of the strategy over that period.

As we've seen, Graham's net-net stock strategy has one of the best long-term records of any strategy, at least when it comes to reported performance. Many researchers have looked at the performance and prevalence of net-nets, and have done so over many decades. Currently, no other strategy can match the great track record shown by Graham's net-net stock strategy.

But while a good past record is a prerequisite for strategy selection, it's not enough. A strategy also has to be viable in terms of real-life application. If investors can't come close to replicating the reported returns, then the strategy may be worthless.

One solid approach to separating practical high performance strategies from those that are mere academic fantasies is to look for investors who have built long track records using the strategy. Both factors are critically important. The investment industry is as much focused on sales as it is on money management, so focusing on trusted professionals is an absolute must. Track records should be long and verifiable – typically a matter of public record where auditors have been involved, as in the case of publicly traded companies and investment funds. The more eyes scrutinising the investment performance of the investment professional, the better.

These standards are hard to meet but important when real money is involved. That's why I assessed both the scholarly record and practical application by trusted professionals before adopting Graham's net-nets.

Earlier, I wrote that investors with large portfolios can't use the strategy, which provides small investors with a strong competitive advantage. Over the past 100 years, there have been a handful of periods in which the strategy was viable for larger portfolios, due to the depressed overall market level. These periods opened up opportunities for professionals, allowing us to assess how well the strategy performs in the real world.

In this chapter, I'll walk you through the unique approaches to net-net investing taken by three investors with solid track records. They pushed me to become a diehard convert to the net-net investing strategy. One of these approaches may resonate strongly with you.

The Graham approach to net-net investing

Considered the father of value investing and security analysis, Graham focused on net-net stocks extensively throughout his career. But while Graham was a prolific writer, he only discussed his net-net strategy in brief. He relegated coverage to short sections in *Security Analysis*, scant mentions in more general articles, and brief comments in published interviews. An enlightening account of Graham's application of this strategy, therefore, requires piecing together fragments from various sources.

Graham used the strategy successfully over a 40-year period, much of it at Graham-Newman. As Graham explained in 1975, "[Net-nets] gave such good results for us over a forty-year period of decision making that we eventually renounced all other common-stock choices based on the regular common stock procedures, and concentrated on these 'sub-asset stocks'."[86] He elaborated further, right before his death in 1976: "We used this approach extensively in managing investment funds, and over a 30-year period we must have earned an average of some 20% per year from this source."[87] Graham's use of the strategy and performance is absolutely clear.

How did he do it?

Graham operated on two different value-investing paradigms. The first, adopted soon after entering Wall Street in 1914, focused on detailed analysis utilising both quantitative and qualitative factors. The second approach, adopted late in life, constituted a radical shift towards quantitative mechanical investing.

---

86 Graham, 'The Decade'.
87 Graham, 'A Conversation with Benjamin Graham'.

Early Graham

Graham's writing suggests a strong analytical mind focused on both quantitative and qualitative facts. Graham started his career as a bond salesman in 1914, working out arbitrage plays before splitting off to manage investment accounts. Graham's gift for mathematics allowed him to work out profitable trades, and he focused a lot of his early effort on bond arbitrage.

But Graham's mathematical focus drifted, and he soon began to employ qualitative elements. This focus on both quantitative and qualitative factors would dominate much of his career. In the 1954 edition of *Security Analysis*, Graham highlighted the importance of each:

> "The analyst's conclusions must always rest upon the figures and upon established tests and standards. These figures alone are not *sufficient*; they may be completely vitiated by qualitative considerations of an opposite import … It is also true that he will be far more confident in his selection of an issue if he can buttress an adequate quantitative exhibit with unusually favorable qualitative factors."[88]

While the investment had to show promise from a quantitative point of view, it wasn't enough. Both promising quantitative and qualitative elements had to be in place for the stock to be considered a sound investment.

Graham's liquidation value assessment

Graham's net-net stock approach was an attempt to buy businesses selling for less than liquidation value. According to Graham:

> "By the liquidating value of an enterprise we mean the money that the owners could get out of it if they wanted to give it up. They might sell all or part of it to someone else, on a going-concern basis. Or else they might turn the various kinds of assets into cash, in piecemeal fashion, taking whatever time is needed to obtain the best realization from each. Such liquidations are of everyday occurrence in the field of private business."[89]

According to Graham, this value could be approximated by assessing a firm's NCAV. In his 1937 edition of *The Interpretation of Financial Statements*, he wrote:

> "Liquidating value differs from book value in that it is supposed to make allowance for loss of value in liquidation … the current assets usually suffer a much smaller loss in liquidation than do the

---

88 Graham and Dodd, *Security Analysis*, 76.
89 Ibid., 559.

fixed assets. Hence the 'NCAV' of an industrial security is likely to constitute a rough measure of its liquidating value."[90]

Unlike most quantitative investors, who confuse mathematical precision with sound investing, Graham only aimed to arrive at a rough assessment of liquidation value. He would simply use numbers to describe the investment situation and then buy when it looked favourable. In the 1954 edition of *Security Analysis*, he explained:

> "The analyst cannot calculate accurately the liquidating value of a given company, since it is ordinarily impossible to estimate what could actually be realized for its fixed assets and what the expenses of liquidation would be. But we do know as a practical matter that most companies could be disposed of for not less than the net working capital if the ladder is conservatively stated."[91]

But while a precise assessment was not necessary for Graham, a conservative assessment of value was. An investor, according to Graham, was to assess the value of each current asset account separately, applying an appropriate discount based on his professional judgement. An investor could go further, applying a large discount to fixed assets, but Graham mostly seemed satisfied that fixed assets would simply step in to make up for any shortfall in NCAV during liquidation.

In the sixth edition of *Security Analysis*, Graham provides readers with a series of approximations that they can use when discounting asset accounts. Contrary to popular practice, Benjamin Graham discounted current asset accounts to arrive at net-net working capital based on business judgement. In this table, Graham suggests a range of discounts (left) that analysts could use when assessing a company and a rough middle ground (right) for each account. Note that he also included fixed assets in this assessment.

By leveraging Graham's framework, net-net investors could arrive at a much more conservative assessment of liquidation value, and therefore a much larger margin of safety.

---

90 Graham, *The Interpretation of Financial Statements*, 38.
91 Graham and Dodd, *Security Analysis*, 485.

Table 5: Ben Graham's net-net working capital current asset value adjustments

Type of asset	% of liquidating value to book value	
	Normal range	Rough Range
Current assets:		
Cash assets (including securities at market)	100	100
Receivables (less usual reserves)*	75–90	80
Inventories (at lower of cost or market)	50–75	66 2/3
Fixed and miscellaneous assets:		
(Real estate, buildings, machinery, equipment, nonmarketable investments, intangibles, etc.)	1–50	15 (approx.)

Source: Graham, *Security Analysis*, 6th ed.

But assets are only one part of Graham's liquidation value formula. Equally important are obligations a would-be acquirer would have to pay. Graham often referred to these as obligations *prior to the common* (total balance-sheet liabilities and the cost of retiring preferred shares). In a liquidation scenario, a liquidator would have to cover all of these costs before reaping any profit. Today, Graham might cite off-balance-sheet items as an important cost to include.

Graham's net-net selection criteria

Graham used quantitative facts as the basis for his stock screening but leaned heavily on qualitative assessment when finalising his purchases. In the sixth edition of *Security Analysis*, he wrote:

> "Much more difficult [than finding cheap stocks] is the task of determining whether or not the qualitative factors will justify following the quantitative indications – in other words, whether or not the investor may have sufficient confidence in the company's future to consider its shares a real bargain at the apparently subnormal price."[92]

Initial screening focused on avoiding specific firm classifications. According to Graham, utilities and railroads were strictly forbidden. According to Graham, it did not make sense to try to determine the liquidation value of these firms. This may have been due to their unique positions in the economy, which may have brought along significant government interference in the liquidation process.[93]

92 Ibid., 675.
93 Graham, *Interpretation of Financial Statements*, 55.

If the company met his basic industry requirement, he would then calculate its liquidation value and exclude firms that were not priced at least one-third below that value.

Graham also wanted to see some sign that the firm's situation would improve. Once distressed, it's not at all certain that a company will quickly recover, allowing an investor to profit. Because of that, Graham looked closely at a company's qualitative situation for hints that a better future was in store, at least for the investor. In the sixth edition of *Security Analysis*, he wrote:

> "Nevertheless, the securities analyst should exercise as much discrimination as possible in the choice of issues falling within this category. He will lean toward those for which he sees a fairly imminent prospect of some one of the favorable developments listed above. [growth in earnings to match asset values through an improvement in the industry or change in management policy, a sale, or merger, or whole or partial liquidation]." [94]

Barring a significant catalyst, Graham looked for other statistical features that suggested a better than average buy. He wrote:

> "Or else he will be partial to such as reveal other attractive statistical features besides their liquid-asset position, e.g., satisfactory current earnings and dividends or a high average earning power in the past. The analyst will avoid issues that have been losing their current assets at a rapid rate and show no definite signs of ceasing to do so." [95]

These additional characteristics provided an extra reason for a stock to rise in price. Spotting a solid dividend, stable earnings, or growing asset base, the investing public may revalue a firm it had given up for dead, bidding its price up and allowing an investor to prosper.

Based on this passage, we can form a solid checklist that Graham could have used when selecting net-nets throughout most of his career. While Graham provided a wealth of information about stock selection, this set of criteria pertains to net-net stocks specifically.

Early Graham net-net checklist

- Company is not a utility or railroad; and has
- minimum one-third discount to liquidation value;
- growth in earnings, sale or merger, or liquidation likely to materialise soon; or
- satisfactory current earnings and dividends;

94 Graham and Dodd, *Security Analysis*, 569.
95 Ibid.

- large past earnings;
- liquidation value not rapidly shrinking.

While short, this simple checklist is also very flexible and therefore provides a powerful framework for net-net investors.

White Motor provides a unique look at one of Graham's early investments. Graham spotted the stock in 1931, when it was traded for just $8 against a book value of $55. The firm was distressed, having suffered a major loss the year prior.

Sifting through the financials, Graham recognised the firm's rather large NCAV of $34, and applied his best judgement to work out the firm's liquidation value. Table 6 shows Graham's net-net working capital assessment of White Motor.

Table 6: Ben Graham's White Motor net-net working capital valuation

Current assets			
Cash	$4,057	@100%	$4,057
Government bonds	$4,573	@100%	$4,573
Net receivables	$5,611	@80%	$4,500
Inventory	$9,219	@50%	$4,600
Total	$23,460		$17,700
Long term assets			
Plant account, net	$8,545		
Subsidiaries	$4,996		
Deferred charges	$388		
Goodwill	$5,389		
Total	$19,318	@20%	$4,000
Liabilities			
Current liabilities	$1,353	@100%	$1,400
Long term liabilities	$0	@100%	$0
Liquidation value			
Net assets			$21,700
Net liabilities			$1,400
Total			$20,300

Source: Graham, *Security Analysis*, 6th ed.

While many investors carry out calculations to three or four decimal places, Graham was content to simply round to the nearest whole number, in most cases.[96]

Also evident here is Graham's preference for including total assets in his liquidation value assessment rather than sticking with the firm's net current assets. This would later change to a preference for simplicity over more detailed figures. In the case of White Motor, Graham highlighted just how similar his liquidation calculation was to the firm's NCAV. While his estimate of liquidation value came out to $31 per share, the firm's NCAV was nearly identical at $34. He explained that "in the typical case it may be said that the noncurrent assets are likely to realise enough to make up most of the shrinkage suffered in the liquidation of the current assets. Hence our first thesis, viz., that the current-asset value affords a rough measure of the liquidating value."[97]

Looking more closely at the firm, we can see that White Motor had other attributes that made it a better than average buy. It had a rock-solid balance sheet with a significant cash balance, a current ratio[98] of 17×, and no debt. The firm was dirt cheap, priced at just 26% of Graham's liquidation value, or 24% of NCAV. A full $11 of that value was made up of net cash (cash and equivalents less total liabilities). This was 38% greater than the firm's stock price! To top it off, management had also decided to seek *strategic alternatives* (corporate speak for a third-party acquisition).

Hit hard by the Great Depression, White Motor continued to lose a significant amount of money in 1931 and 1932. In September of that year, Studebaker agreed to purchase the struggling manufacturer for $5 in cash, $25 in ten-year notes, plus one share of Studebaker stock priced at $10. This amounted to $40 in value. Investors who had purchased White Motor at $8 a couple years earlier nailed a 400% profit.

Graham's shift to mechanical value

Competition in the securities market continued to build throughout Graham's career. By the 1970s, Graham was beginning to rethink his views on investing and security analysis. In a telling interview he gave in 1975, he admitted:

96 A keen student of classical thought, Graham likely based this preference on Aristotle's observation: "It is the mark of an educated mind to rest satisfied with the degree of precision which the nature of the subject admits and not to seek exactness where only an approximation is possible." When assessing intrinsic value, investors should be satisfied with close-enough appraisals and not assume that more precise figures always yield better results.

97 Ibid., 562.

98 The current ratio is a measure of balance sheet liquidity which shows how many times current assets can cover current liabilities. In this case, White Motor has enough in current assets to pay off its current liabilities 17 times. This large figure is both ample and rare – the company should have had no problem paying off its current liabilities that year.

"I am no longer an advocate of elaborate techniques of security analysis in order to find superior value opportunities. This was a rewarding activity, say, 40 years ago, when the textbook *Graham and Dodd* [Graham often referred to *Security Analysis* volumes as his *Graham and Dodd* textbooks] was first published. But the situation has changed a good deal since then. In the old days any well-trained security analyst could do a good professional job of selecting undervalued issues through detailed studies. But in the light of the enormous amount of research now being carried on, I doubt whether in most cases such extensive efforts will generate sufficiently superior selections to justify their cost. To that very limited extent I'm on the side of the 'efficient market' school of thought now generally accepted by professors."[99]

According to Graham, the era of security analysis was over, and investors had to seek new methods by which to profit in the stock market. While Graham had built his career on his ability to dissect balance sheets and discern a quality opportunity from a merely depressed stock, he had clearly moved on. As he revealed at a seminar given in 1975:

"This is far from saying that I think that individual stock prices reflect in general and under most conditions the fair value of each issue. On the contrary, my present emphasis on the tendency of most stocks to fluctuate widely and often wildly in price over the years should show my conviction that stock prices are often out of line with their fair or intrinsic values."[100]

The question Graham now shifted to was how to best exploit those mispricings in the face of so much competition on Wall Street. In his view, old strategies remained viable if investors were prepared to change their tactics. As it turned out, this approach would require radically simplifying stock selection and employing extreme diversification:

"[I now favour] a highly simplified [strategy] that applies a single criterion or perhaps two criteria to the price to assure that full value is present and that relies for its results on the performance of the portfolio as a whole – i.e., on the group results – rather than on the expectations for individual issues."[101]

Referring to his classic net-net stock strategy, Graham observed:

---

99 Graham, 'A Conversation with Benjamin Graham', 20–23.
100 Graham, 'Three Simple Methods of Common Stock Selection', 40.
101 Graham, 'A Conversation with Benjamin Graham', 23.

"I have no doubt that their purchase now, on a diversified basis and without the addition of detailed analyses or forecasts, will prove eminently profitable in the next few years, as it always has in the past ... This approach does certainly meet our three requirements of logic, simplicity and good performance."[102]

Rather than spend significant time assessing a firm's situation, Graham was content to simply buy statistical bargains, so long as they met a few basic criteria. In one of his last seminars given just before his death in 1976, Graham outlined his preferred method of purchasing bargain issues. This seminar was made available in question-and-answer format in the September–October 1976 edition of the *Financial Analysts Journal*. On the question of how to invest in net-net stocks, he noted:

"My first, more limited, technique confines itself to the purchase of common stocks at less than their working capital value, or NCAV, giving no weight to the plant and other fixed assets and deducing all liabilities in full from the current assets ... I consider it a foolproof method of systematic investment – once again, not on the basis of individual results but in terms of the expectable group outcome."[103]

The 1973 publication of *The Intelligent Investor* sheds light on additional criteria Graham employed. In chapter 15, starting with 50 statistical net-nets, he eliminates firms that lost money over the previous 12 months in order to arrive at a better-quality portfolio. While Graham favoured simplicity, it's clear that he found additional criteria advantageous when practical.

Graham's net-net criteria post-1970

From various articles and publications written either by or about Graham in the 1970s, we can put together a concise set of criteria:

- margin of safety
- profitable over the most recent 12-month period
- reasonably good future prospects
- sell at no more than a 100% gain
- maximum holding period of three years

Astute readers will note the inclusion of mechanical sell rules in the set of criteria. Near the end of his life, Graham made it very clear that investors were to set strict

102 Graham, 'Three Simple Methods of Common Stock Selection', 32.
103 Graham, 'A Conversation with Benjamin Graham'.

sell rules consistent with their purchase criteria. Specifically, investors were to sell a stock after a 50–100% gain, or two to three years had passed.[104]

MARGIN OF SAFETY

Graham stayed true to his principle of ensuring a solid margin of safety throughout his career. Even towards the end of his life, Graham was cautioning investors to ensure that a stock's per-share value was at least 50% more than its quoted price.

PROFITABLE OVER THE MOST RECENT 12-MONTH PERIOD

Buried deep within *The Intelligent Investor*, Graham walks readers through a winnowing of the Standard & Poor's stocks guide. In the process, he briefly mentions finding dozens of net-nets. To shrink the number to a manageable group, he suggests eliminating firms that show a loss over the previous 12 months. While it's unclear which other criteria Graham would have adopted when putting together a high-quality net-net portfolio, he clearly favoured profitable firms.

REASONABLY GOOD FUTURE PROSPECTS

Interestingly, while Graham shifted to favouring a simple quantitative approach to stock selection, he retained what are arguably the most qualitative selection criteria he ever used. In September 1974, he gave a talk titled 'The Renaissance of Value'. During the talk, he discussed a couple of approaches designed to provide investors with good returns. While discussing net-nets, he specifically identified good future prospects as a major criterion.[105]

Final thoughts on Graham's net-net investing

It's ironic that Ben Graham invested in net-net stocks so heavily throughout his career but did not provide more information about how he employed this fantastic strategy. What is clear is that he used a great deal of critical thought to craft a highly refined set of selection criteria and then abandoned it just before his death in favour of mechanical or contrarian value investing.

Small investors should think twice about adopting Graham's simplified approach, however. Graham's preferences shifted due to a significant influx of competent security analysts. While the competition has only increased since Graham's passing in 1976, small investors are still buffered from competition when bargain-hunting among the smallest companies. It's in these nooks that security markets retain much of the inefficiency that Graham enjoyed in the 1960s. A small investor sharp

104 Ibid., 22.
105 Graham, 'The Decade', 6.

enough to grasp the basics of qualitative analysis should be able to use it to select more promising investments within this niche, just as Graham did 80 years ago.

Buffett, the gifted protégé

Warren Buffett is a legend. Considered by many to be the best investor of all time, he made a name for himself by buying some of the best companies in existence. But few investors realise that Buffett earned his highest returns investing in *cigar butt stocks*,[106] net-net working capital stocks,[107] the same strategy he used while at Graham-Newman Corp. At his 1998 Berkshire Hathaway annual meeting, Buffett confirmed that the term referred to working capital stocks when he described his initial purchase of Berkshire Hathaway: "It was selling well below working capital, so it was a cigar butt."[108]

He confirmed this at the 2001 Berkshire Hathaway annual meeting when he described the enormous success Walter Schloss had as a net-net investor:

> "And he's done it in, you know, what I tend to call cigar butt companies. You know, you get one free puff and that's about it, but they don't cost anything. And that's – that was – the sub-working capital type situations. Walter's had to extend that somewhat, but it's been a great, great record over a considerable – I mean, 46 years – a very considerable period of time."[109]

Despite writing volumes while managing the Buffett Partnership, Buffett remained elusive about the stocks he was buying. That leaves investors having to piece together his investment strategy from a few stock write-ups he crafted for his partners, brief explanations of his investment strategy in his partnership letters, plus short statements he made years later. Despite the scant evidence, what's available makes it very clear that Buffett focused almost exclusively on sub-liquidation value when buying common stocks and many of those purchases were net-nets.

Buffett's value-investing baptism began by stumbling, as a youth, upon Graham's book *The Intelligent Investor*. He later attended Graham's investing course at Columbia, and then landed a job – combing stock lists by hand to find net-nets – at Graham's investment company, Graham-Newman Corp. This exposure instilled in him a powerful investment framework that Buffett would leverage for his entire career.

---

106 Buffett, 'Berkshire Hathaway 2014 Annual Shareholder Letter', 26.
107 Buffett frequently referred to the cheap stocks he bought for his partnership as cigar butts, a term Graham coined for his working capital stocks (net-net working capital stocks).
108 Berkshire Hathaway, Annual Meetings, 'Afternoon Session – 1998 Meeting'.
109 Berkshire Hathaway, Annual Meetings, 'Afternoon Session – 2001 Meeting'.

Despite Graham's enormous prominence on Wall Street, he wasn't very interested in building wealth.[110] He saw investing as an intellectual puzzle rather than simply a way to get rich. Buffett differed in this respect enormously, having developed an intense interest in money and wealth accumulation from a young age. While Graham wanted to develop a framework that the average investor could follow to earn good returns, Buffett was mostly interested in becoming wealthy.

This difference was reflected in the pair's approach to net-net stock selection. While Graham would filter for net-nets following a simple checklist and then bring a huge number of individual issues into his portfolio at any one time (some positions as small as $1000, a tiny amount for a professional fund manager), Buffett would try to identify a handful of the best buys.[111] By concentrating his portfolio on these stocks, he was convinced he could earn higher returns than Graham had.

Buffett included many of these higher-quality picks in his portfolio in the 1950s. His cigar-butt focus proved so lucrative that he made it his bedrock approach after launching his partnership in the late 1950s. Half of his portfolio comprised just five to ten big companies, and the rest were 15 or so tiny positions. On occasion, he even allocated 25% of his capital in a single net-net stock if he believed it was of high quality or he could wrestle control of the firm.[112]

This approach proved extremely successful over the 13 years that he managed the Buffett Partnership. At the end of 1969, his portfolio's unleveraged compound annual growth rate was 29.5% versus the Dow Jones' 7.4% showing.[113] This was 50% higher than the 20% compound annual return Graham earned at Graham-Newman. Buffett amassed so much money investing in cigar butts that his large portfolio size eventually made them impossible to buy, so he was forced to radically change his strategy. Buffett writes in his 'Berkshire Hathaway 2014 Annual Shareholder Letter':

> "My cigar-butt strategy worked very well while I was managing small sums. Indeed, the many dozens of free puffs I obtained in the 1950s made that decade by far the best of my life for both relative and absolute investment performance. Most of my gains in those early years ... came from investments in mediocre companies that traded at bargain prices. Ben Graham had taught me that technique, and it worked. But a major weakness in this approach gradually became

---

110 Schroeder, *The Snowball*, 186.
111 Ibid., 185.
112 Buffett writes at length about his portfolio construction in his Buffett Partnership letters, which are easily found online via a simple search.
113 Buffett, 'The Superinvestors of Graham-and-Doddsville', *Hermes* (Fall 1984). This article was based on a speech Buffett gave on 17 May 1984 at Columbia Business School.

apparent: Cigar-butt investing was scalable only to a point. With large sums, it would never work well."[114]

As long-time friend and business partner Charlie Munger recounted in 2017, "He just made so much money in this other stuff and he had been taught it by Ben Graham. It was hard for him to quit when he was just coining money."[115]

Given Buffett's enormous success with net-nets in the 1950s and 1960s, it's worth trying to distill his approach in order to refine an already great strategy.

How exactly did Buffett approach net-net investing?

Buffett's net-net stock approach

Buffett's main focus was on purchasing undervalued stocks, which he dubbed "generals". Writing in early 1964, he outlined this approach for investors:

> "Generals – A category of generally undervalued stocks, determined primarily by quantitative standards, but with considerable attention also paid to the qualitative factor. There is often little or nothing to indicate immediate market improvement. The issues lack glamour or market sponsorship. Their main qualification is a bargain price; that is, an overall valuation on the enterprise substantially below what careful analysis indicates its value to a private owner to be."[116]

Buffett's fundamental quantitative criteria focused on buying firms well below their value to a private businessman. He wasn't just looking for a simple one-third margin of safety, however. His aim was to spend as little as possible to acquire as much value as possible. As he explained to his partners, "This is the cornerstone of our investment philosophy: Never count on making a good sale. Have the purchase price be so attractive that even a mediocre sale gives good results. The better sales will be the frosting on the cake."[117]

According to Buffett, when you buy at a price low enough relative to value, often there will be some bump-up in the stock price that will allow you to cash out at a decent profit even if the firm's long-term prospects are terrible.[118] Reviewing Buffett's highest-conviction buys shows just how undervalued his purchases were. Buffett often demanded an enormous 50 to 67% discount to fair value.[119]

---

114 Buffett, 'Berkshire Hathaway 2014 Annual Shareholder Letter'.
115 Ross, 'A Conversation with Charlie Munger'.
116 Buffett, '1963 Letter', Buffett Partnership.
117 Buffett, '1962 Letter', Buffett Partnership.
118 Buffett, 'Berkshire Hathaway 1989 Annual Shareholder Letter'.
119 This is equivalent to buying firms at a price to some source of value of 0.5 to 0.33.

Buffett typically applied this principle by buying below a highly conservative assessment of liquidation value, Graham's net-net working capital value. He walked partners through its use in the case of Dempster Mills in 1962, and later explained how shifts in the firm's asset make-up influenced the firm's intrinsic value.[120] Buffett's purchases below net-net working capital amounted to a strong margin of safety that he could count on if he needed to liquidate assets.

Another pillar of Graham's philosophy that rubbed off is what Buffett termed "very strong defensive characteristics" in his 1958 letter.[121] Because Graham was obsessed with capital preservation, having almost gone bankrupt during the Great Depression, he employed a number of quantitative checks to ensure a strong margin of safety, and wide diversification to keep from losing money.[122] While Buffett didn't see the need to diversify as widely as Graham and didn't specify the sort of defensive characteristics Graham preferred, it's likely that he followed Graham's approach by demanding strong balance sheets and significant interest or dividend coverage.

Strong moats, on the other hand, were almost never a priority. While Buffett purchased Geico and American Express in part due to their strong competitive advantages, the rest of his investments lacked any competitive advantage whatsoever. Some, such as Berkshire Hathaway and Cleveland Worsted Mills, even operated at a competitive disadvantage. At the time, both were plagued by higher-than-average manufacturing costs, paying higher prices for electricity in comparison to their southern peers.[123]

Despite this, qualitative elements were still an important consideration, as Buffett reiterated in 1964: "Again let me emphasise that while the quantitative comes first and is essential, the qualitative is important. We like good management – we like a decent industry – we like a certain amount of 'ferment' in a previously dormant management or stockholder group. But we demand value."[124]

Buffett's early writings for *The Commercial and Financial Chronicle* reveal his early thoughts on management. In his write-up on Western Insurance Securities, for example, he praised Ray DuBoc's reputation for integrity and ability. Good management, in Warren's eyes, comprised individuals who made wise business decisions which increased a firm's value (or at least maintained it in a bad industry).

---

120 Buffett, '1962 Letter', Buffett Partnership.
121 Buffett, '1958 Letter', Buffett Partnership.
122 Carlen, *The Einstein of Money*, 50.
123 Schroeder, *The Snowball*, 268; Arnold, 'Warren Buffett: Learning through the School of Hard Knocks', www.MoAF.org.
124 Buffett, '1963 Letter', Buffett Partnership.

Buffett's early writings also show a strong preference for industries with a favourable outlook. The better the industry were to perform, the better the company and stock would do.

Buffett was not forthcoming about what he meant by "a certain amount of 'ferment' in a previously dormant management or stockholder group", but we can assume he was referring to the desire by insiders or activists to improve the business or help shareholders realise fair value. The latter could be accomplished through a redistribution of capital, share buy-backs, or by forcing management to take corrective action. Buffett often referred to his preference for coat-tail riding: buying stock in a business where activists exert their influence for the betterment of shareholders.

Also present in many of Buffett's early buys were significant fixed or hidden assets, additional items that boosted a company's value beyond mere net-net working capital. Buffett's partnership letters and articles for *The Commercial and Financial Chronicle* typically list bonus items that would boost value obtained from a liquidation. For example, Union Street Railway owned property and had special reserves that would step up the value in liquidation from simply NCAV.[125]

Aside from good management, industries, activists, and assets, Buffett also preferred growth. In 1957, while discussing Commonwealth Trust Co., he emphasised its "good solid value building up at a satisfactory pace" which "would presumably have been built up to a considerably larger figure" if the stock had remained stagnant for some time.[126] Other top picks selected for *The Commercial and Financial Chronicle*, such as Geico, Western Insurance Securities, and Home Protective Co., really drive this home.[127] According to Buffett, all had solid growth ahead, which would benefit investors. While none of these were technically net-nets, all were trading below liquidation value, so Buffett's enthusiasm for their growth prospects should be considered an important investment factor. Interestingly, Buffett never mentioned promising growth ahead for any of the net-nets that he purchased. Most were simply troubled firms.

From these and other scattered bits, we can piece together a checklist that reflects how Buffett could have selected high-quality net-nets while managing his partnership.

---

125 Schroeder, *The Snowball*, 195.
126 Buffett, '1957 letter', Buffett Partnership.
127 Buffett, 'The Security I Like Best'.

Buffett's cigar-butt scorecard

CORE CRITERIA

- priced below net-net working capital
- strong defensive characteristics as determined by balance sheet ratios

RANKING CRITERIA

- very cheap price relative to net-net working capital
- good management
- decent industry prospects
- very cheap price relative to earnings
- other assets that significantly increase value
- activists intent on improving the firm
- activists intent on helping investors realise value
- strong earnings growth
- strong asset value growth

The core criteria specified here are the criteria that Buffett would demand as a basic requirement for purchase. When selecting net-nets, he'd simply pass on firms not meeting these basic stipulations.

Ranking criteria, on the other hand, are features that Buffett would prefer in an investment. Each has been selected from Buffett's early writings, whether stated directly or alluded to in examples. While none of these criteria are necessary for a solid investment, each of Buffett's early known investments included at least one of these characteristics. It's also fair to assume that the more of these factors that the criteria had in place, the better the stock was as an investment.

Buffett's cigar-butt investments

CLEVELAND WORSTED MILLS

While Berkshire Hathaway stands out as one of Buffett's worst blunders, his venture into textile manufacturing started at a much younger age. In 1951, Buffett identified a promising purchase for his partners, Cleveland Worsted Mills.

The company had $146 per share in net current assets against a stock price of $115. This represented a shallow 21% discount to NCAV, but Buffett spotted significant value in long-term assets, specifically the firm's ownership of "several well-equipped mills".[128]

---

128 Schroeder, *The Snowball*, 168.

He also liked the firm's 7% yield, representing a significant amount of the firm's earnings. Despite the solid payout ratio, he thought the dividend was well protected due to its excess of profit over declared dividends.[129]

Long-time value investor Glen Arnold explains what happened next: "After buying in, Buffett discovered that the company faced intense competition from textile plants in the southern US states and from synthetic fibers. It made large losses, cut its dividend and its share price dropped."[130]

Buffett was dismayed. He had backed the firm and encouraged others to invest in the company, only to watch the stock crater. He had to find a way to see what was going on and rescue the investment:

> "I flew all the way to Cleveland [to an annual meeting]. I got there about five minutes late, and the meeting had been adjourned. And here I was, this kid from Omaha, twenty-two years old, with my own money in the stock. The chairman said, 'Sorry, too late.' But then their sales agent, who was on the board of directors, actually took pity on me, and so he got me off on the side and talked to me and answered some questions."[131]

It didn't help. But as Glen Arnold wrote, "Buffett learned the importance of strategic competitive positioning and pricing power."[132] Buffett also began to show a preference for good industries, solid business growth, and deep discounts.

UNION STREET RAILWAY

Union Street Railway is a good example of a terrible business that paid off handsomely for Buffett. The business prospered during the war years as rubber, steel, and other commodities were diverted from consumer goods to military equipment. As a result, consumers bought fewer vehicles so Union Street's ridership was strong. The company experienced a significant drop-off in revenue passengers, from 27 million in 1946 to just 14 million by post-war 1953. Profits eroded and the firm started losing money.[133]

The stock dropped in sympathy with the firm's poor post-war showing, from a high of $50 in 1949 to $25 two years later. When Buffett found it, its price had recovered to $30 per share, but he still felt value dwarfed the market price: "I started buying the stock because they had eight hundred thousand dollars in treasury bonds, a

---

129 Ibid.
130 Arnold, 'Warren Buffett: Learning through the School of Hard Knocks'.
131 Schroeder, *The Snowball*, 168.
132 Arnold, 'Warren Buffett: Learning through the School of Hard Knocks'.
133 *Moody's Transportation Manual*, 1492.

couple of hundred thousand in cash, and outstanding bus tickets of ninety-six thousand dollars. Call it a million dollars, about sixty bucks a share."[134]

Buffett was buying in at less than 50% of net-net working capital, but he had other reasons to be optimistic. Aside from working capital, the firm owned a significant amount of fixed assets: 116 buses, an amusement park, plus special reserves, other land and buildings, and car barns where it stored old streetcars.[135]

It was clear that the firm had a massive amount of value on offer for a very cheap price, so Buffett began buying heavily. But he wasn't alone. Management were keen to exploit the situation and began buying back shares, running an advertisement in the local paper to attract sellers.[136] This amounted to buying undervalued assets for remaining shareholders, a tactic that would disproportionately increase the value of their shares and attract investor interest. Buffett, keen to buy as much of the stock as he could, matched management by running his own ad. Eventually he obtained a list of the firm's largest holders and contacted them directly.[137]

Not yet satisfied with management's actions, Buffett decided to pay company head Mark Duff a visit to see if he could get his hands on some of the firm's cash:

> "I got up at about four a.m. and drove up to New Bedford. Mark Duff was very nice, polite. Just as I was about ready to leave, he said, 'By the way, we've been thinking of having a return of capital distribution to shareholders.' That meant they were going to give back the extra money. And I said, 'Oh, that's nice.' And then he said, 'Yes, and there's a provision you may not be aware of in the Massachusetts statutes on public utilities that you have to do it in multiples of the par value of the stock.' The stock had a $25 par value, so that meant it would be paying out at least $25 per share. And I said, 'Well. That's a good start.' Then he said, 'Bear in mind, we're thinking of using two units.' That meant they were going to declare a fifty-dollar dividend on a stock that was selling at thirty-five or forty dollars at that time."[138]

That special dividend provided Buffett with an enormous short-term profit. Having bought in at $30 per share, his $50 dividend amounted to a 167% yield. Even better, he still hung on to the stock which represented a significant amount

134 Schroeder, *The Snowball*, 194.
135 Ibid.
136 Ibid.
137 Ibid.
138 Ibid.

of value in fixed assets. Alice Shroeder notes that Buffett's $20,000 in profit was several times the average American's yearly salary.[139]

Was Buffett instrumental in management's decision to redistribute capital? Nobody can know for sure, but the experience encouraged him to become more active in the firms he bought.

DELTA DUCK CLUB

While primarily thought of as a stock investor, Buffett proved extremely flexible in his early career, buying preferred shares, bonds and even hunting club memberships.

As Buffett and Charlie Munger described it at the 1995 Berkshire Hathaway annual meeting:

> Charlie Munger: "Well, I can remember when you bought one membership in some duck club that had oil under it, when you were young."
>
> Warren Buffett: "Yeah, that was a company called Atled —"
>
> Charlie Munger: "When you get down to one duck club membership, well, you're really scavenging for cigar butts. [laughter] But —"
>
> Warren Buffett: "Not a bad cigar butt. There were 98 shares outstanding. It was the Delta Duck Club. And the Delta Duck Club was founded by a hundred guys who put in 50 bucks each, except two fellows didn't pay, so there were only 98 shares outstanding. They bought a piece of land down in Louisiana, and one time, somebody shot downward instead of upward, and oil and gas started spewing forth out of the ground. So, they renamed it Atled, which is delta spelled backwards, which was – sort of – illustrated the sophistication of this group."[140]

The duck club is an extreme example of the off-the-beaten-track investments Buffett made in the 1950s. With small amounts of capital, even a hunting membership could pay off handsomely.

At $3 per barrel of oil, the company was taking a million dollars' worth of royalties out of the ground each year. Buffett wrestled someone for a share, paying $29,000 for the ownership stake, but that stake represented $20,000 in cash plus $7,000 in after-tax income. At that figure, nearly Buffett's entire purchase price was covered

---

139 Ibid.
140 Berkshire Hathaway, Annual Meetings, 'Afternoon Session – 1995 Meeting'.

in his first year of ownership. To top it off, the asset was a long-lived field, so Buffett had many years of royalties ahead.

> "So, you know, I use that sometimes as an example of efficient markets, because somebody called me and offered me a share of it, and those things, you know – is that an efficient market or not? You know, 29,000 for 20,000 of cash, plus 11,000 of royalty income at 25 cent gas and $3 oil? I don't think so. You can find things out there. I'll give you hunting rights on all my duck clubs in the future."[141]

DEMPSTER MILLS

Buffett first purchased Dempster Mills, a struggling farm implement and water pump manufacturer in 1956. Dempster would prove to be one of Buffett's longest holdings while running his partnership and would suck up a massive amount of his time and energy after gaining control in 1961. Given Buffett's involvement, it's also one of most documented investments.

Buffett gained control of Dempster in 1961 for a total of $1.26 million, which made up 21% of partnership assets. The company had $50 per share in NCAV, and another $25 per share in long-term assets. Despite these figures, Buffett assessed the firm's NNWC value at $35 per share,[142] applying a heavy discount based on what

---

141 These incredible bargains are still available in the US, and you don't have to buy hunting memberships to take advantage of them. In December 2019, for example, investors could have purchased shares of NASDAQ listed Support.com. A group of activist investors had wrestled control of the company from management in a proxy battle a few years prior, and then got to work bringing the firm back from the grave, reducing its enormous losses until it started producing ample profits. At the start of December, the firm was trading for $1.95 per share, but had earned $0.21 per share over the trailing 12 months and was sitting on $2.56 in net current asset value. A full $2.07 of that value was made up of net cash (cash less all of the firm's liabilities and off-balance-sheet items). Even more interestingly, the firm's new management team was being held in check by additional activist investors, who had pressured the company to distribute $1 of the firm's cash in a special dividend to be paid on the 26th. Throughout December, an investor could have purchased shares for under $2, obtaining a near-immediate 50% purchase refund. Post-dividend, the stock still represented $1.07 in net cash, but now had a PE of just 4.8×. Having distributed half of the firm's net cash to shareholders, investors had good reason to suspect that management may distribute a good chunk of the remainder, or take other shareholder value-maximizing actions. While the firm would not have benefited from rising oil prices, as was the case with Buffett's duck club, Support's Harvard graduate-lead marketing team had just launched an interesting new online third-party tech support solution startup for retail customers and small businesses. While still in its infancy, the new venture's website traffic was growing at an incredible rate. While success is seldom obvious, effectively paying $0.95 for $1.56 in NCAV, $1.07 of that in net cash, plus $0.21 in ongoing earnings, and an interesting new tech start-up was an incredible bargain.

142 Buffett, '1961 Letter', Buffett Partnership.

he thought a quick asset sale might bring.[143] With an average cost of $28 per share, Buffett purchased the investment at a 20% discount to his assessment of fair value.

Despite sales of about $9 million, Dempster was only earning token profits. Buffett's plan was to improve profitability, which would justify a higher valuation and raise the stock price.[144] He was sure that his significant margin of safety and the strength of the firm's balance sheet would allow him to cash out at a profit. As he explained to investors in early 1962, "Certainly, if even moderate earning power can be restored, a higher valuation will be justified, and even if it cannot, Dempster should work out at a higher figure."[145]

But despite Buffett's instructions, management kept spending cash on inventory, weakening the firm's balance sheet liquidity. The situation got so bad that the firm's creditors considered shutting the business down. Dempster was just months away from disaster.[146]

> "Initially, we worked with the old management toward more effective utilisation of capital, better operating margins, reduction of overhead, etc. These efforts were completely fruitless. After spinning our wheels for about six months, it became obvious that while lip service was being given to our objective, either through inability or unwillingness, nothing was being accomplished. A change was necessary."[147]

In desperation, Buffett turned to his friend Charlie Munger, who recommended an accountant named Harry Bottle. As Munger recalled, Buffett asked him, "'Who can you get to help me?' And I said, 'I've got just the man for you.' And so one of my old colleagues from a transformer business who was an accountant, I said, 'He will fix your windmill company.' Warren was desperate; he hired him on the spot.

Harry walked in on the first day, into this town with this big collection of windmills and so forth, and a whistle blew. The whole plant stopped for 15 minutes. And he said, 'What the hell is this?' They said, 'Well, it's respect for the town – anybody who has a funeral we blow this whistle and stop for 15 minutes. And Harry said, 'That'll be the last time.' He just approached everything that way."[148]

Bottle immediately began converting assets to cash by shrinking inventory, which reduced carrying cost and obsolescence risk significantly.[149] He eliminated

---

143 Buffett, '1963 Letter', Buffett Partnership.
144 Buffett, '1961 Letter', Buffett Partnership.
145 Ibid.
146 Arnold, 'Warren Buffett: Learning through the School of Hard Knocks'.
147 Buffett, '1962 Letter', Buffett Partnership.
148 Ross, 'A Conversation with Charlie Munger'.
149 Buffett, '1963 Letter', Buffett Partnership.

unprofitable lines of business, and began squeezing inefficiencies out of the company, often by firing staff. He found products for which Dempster was the sole supplier and raised prices significantly without suffering a drop in volume. Soon, Dempster began producing meaningful profits, which Buffett began reinvesting in marketable securities.[150]

By mid-1963, Buffett was ready to sell the company. Highlighting the partnership's success, Buffett explained to his investors:

> "B.P.L. owns 71.7% of Dempster acquired at a cost of $1,262,577.27. On June 30, 1963 Dempster had a small safe deposit box at the Omaha National Bank containing securities worth $2,028,415.25. Our 71.7% share of $2,028,415.25 amounts to $1,454,373.70. Thus, everything above ground (and part of it underground) is profit."

Buffett had managed to turn a small struggling net-net company into a lean, profitable enterprise with a significant securities portfolio. Spotting a chance to unload the partnership's holdings, he sold the business for a price approximating the firm's book value, earning $80 per share.[151] His effort had been rewarded with an investment gain amounting to 186%.

BERKSHIRE HATHAWAY

Buffett often labels Berkshire Hathaway one of his greatest investing mistakes, but a closer look at the situation shows a much different story. Buffett picked up the troubled New England textile manufacturer in 1962 after studying the situation in detail. While he wasn't hopeful about the firm's future prospects, he spotted a quick way to earn a significant return.

Berkshire was without question a poorly run business, but it was also cheap. Trading at $7.60 per share, NNWC came in at $19 for an enormous 60% discount to fair value. As Buffett explained to partners in his 1965 partners letter:

> "This price partially reflected large losses incurred by the prior management in closing some of the mills made obsolete by changing conditions within the textile business (which the old management had been quite slow to recognize)."[152]

Despite the problems, Buffett saw a way to earn a quick profit. The firm's CEO, Seabury Stanton, had been spending whatever cash was not used for equipment purchases on tender offers, buying back stock.[153] Buffett began acquiring the stock

150 Ibid.
151 Ibid.
152 Buffett, '1965 Letter', Buffett Partnership.
153 Schroeder, *The Snowball*, 269.

at a deep discount, hoping it would spook management which would then offer to buy him out at a premium. It worked.[154]

Stanton treated Buffett's buys as if a takeover were about to ensue, so Buffett used the opportunity to enquire about the next tender. When Stanton asked Buffett's price, Buffett replied, "$11.50, so long as it's in a reasonable amount of time." Stanton agreed.

But as Buffett recalls in Schroeder's biography, "I went home, and not too long after, a letter comes … offering $11 3/8 per share to anyone who would tender their Berkshire."[155]

Buffett was furious.[156] Stanton had tried to squeeze the last nickel out of Buffett, reneging on their agreement. Warren began buying as many shares as he could get his hands on in order to take control of the firm away from Stanton.[157] In 1965, he succeeded, at an average price of $14.86, but soon came to realise that he'd made a serious mistake.[158] In 1989, he explained to Berkshire shareholders, then a much different business:

> "If you buy a stock at a sufficiently low price, there will usually be some hiccup in the fortunes of the business that gives you a chance to unload at a decent profit, even though the long-term performance of the business may be terrible. I call this the 'cigar butt' approach to investing. A cigar butt found on the street that has only one puff left in it may not offer much of a smoke, but the 'bargain purchase' will make that puff all profit.
>
> Unless you are a liquidator, that kind of approach to buying businesses is foolish. First, the original 'bargain' price probably will not turn out to be such a steal after all. In a difficult business, no sooner is one problem solved than another surfaces – never is there just one cockroach in the kitchen. Second, any initial advantage you secure will be quickly eroded by the low return that the business earns. For example, if you buy a business for $8 million that can be sold or liquidated for $10 million and promptly take either course, you can realise a high return. But the investment will disappoint if the business is sold for $10 million in ten years and in the interim has

---

154 Ibid.
155 Ibid.
156 Ibid.
157 Ibid., 273.
158 Buffett, '1965 Letter', Buffett Partnership.

annually earned and distributed only a few percent on cost. Time is the friend of the wonderful business, the enemy of the mediocre."[159]

Buffett had abandoned his initial sound strategy of buying Berkshire stock and selling it at a profit, due to a bump-up in price. Instead, he acquired control of the actual business, a business that was operating in an industry with a bleak future. To make matters worse, because he had been scared from the public attacks made against him during the Dempster restructuring, he was not about to liquidate the business. He was forced to run it.

Charlie Munger summed up the situation in 2017:

> "You can't imagine a more lousy business than New England textile mills because a textile is a congealed electricity and the electricity rates in New England were about 60% higher than TVA rates. So, it was absolute, inevitable, certain, liquidation. Now, Warren should have known better than to buy into a totally doomed enterprise, but it was so damn cheap he could buy it at a big discount to liquidating value. So he bought a big chunk and he finally ended up in control of the business. But the business was going to die, so the only way to go forward from there was to ring enough money out of the declining textile business to have more money than he paid to get in and he could use it to buy something else."[160]

No sooner did Buffett take control than he was forced to begin shutting down unprofitable production lines. The first closure resulted in the layoff of 450 people.[161] Buffett would spend the next two decades cutting back costs and avoiding capital expenditures, forcing the business to operate as efficiently as possible using its ancient equipment.

> "The textile business would make money for about ten minutes each year. We made half the men's suit linings in the country, but nobody ever went to a tailor and said, 'I'd like a pin-striped gray suit with a Hathaway lining.' A square yard of cloth that came out of our mill cost more than a square yard from somewhere else, and capitalism's frugal that way. We'd get awards from Sears, Roebuck as supplier of the year, and we took them fishing, and supplied them during World War II, and I was personal friends with the chairman of Sears, and they'd say, 'Your products are wonderful.' And we'd say, 'How about

159 Buffett, 'Berkshire Hathaway 1989 Annual Shareholder Letter'.
160 Ross, 'A Conversation with Charlie Munger'.
161 Schroeder, *The Snowball*, 298.

another half a cent a yard?' And they'd say, 'You're out of your mind.' So it was a terrible business."[162]

Finally, in 1985, he decided that the enterprise could not produce a dollar more of cash for its owners without spending another $50 million on equipment. He had to shut it down. Placing the remnants of the plant on the auction block brought in just $163,122.90.[163]

Berkshire Hathaway is a great example of how a shift in strategy can bring about vastly different results. As Buffett wrote in 2014:

> "Though marginal businesses purchased at cheap prices may be attractive as short-term investments, they are the wrong foundation on which to build a large and enduring enterprise. Selecting a marriage partner clearly requires more demanding criteria than does dating. (Berkshire, it should be noted, would have been a highly satisfactory 'date': If we had taken Seabury Stanton's $11.375 offer for our shares, BPL's weighted annual return on its Berkshire investment would have been about 40%.)"[164]

Buying a net-net stock may be a great short- to medium-term investment. But the same poor economics that often lead a business to trade below liquidation value in the first place prevent it from being a solid long-term investment.

Peter Cundill: Graham's second coming?

Peter Cundill is a legend in some circles but largely unknown by the wider investing community. A die-hard Grahamite, his focus on sub-liquidation value investing helped him achieve one of the best mutual fund records in history.

Cundill's first brush with investing started as an intern at the Canadian investment firm Wood Gundy. Enchanted by a speculative mining stock, Cundill invested $500, a sizeable amount for a university student in 1959, and then he lost it all within a span of 48 hours.[165]

Cundill was smart and hard working and had a natural understanding of value, but lacked a solid philosophical framework. That would all change 14 years later when a colleague handed him the book *Supermoney* just before Cundill boarded a flight home to Montreal. Leafing through its pages on the plane, the term *margin of safety* immediately caught his eye.

---

162 Ibid., 481.
163 Ibid., 508.
164 Buffett, 'Berkshire Hathaway 2014 Annual Shareholder Letter'.
165 Morton, *The Financial Times Global Guide to Investing*, 644.

"Goodman devotes chapter 3 to Benjamin Graham and Warren Buffett and 'the margin of safety'," Cundill wrote in his diary that night. "It struck me like a thunderbolt – there before me in plain terms was the method, the solid theoretical back-up to selecting investments based on the principle of realisable underlying value. My years of apprenticeship are over: THIS IS WHAT I WANT TO DO FOR THE REST OF MY LIFE!"[166]

In 1975, Cundill would have a chance to put that philosophical framework to good use, having just taken over management of a struggling Canadian mutual fund. By then, he had studied Graham's work intensely, even attending the great man's 'Renaissance of Value' lecture in 1974, and he was a devoted disciple of the church of Graham and Dodd. Writing to investors, he explained his intent to leverage Graham's net-net stock strategy, which had helped both Graham and Buffett achieve exceptional records.

"The essential concept is to buy under valued, unrecognised, neglected, out of fashion, or misunderstood situations where inherent value, a margin of safety, and the possibility of sharply changing conditions created new and favourable investment opportunities. Although a large number of holdings might be held, performance was invariably established by concentrating in a few holdings. In essence, the fund invested in companies that, as a result of detailed fundamental analysis, were trading below their 'intrinsic value'. The intrinsic value was defined as the price that a private investor would be prepared to pay for the security if it were not listed on a public stock exchange. The analysis was based as much on the balance sheet as it was on the statement of profit and loss."[167]

Over the first ten years, strictly employing Graham's net-net approach, Cundill achieved a compound growth rate of 26%, with no down years, for the Cundill Value Fund, and he grew shareholder equity to C\$126 million.[168] While the compound annual growth rate was lower than that of Buffett's partnership, Cundill achieved his record during one of the most devastating stock market periods since the Great Depression. During the Cundill Value Fund's first ten years, the US markets produced a small overall loss, while the Dow Jones produced a 7.4% compound rate of return over the 13 years that Buffett ran his partnership.[169] This

---

166 Risso-Gill, *There's Always Something to Do*, 4.

167 Ibid., 23.

168 Cundill, Presentation at The Ben Graham Centre for Value Investing, Richard Ivey School of Business (28 March 2005), www.youtube.com/watch?v=UWMrBJxy3us; Risso-Gill, *There's Always Something to Do*, 57.

169 Buffett, 'The Superinvestors'.

puts Cundill's market-relative performance ahead of Buffett's, enough to dub him the king of net-nets.

Cundill's net-net selection criteria

Cundill's strategy seemed to be lifted straight from Graham and Dodd's *Security Analysis*. Writing in 1995, Cundill outlined his investment framework this way:

> "I'm searching for securities that trade below their seeming liquidation value. The framework is really the one set by Benjamin Graham. He took the current assets less all the liabilities, including preferred shares, at their liquidation value and divided that number by the number of shares outstanding. If the price of the security is less than that, you examine the business."[170]

Cundill's personal diary reveals a strong preference for detailed analysis to establish fair values, while incorporating qualitative aspects that would influence the investment. In this respect, his philosophy was very similar to Buffett's.

Cundill's quantitative checklist

Soon after taking over the value fund, he noted in his diary the investment checklist that would help him earn outstanding returns:

> "Based on my studies and experience, investments for the Venture Fund should only be made if most of the following criteria are met:
>
> - The share price must be less than book value. Preferably it will be less than net working capital less long-term debt.
> - The price must be less than one half of the former high and preferably at or near its all time low.
> - The price earning multiple must be less than ten or the inverse of the long-term corporate bond rate, whichever is the less.
> - The company must be profitable. Preferably it will have increased its earnings for the past five years and there will have been no deficits over that period.
> - The company must be paying dividends. Preferably the dividend will have been increasing and have been paid for some time.

---

170 Cundill, *The Financial Times Global Guide to Investing*, 644.

- Long-term debt and bank debt (including off-balance-sheet financing) must be judiciously employed. There must be room to expand the debt position if required."[171]

While most are simple to understand, why demand an inverse PE ratio that's less than the corporate bond yield?

The lower a firm's price to earnings ratio, the more attractive the investment, all else being equal. The inverse of the PE ratio, known as the earnings yield, allows an investor to compare a firm's income to the income of other assets. Cundill's PE of 10 amounts to an earnings yield of 10%, while a PE of 20 equals an earnings yield of 5%.

Investment yields tend to move in sympathy with changes in the prime rate, so when the prime rate is high, so are investment yields. In fact, yields may rise to such an extent that a PE of 10 is merely average rather than cheap. In these situations, Cundill's PE of 10 requirement would not specify a cheap stock. If interest rates rose even higher, Cundill would demand a greater earnings yield (or lower PE) and would use a corporate bond yield as a benchmark. If corporate bond yields were 20%, as they were in Canada in the early 1980s, Cundill would aim to buy companies with earning yields of 20% or higher (PEs of 5% or lower). This would ensure that he'd be buying at a lower valuation relative to earnings.

But Cundill didn't just seek firms priced cheaply relative to earnings; he also used earnings records to screen for higher-quality investments. All three gurus presented here considered growth an important factor. Growth, without a corresponding deterioration in operating ratios, leads to higher valuations and increasing stock prices. Cundill's preference for sustained profitability also meant buying firms that were less affected by business challenges to help him select more stable businesses, which provided him with additional downside protection.

Firms suffering large business problems are in a much trickier spot if their balance sheets are overloaded with debt. As Cundill wrote in *The Financial Times Global Guide to Investing*, "[a] strong balance sheet with very little debt gives you the margin of safety. Even if the business is deteriorating, as long as it's not too badly, that allows you to fight another day," since the business is less likely to slip into bankruptcy. When facing a crisis, management also have a much easier time righting operations if they're free from the worry of covering interest or principal payments.[172]

---

171 Risso-Gill, *There's Always Something to Do*, 24.
172 Ibid.

Cundill's qualitative assessment

Far from being a purely quantitative investor, Cundill incorporated qualitative aspects in his approach to investing in terms of assessing both ultimate liquidation value and where the business would end up. Highlighting this approach in his diary, right after taking control of The Cundill Value Fund, he wrote:

> "Studies should be made of past and expected future rates of profitability, the ability of the management, and the various underlying factors and hypotheses that govern sales volume, costs, and profit after taxes. Of course, one should never become an absolute slave to the above criteria [Cundill's selection criteria discussed above], but they have proved to my satisfaction to be a vital starting point."[173]

In this respect, Cundill echoed Graham's preference for firms that had a solid record of earnings in the past, and were expected to return to that level of performance again in the future. But he also adopted elements of Buffett's in-depth assessment of the business in taking apart a firm's operations and trying to determine where the business could be in the future.

Cundill's early investments

CREDIT FONCIER

Credit Foncier was a Canadian finance company that had enjoyed a good business lending to farmers in Western Canada in the 1920s. But these loans came to haunt the company as the nation entered the 1930s recession. Struggling to cover interest payments, Credit Foncier was forced to foreclose on many of the people it had spent a decade building customer relationships with.

Rather than force farmers off the land, only to liquidate properties at fire sale prices, the firm kept them as tenants, charging manageable rents so the properties would remain occupied. When the economy recovered years later, the firm resold the properties but kept the associated mineral rights.

This proved fortuitous when commodity prices began to rise significantly in the 1970s. It added significantly to shareholder value, which shareholders were unaware of, due to the firm's highly conservative accounting. Foncier maintained its owned real estate and associated mineral rights at cost on its balance sheet. While value had built up enormously over 50 years, the firm's accounting didn't reflect that fact.[174]

173 Risso-Gill, *There's Always Something to Do*, 24.
174 Ibid.

The firm's ongoing profitability was apparent, however. It was consistently profitable and had paid dividends for decades, satisfying two of Cundill's basic criteria.[175]

There was another quirk that made the investment interesting: its unusual board structure. Paribas, an elitist French bank, owned majority control of the Montreal-based firm. While Fontier's main board ran the company in Canada, Paribas had instituted an auxiliary board which drew high salaries but added little in terms of value to the company or minority shareholders. In fact, shareholders were particularly short-changed by the deal. The French auxiliary board (some called them leeches) personally took home 20% of the Canadian firm's profits.[176] A seat on the board had become highly sought after over the years and was regarded as a retirement perk for exemplary service. But the company's shareholders had become unhappy with the arrangement. To Cundill, it looked increasingly likely that the two camps would clash, which would draw attention to the firm's enormous unrecognised value, ultimately boosting the stock price.

Cundill assessed the firm's net-net value at $150, and acquired his position at an average cost of $43. This was an enormous 71% discount to fair value. By the time he was finished, he owned 2% of the company and the investment made up a very large chunk of his portfolio.[177]

The stock crept up persistently as word about Cundill's discovery spread throughout the Canadian financial establishment. Within two months, the stock was up 25%, but Cundill remained enthusiastic about his investment. As Christopher Risso-Gill noted in his outstanding biography of Cundill, Cundill considered Foncier to be one of the one or two outstanding opportunities any investor might ever have:

> "I believe that there is probably one opportunity in every man's life which demands his knowledge, his guts, his self-esteem, and his judgement. If he seizes it with both hands and it is successful, he joins the first rank; if not he remains a mortal with feet of clay. Credit Foncier may well be my test."[178]

While Christopher Risso-Gill does not reveal just how much Cundill made from the investment, it developed into one of Cundill's best investments.

175 Ibid.
176 Ibid.
177 Ibid.
178 Ibid.

J. WALTER THOMPSON

The advertising company J. Walter Thompson (JWT) leapt on to the public markets at $20 per share in 1972, just in time to experience one of the largest market downturns in modern times.[179] As the 1970s drew on, the developed world's enormous economic stress hit advertisers particularly hard. JWT's revenue tumbled, resulting in layoffs, and particularly acute negativity regarding the company's future. Advertising companies were a luxury that businesses couldn't afford, and their earnings were expected to remain depressed for years to come.[180]

To make matters worse, JWT's former Los Angeles branch head H. R. Haldeman had been imprisoned for his role in the Watergate scandal. The firm's stock tumbled 80% from its initial IPO price to just $4 by 1976.[181]

Cundill quickly spotted an enormous opportunity. The firm's liquidation value came in at $18 per share, excluding high-priced real estate in Paris and Tokyo and a long-term lease in Berkeley Square in London.[182] The firm was free of debt and most of the firm's liquidation value, $10 per share, was made up of cash and marketable securities.[183]

Qualitative assessment revealed another striking fact. JWT was a household name, which meant the brand had to be worth something in liquidation.[184] But if the firm were not to be liquidated, its brand power would help it earn significant profits again in the future.

In fact, its brand power was likely helping the company during the mid-1970s. The firm was profitable and, despite its troubles, still paying a dividend. Cundill began buying, eventually filling 10% of his fund at an average price of $8 per share.[185]

Cundill didn't have to wait long for his keen judgement to pay off. Within months, First City Financial filed a 13D with the Security and Exchange Commission. (A 13D is a form investors are required to submit after obtaining ownership stakes above 5%.)[186] In effect, this was a flare in the dark, alerting management and investors of a potential takeover attempt. The resulting bump-up in the firm's stock price allowed Cundill to exit his position at $20, for a 150% capital gain in just over a year.

179 Ibid.
180 Ibid.
181 Ibid.
182 Ibid.
183 Cundill, *The Financial Times Global Guide to Investing*, 645.
184 Ibid.
185 Risso-Gill, *There's Always Something to Do*, 29.
186 Ibid.

AMERICAN INVESTMENT COMPANY

Personal finance companies were suffering under the weight of the mid-1970s crisis, as the cost of money rose and borrowers found it tougher to cover their interest payments. As one of the largest consumer finance companies in the USA, American Investment Company (AIC) was struggling. Founded in the 1930s, the company had enjoyed a long history of profitability, but the 1970s crisis led to losses and knocked the firm's shares down by 90%, from $30 to just $3.

Value, however, was not in question. Cundill assessed the firm's liquidation value at $12 per share, three times greater than the firm's share price. This excluded a significant real estate portfolio and tax-loss carry-forwards that the company could use to offset future tax liabilities.

It was also evident that the company would be able to put those carry-forwards to good use. The retail loan market had already recovered, and AIC was back to pumping out profits for shareholders. While the firm had not yet resumed paying dividends, Cundill had reason to think that reinstatement was just around the corner. Spotting opportunity, he pounced, buying over 5% of the firm, which required him to file a 13D.

Other investors took note. Soon the company had a pair of suitors, Household Finance and Gulf and Western, which offered competitive bids for the firm, only to be stonewalled by regulators. Shortly after, Leucadia National made an offer of $13 for the shares, allowing Cundill to cash out at a 333% gain in just two years.

CLEVELAND CLIFFS

Modern value investors often turn their nose up at widget makers, preferring companies with strong franchises or moats. That competitive barrier helps firms fend off competition, so they're much more likely to produce significant profit for their owners over a long period of time.

Cundill was different. As a net-net investor, he was primarily concerned with the value of tangible assets; the more liquid those assets were the better. It's no surprise, then, that he found Cleveland Cliffs such a compelling buy.

Cleveland Cliffs was the quintessential widget producer, manufacturing a pure commodity: iron ore pellets. As the 1980s pressed on, investors were becoming more enchanted with technology companies that showed significant growth potential. Firms such as Cleveland Cliffs held less and less interest for them. When the firm's performance began to slide, investors dubbed it a total dog and began exiting the stock in droves. Shares traded down from $40 to $18 by mid-1985.[187]

---

187 Ibid.

That dog still retained $22 in book value, according to Cundill. If its holdings in various joint venture investments were included in its current assets, investors could consider the firm a net-net.[188] Even more enticing, Cundill spotted what looked like a hidden asset buried deep within the notes to the financial statements: ownership of a Michigan power plant it was carrying at a trivial amount on the books.[189]

Cundill reached out to one of his fellow net-net hunters, Alan Kahn, who had spent a considerable amount of time assessing power plants in Arizona. According to Kahn, the plant was worth an enormous amount of money. Immediately interested, Cundill reached out to another deep value investor, Don Kennedy, who confirmed the significant hidden value on the firm's balance sheet.[190] This hidden asset boosted the firm's valuation far above book value.

Cundill started buying at $15 per share, only to watch the firm's market value continue to slide. By November of that year, the trio had bought the stock all the way down to $6 per share.[191] At that price, the company was trading at 67% discount to book value, and the discount to net-net value was nearly as large. The position now made up 4% of Cundill's fund, at an average cost of $9.75.[192]

Stock prices surged in 1987, the product of a euphoria that had built up throughout the 1980s. Scrambling to find value, investors latched on to Cleveland Cliffs, bidding its stock price up to $20. This triggered Cundill's automatic sell rule, so the fund began to unload its shares. Cundill had nailed a 90% gain in roughly a year and a half.[193]

By the end of the summer, the Cundill Value Fund had unloaded 15% of its position and was set to unload a significant amount more.[194] On 19 October 1987, after a few volatile trading sessions, the American markets collapsed, recording their largest one-day loss ever.[195] The market's 20%+ drop hammered Cleveland Cliff's stock price, pulling it back down to Cundill's average cost, well below net-net value. In characteristic fashion, Cundill checked the numbers and rebuilt his position at the newly depressed prices. His persistence paid off. By the time his

188 Ibid.
189 Ibid.
190 Ibid.
191 Ibid.
192 Ibid.
193 Ibid.
194 Ibid.
195 Black Monday, on 19 October 1987, was when a sudden and unexpected global market crash occurred.

fund exited the position in the early 1990s, he'd recorded a compound annual return of over 30%.[196]

What to take away from Graham, Buffett, and Cundill

While all three gurus presented here employed Graham's net-net strategy differently, there are still striking similarities in their approaches.

A broad look at all three highlights significantly different diversification strategies. While Graham would often hold over 100 net-nets, both Buffett and Cundill preferred highly concentrated portfolios comprised of their highest-conviction picks. And though Graham shifted from detailed security analysis to a radically simplified mechanical approach in the mid-1970s, Cundill successfully employed detailed security analysis to achieve world-class returns.

All three agreed, however, on the need for both qualitative and quantitative analysis. Assessing a firm's future performance was a key consideration for each investor when it came to qualitative analysis. On the quantitative front, all three preferred strong defensive characteristics primarily comprised of rock-solid balance sheets. They also sought to assess a firm's real-world liquidation values and then buy well below that figure. After all, buying below a conservative assessment of liquidation value is the core principle of Graham's classic net-net strategy.

196 Risso-Gill, *There's Always Something to Do*, 75.

9

My Own Net-Net Stock Portfolio Returns

SELECTING AN INVESTMENT strategy is arguably more important than selecting individual stocks. Investment strategies guide decision making and provide an overall roadmap for long-term success. Select a sound high performance strategy and you'll accumulate more wealth, faster. Select a poor strategy, on the other hand, and you can lose a lot of money very quickly.

Smart strategy selection requires a focus both on the strategy's performance record as provided by high-quality sources, and evidence that the strategy has been used successfully in practice. Typically, this means sourcing academic studies and, to a lesser extent, high-quality industry studies, and identifying professional money managers (or reliable, small, private investors) who have used the strategy to produce comparable returns.

Neglecting to take these steps can result in embarking down a long road that ends in financial pain. Academic studies or industry white papers from trusted sources are necessary to establish a base rate for the strategy: an average rate of return attributable to stocks that fit the criteria. Without a solid long-term record, any market-beating outperformance will be more a matter of luck. On the other hand, without evidence that a strategy can be used effectively in practice, a solid academic record remains simply an academic exercise that may not yield comparable results in the real world.

This book has discussed the history of net-nets, why people fail to use the strategy, why net-nets are so profitable, and the sort of base rate returns net-nets have shown in academic studies. We've also covered returns achieved by three outstanding investors, Graham, Buffett, and Cundill, highlighting the fact that the strategy can be used successfully in practice.

While I do not consider myself to rank alongside Graham, Buffett, or Cundill, it's fair to ask how an everyday investor without any real professional training fares when adopting Graham's famous strategy. We've included this chapter to provide some insight into that question.

My performance over the previous nine years can be divided into two periods:[197]

1. The first period covers my first few years using the strategy. During this period I had not yet fully transitioned to a portfolio comprised only of net-net stocks. Despite realising that I had stumbled onto a terrific strategy, I still hung on to some past picks – and, in hindsight, held on much too long. To make matters more complicated, my broker lacked any sort of portfolio reporting tool (maybe by design), so I could not track my portfolio performance relative to the market.

2. The second period marks my transition to international net-net investing in order to source a wider range of high-quality net-nets. To do so, I shifted to using a much better broker and gained access to robust reporting tools that I still use to track my performance versus the market. During this period, all but two of my stocks were net-nets (and those two stocks added nothing to my returns on balance).

My early net-net stock returns

The table below lists all of my positions from 2010 to 2014. It shows real money returns net of fees as reported by my broker. It should provide some idea of the returns on offer for small investors.[198] Not all net-nets provided positive returns, but many did and the average return was excellent.

Some firms are listed twice. In some cases this is because I purchased an initial block of shares and then later a second block at a different price. Other firms are

---

197 For a more up-to-date performance report, visit www.netnethunter.com/hunter-fund or www.evanbleker.com.

198 It's important for readers to take my stated returns with a grain of salt. The published returns have not been (and will not be) audited – I present them here to give some idea of how a small investor may fare using the strategy. Ultimately, investors should not choose to adopt the strategy based on the opinion or stated performance of any one investor. A rational approach requires a thorough assessment of the empirical evidence for the strategy, mostly found in academic studies and industry white papers, plus the opinion of a number of trusted (and very successful) professional investors who have actually used the strategy. Investors need the first to get some idea of how the strategy has performed on a purely statistical basis, while the second is needed to confirm that the strategy can be used successfully in practice. Finally, due to the methodological limits of any study, the biases inherent in industry white papers, the varying skill of successful individual investors, and even the ability of professional investors to "shape" audited results, investors need a little faith before adopting any investment strategy.

listed twice because after initially selling them for a gain I saw them drop back in price, sparking a second purchase.

Table 7: Evan Bleker's net-net investments, 2010–14

Company	Percentage change	Months
Trans World Entertainment	193.70%	27 months
BFS Entertainment	–4.80%	36 months
Mead Instruments	1.40%	29 months
InfoSonics	46%	14.3 months
Total Telcom	–75%	35 months
Paulson Capital	72.5%	28.3 months
Jemtech	–11.1%	35.5 months
InfoSonics	103.1%	8.5 months
BFS Entertainment	33%	26.3 months
GTSI Corp.	84.90%	6 months
InfoSonics	73.4%	10.6 months
IGo Inc	65.2%	3.3 months
IGo Inc	–1.6%	6 months
InfoSonics	146.6%	7 months
Sangoma Technologies	85%	4.3 months
Jemtech	7.4%	3.5 months
Sangoma Technologies	85%	4 months
Universal Power Group	5.1%	2.3 months

Source: Scotia iTrade brokerage account reports

Despite having little experience with the strategy initially, my early performance was excellent. In the next table, I have presented the position's average return over the period and the average holding period length. These positions averaged a 51% return, and each position was held for 16 months, on average.

The average annualised return adjusts each position to set it to a 12-month holding period. The return of each stock is divided by the number of months I held the position, and multiplied by 12 to obtain an annualised figure. I held some of these positions for under a year, so their annualised returns are higher than their actual returns shown above. In other cases, stocks were held for more than a year so their annualised performance is shown as smaller than their actual realised returns over the holding period.

On a 12-month basis, positions averaged a 38% return. That's quite good, but remember that the 38% return is not my portfolio's compound average return over the period. It is simply the average annualised return of each one of my NCAV stock picks.

Finally, my portfolio's overall win rate (the percentage of stocks that produced positive returns) was nearly 78%. This figure was likely inflated as the markets came out of the Great Financial Crisis, and later dropped to around 70%.

Table 8: Summary statistics for Evan Bleker's early net-net stock returns, 2010–14

Average	50.54%	15.94 months
Average annualised	38.04%	12 months
Win percentage	77.8%	14 of 18 positions

Source: Scotia iTrade brokerage account reports.

A fatal early investing mistake

My early success as a net-net investor masks a major mistake I made when first starting out in 2010. As you saw above, I had a total of 18 NCAV positions over the three-year period and rarely held more than eight positions at any one time. Concentrating on a small number of high-quality investment opportunities boosted both returns and volatility. But when first starting out, I took a risky approach to testing the strategy before fully embracing it.

Net-net stock investing is what I've come to call a statistical strategy. The strategy works well so long as you focus on the group return rather than the return of any one position. The base rate highlighted earlier is an average return for all net-nets over all years studied. It's not the return an investor can expect from each and every net-net pick. Within a portfolio, net-net stocks will produce a wide range of results, from heavy losses to unbelievable gains. It's the average return of all of these stocks that produce your yearly performance figures.

Likewise, a long string of yearly results produces an overall performance record. All the years – both good and bad – work together to produce your eventual result.

It's easy for investors to miss these crucial facts, just as I did when first starting out. Rather than buy a basket of net-nets and employ the strategy for a good number of years, I made the mistake of trying to tiptoe into the strategy by buying only two or three net-nets "to see how they would do". In reality, I was playing Russian roulette with my financial future. The two or three stocks I purchased could have produced returns anywhere along the distribution of returns attributable to net-net stocks. Had I rolled the dice and picked up three losing stocks, I would have concluded that net-net investing doesn't work, and would have missed the exceptional returns on offer to long-term investors.

As luck would have it, my early experience proved very lucrative and sold me on the strategy. As I studied net-net investing in depth over the next couple of years, I gradually woke up to the near-fatal mistake I had made. Luckily, I kept digging up winners and producing good yearly returns, which kept me hooked on the strategy.

New investors should keep this lesson in mind: you can't simply buy a few net-nets to test out the strategy. That cautious approach will provide you with no insight into how the strategy performs over the long run. At best, you'll be happily misled, as I was during this early period. At worst, you'll stumble onto two or three terrible stocks which will lead you to abandon the strategy. Likewise, assessing the strategy's performance over a single year or two provides you with misleading information because, like individual stocks, a net-net portfolio will produce a range of outcomes. Assessing the merits of a strategy can only be done by referencing academic or industry studies, and checking to see if the strategy has been used successfully in practice.

New era: my experience with international net-nets

February 2019 marked the end of my fifth fiscal year investing internationally with my new broker. Employing a strategy over five years provides a reasonable amount of data, really the minimum necessary, to assess your performance as an investor. Any shorter and it becomes difficult to parse skill from luck.

How has value performed this past decade?

First, some context: The last ten years have been outstanding for stocks generally. Indices have risen fairly steadily over this period, one of the longest stretches of uninterrupted market growth in the last 100 years. Firms like Facebook, Amazon, and Netflix have taken the market by storm, and quantitative easing has flooded the market with cash, pushing up the price of high-flying growth companies.

For some reason, however, it's been a terrible decade for value. The chart below shows the performance of value indices in the US from 2007 to 2016, a period of underperformance relative to growth investing and the overall market. A $100 investment in US value indices in 2007 would be worth less than $100 in 2017.

Fig. 4: Cumulative total relative return for value indices, 2007–2016

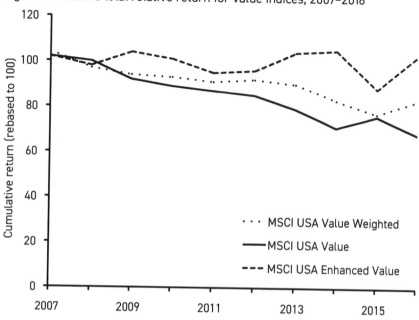

Source: S. Markowicz, 'Where Is the Value in Value Investing?', Schroders (December 2018).

American value indices underperformed from 2007–2019 and actually produced losses during one of the greatest bull markets in history.[199]

Performance has not improved since 2017, and this marks the longest period of time that value investing has underperformed growth investing (and by the greatest degree).

Despite the recent underperformance, value investing has almost always outperformed growth investing over rolling ten-year periods. In 2007, smart value investors would have had every reason to expect great performance going forward based on the historic record. Returns have proven lacklustre at best, however. This highlights the fact that, while necessary for success, a rational approach to investing does not always yield great returns.

199 Markowicz, 'Where Is the Value in Value Investing?', Schroders (December 2018).

Fig. 5: The return of value stocks relative to growth stocks, 1936–2016

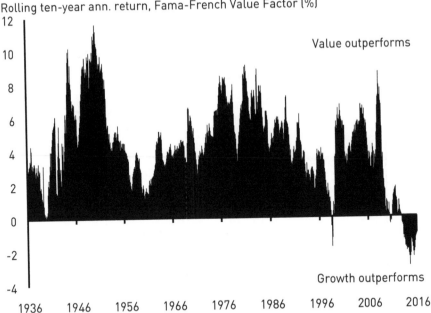

Source: Markowicz, 'Where Is the Value in Value Investing?', Schroders (December 2018).

The performance of American net-net stocks since 1999

Where does the poor performance of value leave American-only net-net investing?

Not in much better shape. Research conducted by Net Net Hunter revealed that while net-nets outpaced value indices as expected over the last ten years, American net-nets failed to beat the market. This marks the worst showing for net-nets in any single country that I'm aware of, highlighting the importance of sourcing the best net-nets from a diverse group of global markets.

Figure 6 shows that American net-nets have performed very well relative to the NASDAQ on a cumulative basis, since 1999. Even with the recent underperformance, an investor would have experienced life-changing results. The total return of around 1750% would not have been smooth, however.

Fig. 6: Cumulative American net-net stock returns versus the NASDAQ, 1999–2016

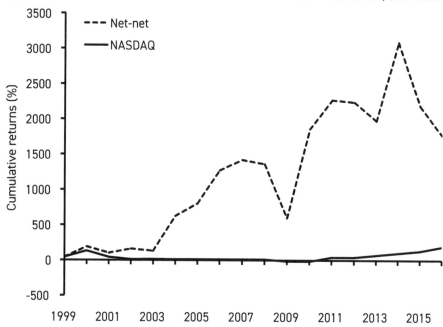

Source: Net Net Hunter.

Part of the reason for the recent underperformance is likely due to the flood of Chinese reverse mergers that hit the market in the 2010s. Many China-based frauds that looked great on paper were ultimately classified as net-nets which dragged down performance. Back tests Net Net Hunter has conducted show a meaningful jump in performance when excluding Chinese companies. When picking net-nets, it really pays to know what you're doing. A lot of investors got sucked into the Chinese reverse merger scam, a problem that Net Net Hunter members easily avoided. More on this disturbing phenomenon in a later chapter.

It's anyone's guess when value will turn the corner in the USA, but three facts are clear:

1. While value has significantly outperformed growth (glamour) long-term, this hasn't been the case during raging bull markets. But value also tends to come back. This may mean that just as value massively underperformed during the late 1990s tech bubble and then dominated the market over the next decade, we could also be on the cusp of a great bull run for value stocks. Graham would agree, citing the law of compensation.[200]

---

200 Kahn and Milne, 'Benjamin Graham, the Father of Financial Analysis', The Financial Analysts Research Foundation (1977).

2. All intelligent investing is value investing. As Munger says, why would you want to pay more for something than it is worth?[201] Eventually those holding on to overpriced stocks will pay the cost of their foolishness. As the performance of a high-flying growth company weakens, investors rush for the exit, causing the stock price to crash. It's an age-old pattern that trips up a lot of investors.

3. Smart value investors who think critically about what they're doing and are investing with a long-term time horizon will earn great returns over the long term. Net-nets are the best way to make that happen as they're at the top of the available value strategies. Even in Japan, value stocks performed very well after the 1989 crisis if you were in it for the long term.[202]

My five-year performance

With all of this in mind, let's look at my five-year returns. The following charts show my account's performance against the NASDAQ and the Russell 2000 small cap index.

Figure 7: Evan Bleker's portfolio performance relative to the NASDAQ and Russell 2000, 2014–2018

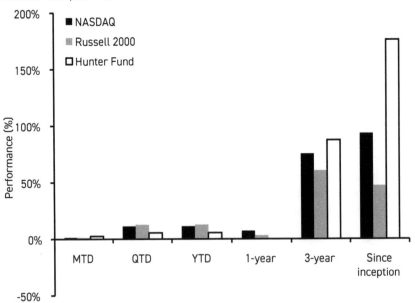

201 Munger, 'All Intelligent Investing Is Value Investing', youtu.be/Lsaj6fmAtNk.
202 Bleker, 'Benjamin Graham, Is Japan Where Money Goes to Die?', netnethunter.com.

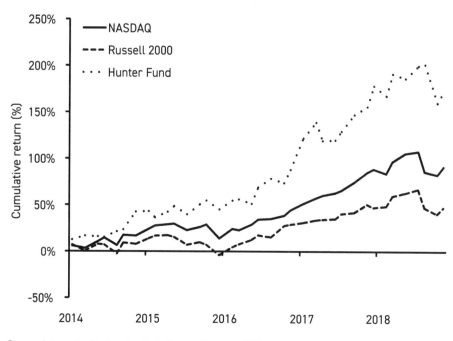

Source: Interactive Brokers Portfolio Report, February 2019.

My portfolio has performed very well relative to the market over the last five years. While the NASDAQ has had an amazing run, my own portfolio has far outpaced it. My total and compound average annual returns were actually better during the summer, but one of my stocks took a major drop, which hit my portfolio hard. Luckily, I ended the year in positive territory.

My portfolio is up 176% total over the five-year period, amounting to a CAGR of 22.5%. This is well above the NASDAQ's 93% total return, which came in at a 14% CAGR. My performance is net of fees and commissions, but not taxes, while the NASDAQ is a no-fee, no-tax index. The Russell 2000 wasn't close.

No single stock accounted for a large percentage of my gains. In fact, I haven't had any big winners but have consistently seen 100% gains on many stocks held for one to three years. My portfolio is also 95%+ invested in net-nets. Where I have deviated, I've bought near-net-nets which, on balance, haven't added to my performance. Overall, my performance relative to American net-nets is due to location, selecting top picks, and concentration:

- **Location.** I invest internationally, so my returns will differ from those of US net-nets. American net-nets have made up between 20 and 70% of my portfolio. I sourced the rest from developed markets.

- **Top picks.** Investing internationally allows me to invest in the best net-nets available because I simply have more net-nets to choose from. The larger your investment universe, the better the stocks on offer. At any one time there have been roughly 1000 international net-nets available. As you might expect, filtering through the list is a Herculean task. That's why Net Net Hunter hired a professional analyst to hand-filter the list to arrive at 40 to 50 of the best net-nets to research. This has been an enormous time-saver, allowing me to focus on the best picks rather than simply filling a plain-vanilla, widely diversified portfolio.

- **Concentration.** I manage a more concentrated portfolio which still leverages the statistical returns associated with net-nets but also allows me to overweight the better opportunities. My portfolio has typically ranged between eight and ten positions, a level of concentration that I feel comfortable with, given my skill and experience. As I learn more and become more skilled, I may concentrate even more to make the most of truly exceptional gems.

While I'm not happy with my current portfolio returns over the last five years, they're very healthy when put into context. Few investors even match the market, let alone beat it. Over the last five years my returns have been exceptional.

Net-net performance over the next five years

One common piece of advice from outstanding value investors is that you can't predict the market.

With that in mind, it's also impossible to predict the future performance of my net-net portfolio. Investing returns do not correlate perfectly with effort, good judgement, and skill over the short or even medium term. As with most long-only strategies, the direction of the market plays a large role in the performance of the strategy. If the market drops, my own portfolio is likely to drop as well. It's also impossible to tell whether I'll be able to maintain the recent outperformance while net-nets in general languish. Again, part of the reason for my outperformance has been concentrating on a smaller number of picks that seem to have better prospects than net-nets in general. Even if I'm able to identify these picks going forward, my own performance depends on the market's ability to spot these opportunities over time and its willingness to bid the price of my stocks up. If the market loses its appetite for tiny companies trading for depressed prospects, my portfolio will not perform well.

Strong effort, good judgement, and skill do, however, play a large role in long-term performance. To that end, I'm focused on continually improving my knowledge of net-nets, qualitative analysis, and accounting, plus my own temperament and psychology, in order to achieve better returns. Aiming to improve little by little each week has a massive impact over time, which will eventually translate into even better investment decisions. Over the long term, I'm confident that Graham's 90-year-old strategy will continue to achieve great results. Human nature does not change and there remains plenty of opportunity for small investors among tiny cheap companies.

PART 3

NET–NET INVESTING METHOD

10

The Net–Net Hunter Scorecard

ONE OF THE most valuable, but least utilised, tools in investing is the investment checklist. A checklist is a list of items used to systematically approach a complex task. They have been tremendously valuable in all sorts of industries for reducing or eliminating human error. Pilots, for example, go through a pre-flight checklist to ensure an aircraft is safe and prepared for flight.

Professionals such as Monish Pabrai have incorporated checklists into their investment process to make sure they don't leave out critical pieces of information when researching a stock. Buffett and Munger are no different, though they call their checklist items filters.

While it's not possible to eliminate all human error, investors can go a long way towards reducing their mistakes and choosing better stocks by referencing a checklist during the research process.

Background to a solid scorecard

I've spent a considerable amount of time combing through Graham's books, Buffett's partnership letters, and a large number of net-net stock studies to assess what works and the pitfalls to avoid. In the process, I've kept notes on the investment characteristics that produce the highest possible returns using this strategy and put these best practices into a list I call the Net Net Hunter Scorecard.

Investors should keep in mind, however, that there are a number of different ways to implement a net-net stock strategy. Academic studies reveal the best characteristics to focus on from a statistical perspective. Focusing on these forms the basis for a solid mechanical net-net strategy.

But we've also looked at how a few choice professionals have implemented Graham's net-net approach. While these pros have based their strategy on sound quantitative characteristics such as a low price to NCAV, they have also incorporated qualitative characteristics to separate the wheat from the chaff.

New investors are unlikely to go wrong using a purely quantitative, mechanical approach to net-net selection. So long as net-net investors maintain a fully stocked portfolio at all times, ensure a good amount of diversification, run the strategy for the long term, and avoid major mistakes, they should obtain market-beating returns.

More advanced investors, on the other hand, will perform better by incorporating qualitative characteristics to identify particularly attractive investments. To use this approach, investors should have a strong understanding of their own abilities. Without a clear understanding of their ability to profit by employing qualitative analysis, they should not forego sound quantitative characteristics in favour of an attractive qualitative picture.

Like many Net Net Hunter members, I use a mixed approach based on identifying stocks that are statistically cheap, have stable NCAV and a solid balance sheet, and sweeteners in terms of a solid near-term catalyst, significant share buy-backs, or expected future growth.

The Net Net Hunter Scorecard was developed for both quantitative investors as well as those who employ a mix of quantitative and qualitative criteria. The approach you take to net-net investing depends a lot on your own temperament, skills, ability, and philosophy.

Temperament – Some investors feel more comfortable owning a lot of positions that are cheap and safe as judged by statistical measures, such as a very low price to NCAV, a small debt to equity figure, and solid balance sheet liquidity. Others will only feel secure if they own net-net investments that have a strong 'story'. This necessitates more qualitative analysis and a more concentrated portfolio as a result.

Investment skill – Newer investors lack the skill and experience needed to identify stronger investment candidates on qualitative grounds, so are better off sticking to a diversified portfolio selected on quantitative grounds. By contrast, some investors will have extensive stock picking skill and investment experience. These investors can leverage this skill and experience by identifying great prospects and concentrating on the better qualitative situations.

Philosophy – Some investors feel that investments should only be selected by use of quantitative data. Jim Simons of Renaissance Technologies may fall into this camp. Other investors, such as Charlie Munger, feel that investments should be selected only if they also possess a very strong qualitative profile. Clearly money can be made with either approach and far be it for me to try to dissuade anyone from their natural leanings. My own approach is to select investments which satisfy both a strong quantitative and qualitative showing.[203]

The Net Net Hunter Scorecard is broken up into three sections: core criteria, quantitative ranking criteria, and qualitative ranking criteria. While investors should only pick net-nets that meet the core criteria, quantitative investors can stick with the quantitative ranking criteria. Those who want to employ both quantitative and qualitative characteristics can employ both sets of ranking criteria. In this way, the scorecard can accommodate both camps.

Long-time mechanical investors will spot a discrepancy in terms. The Net Net Hunter Scorecard is not a checklist, per se, in that firms do not have to satisfy all criteria. In fact, the scorecard incorporates a hard initial checklist in core criteria, but the rest amounts to a scorecard. The more ranking characteristics the company meets, the better the firm is as an investment.

The Net Net Hunter Scorecard: core criteria

The Net Net Hunter Scorecard's core criteria are a set of characteristics that have to be in place before considering a stock for investment. If any of these characteristics

---

203 At this point it's important for me to point out the work of Daniel Kahneman, author of *Thinking, Fast and Slow*. In the book, Kahneman discusses the result of experts going off script by making decisions that are inconsistent with a well put together checklist. In almost all cases, the experts perform worse by introducing their own judgement on individual cases. This seems to be a strong argument against using any sort of qualitative factors in stock selection. After all, if the facts are known and can be put into a checklist, then making investment decisions counter to that checklist seems like a losing bet. Since we have decent quantitative data on which factors lead to great performance with net-nets, we should simply stick to it rather than going off script with factors that can't be measured. This is a strong argument for quantitative investing. Joshua Foer hints at a potential counter-argument, however, in his book *Moonwalking With Einstein*. In the book, Foer writes that superior pattern recognition gained by examining past games played by former grandmasters determines the amount of skill a future grandmaster acquires. The more time a player spends thinking through these past games, the more patterns the player stores in memory for later use when confronted with relevant new situations. It's reasonable to think that acquiring outstanding skill in investing works the same way – that it's a function of internalising a large number of high quality patterns and using that knowledge as an internal checklist when confronted with new investment cases. Studying the early investments of Warren Buffett and Charlie Munger, for example, and reading a significant amount of business literature, could provide investors with new mental frameworks, or 'checklists', that they can apply to new situations. Again, the key is internalising high quality patterns, so filtering for high quality sources of information is critically important. Incidentally, Warren Buffett is widely reported as saying that he would be able to earn a CAGR of 50% if he were investing small sums of money today. Given Buffett's extensive experience, and his scepticism towards mere formulaic investing, he would be achieving this performance through superior pattern recognition, not superior quantitative algorithms.

are missing, the stock should not be considered. Each criterion is important. Some net-nets will seem attractive buys but lack the volume necessary to buy a full position. In other cases, seemingly benign characteristics can lead to unusually poor outcomes. For that reason, all of these criteria have to be met before moving on with a full assessment.

Suitable average daily volume

Investments that can't be purchased have no utility, so investors should first assess whether a stock has enough volume to put together a decently sized position. Net-net firms are usually tiny businesses, which means their stock usually trades infrequently. This thin volume allows small investors to use the strategy but keeps larger investors out.

Sometimes a stock trades so infrequently that even retail investors managing just a few thousand dollars have trouble buying. For that reason, volume assessment is a must.

When assessing volume, we're specifically after average daily dollar volume. Average daily dollar volume is the dollar amount of stock traded on average each day over the recent past. Note that this is different from average daily volume, which only looks at the number of shares traded on average per day, without calculating the value of stock being traded. To find the average daily dollar volume, simply multiply the average daily volume by the stock price.

Minimum standards have to be set by investors' portfolio size, and the size of the position they want to buy. Someone investing $100,000, for example, will have to look for much higher average daily dollar volume minimums than would someone investing $10,000. Because of this, all investors must arrive at a suitable standard for themselves. The $100,000 investor, if buying 20 equally sized positions, would benefit from an average daily dollar volume of at least $1,000. This would help ensure that the investor could build a full position over a reasonable length of time. The $10,000 investor could get away with a much lower average daily dollar volume, while an investor managing $1 million should look for a minimum of perhaps $10,000.

Price to NCAV below 100%

The defining characteristic of net-net investing is buying stocks below their NCAV, which Graham regarded as a rough real-world assessment of their liquidation value. While purists would scoff at buying net-nets without a sufficient one-third discount to NCAV, studies show that net-nets which trade at, or just over, NCAV can still work out beautifully. To balance Graham's philosophy with academic findings, we simply limit the pool of candidates to those trading below NCAV.

Part of the reason why net-nets without a minimum one-third discount work out so well may be due to the put-like nature of net-net investing. An ultra-conservative assessment of liquidation value acts as a rock-bottom minimum valuation when assessing failed businesses. But many firms will ultimately recover and a few will actually thrive. Those that do will be revalued based on a multiple of earnings, book value, and so on, providing enormous returns. This pattern is likely responsible for the excellent returns of more expensive net-nets.

Demanding a more lenient discount has two major benefits. First, investors maintain a larger pool of stocks when the market is trading at higher valuations. This allows them to maintain a portfolio full of high-performance net-nets. Second, this tactic allows investors to pick the few exceptional buys that may not be trading at a minimum one-third discount. Some exceptional buys, such as growth stocks trading below NCAV, stocks with solid near-term catalysts, or firms with executives vacuuming up shares, can provide exceptional returns even if not trading with a minimum discount. When it comes to investing real money, there's little value in hanging on to dogmatic beliefs.

Market capitalisation below $100 million

While studies have shown that net-nets trading at or just above NCAV can still work out very well, the same is not true of larger firms trading below NCAV. In fact, studies that assess the relationship between net-net firm size and return show a significant negative correlation between the two. The larger the firm trading below NCAV, the lower the return.

While there is no clear demarcation line, most net-net firms have market caps below $100 million. Returns drop gradually as market capitalisations tick upwards, so it's unwise to buy larger net-net firms. Setting the cut-off here allows us to maintain a large pool of candidates while screening out a smaller number of statistically terrible buys.

Market capitalisation above $1 million

Despite the negative correlation between firm size and stock returns, as market capitalisations drop, management quality becomes more questionable. Publicly traded companies with market capitalisations below $1 million are not likely to have the financial resources to attract reasonably competent managers and are therefore best avoided.

It's curious why these firms are publicly listed in the first place. Maintaining a listing can cost over $100,000, making it prohibitively expensive for them to maintain a public listing. Small, successful, private businesses will seldom seek a public listing, opting for a private sale if an owner wants to monetise his investment. While it's true that some formerly profitable firms will stumble below NCAV and drop to a market cap of $1 million or less, it's often also the case that a firm went public as a shaky start-up, and subsequently failed to grow.

Firms with market capitalisations below $1 million are probably best avoided by amateur investors unless they have a keen understanding of business and can assess management skill and integrity.

Not a prohibited classification

Exceptional buys can be found in all industries, but some investments make for particularly poor net-nets. When assessing net-net candidates, we want to avoid financial, regulated, real estate, resource exploration, early stage bio, and early stage pharmaceutical firms, as well as closed funds and ADRs.

These categories are excluded in many academic studies, and therefore don't have the same academic backing as other net-net firms. Each classification listed here poses unique problems that inhibit an investor's ability to profit while running a net-net stock strategy. For example, financial firms require specialists to assess, since the range and nature of financial products have changed significantly over the last 50 years. Regulated firms, on the other hand, can face barriers to third-party takeovers and actions that could improve the business.

Real estate firms, resource exploration firms, as well as early stage bio and pharma companies often rapidly destroy NCAV. Real estate firms in particular can see debt ratios balloon and cash evaporate when projects are started, while resource exploration, early stage bio, and early stage pharmaceutical firms spend cash trying to obtain a viable economic asset. Many fail, completely eroding shareholder value, and then come back to shareholders for more money. Suffice it to say, Net Net Hunter has found that firms operating in these industries perform very poorly in its proprietary back tests.

No significant Chinese operations

China is a rich and vibrant country with an enormous depth of culture and an incredibly interesting history. Its people are intelligent and seem poised to lead the world both politically and economically.

But while tourists can gain a lot by venturing east, investors should stay clear of Chinese stocks. The short-selling firm Muddy Waters Research, headed by Carson Block, brought issues with Chinese reverse merger firms to public attention in the early 2010s. Since then, the firm has made a solid living shorting Western-listed Chinese firms that the firm thought were frauds.

Muddy Waters cites the Chinese proverb "Muddy waters makes it easy to catch fish" to explain the attitude of some unscrupulous Chinese businessmen. According to the team, some Chinese firms take advantage of investors ignorant of Chinese culture, language, and business practices by publishing fraudulent financial statements. These financial reports grossly inflate asset values and reported earnings. Rather than act as a watchdog, Western auditors and regulators have largely abdicated their responsibility, leaving short sellers like Muddy Waters to uncover the scams.

Unfortunately, many of these companies trade well below their claimed net asset values. Lured by a seemingly solid balance sheet, solid record of growth, and a dirt cheap valuation, many uninformed net-net investors scoop up shares only to lose most of their principal investment.

There are serious bargains on offer in Chinese public companies, but small investors do not have the skill and experience to avoid the frauds. For that reason, avoiding listed Chinese firms is a must.

Not selling shares

Firms that sell shares below NCAV provide terrible investment returns, as a group. The reason is obvious: either management disregards shareholder value, or the firm's very survival is in question.

Nothing is worse than a management team that disregards shareholder value so much that they give away the firm at a price below liquidation value. As Graham said nearly 100 years ago, if a firm trades below liquidation value, management should liquidate the company or work to correct the issue. Because the voluntary sale of shares below liquidation value destroys shareholder value, it is likely to be a breach of fiduciary duty.

In situations where the firm lacks liquidity to meet near-term obligations, share sales may be the last resort. In these cases, management may suspect that the liquid assets they have on hand are not of sufficient quality to cover near-term liabilities, so they will attempt to raise cash through a share sale. In other cases, management may feel that the firm's business issues are serious enough to warrant raising capital while they can to survive the coming storm.

Whatever the case, selling shares below NCAV is a clear red flag, and investors should act accordingly. In Net Net Hunter's own backtests, firms that trade below NCAV and have sold shares have performed particularly badly.

Current ratio above 1.5×

Current ratios assess a company's ability to meet its short-term obligations. They're measured by dividing a company's current assets by its current liabilities. Distressed firms should have ample current assets to cover any liability that has to be paid over the near term. Failing to meet these obligations could lead to a range of sanctions, from suppliers refusing to sell to the company to the firm filing for bankruptcy.

While current ratios can be neatly stated as a mathematical formula, their composition and implication is messier. Strong firms such as Wal-Mart often have current ratios below 1×, as they're able to demand favourable payment terms from suppliers. But distressed firms with current ratios near 1× are typically in serious trouble, since they lack the earnings or cash flow needed to cover near-term obligations.

While net-net investors should favour large current ratios, setting a limit is necessarily arbitrary. Graham's opinion regarding a specific standard shifted markedly over the course of his career. In mid-career, he explained that hurdles differ based on industry and investor taste, but he offered no clear means of determining an ideal minimum.[204] Towards the end of his life, he favoured the simple rule that a company should own twice what it owes.

My hurdle rate is more lenient. When assessing net-nets, we want to focus on companies that have current assets at least 1.5× their current liabilities. This provides investors with a one-third margin of safety, as current assets can shrink by one-third before the company runs into problems. Luckily, few companies fail this standard in practice.

Reasonable burn rate

Burn rate refers to the rate of shrink in NCAV between two reporting periods. If the firm reported a NCAV of 100 in the previous quarter, and a NCAV of 90 in the most recent quarter, it has a –10% quarter-over-quarter burn rate.

From a qualitative point of view, it makes sense to demand a stable NCAV. All value investors base their investment decision on referencing some source of value, whether earnings, cash flow, or a firm's private market value. Net-net investors reference NCAV, and a discount below this value provides the investor with both safety of principle and profit potential. When a firm's NCAV shrinks, so does an investor's margin of safety and profit potential.

In core criteria, we demand that firms have not shed NCAV by more than –25% over the most recent quarter or most recent 12 months.

---

204 Graham and Dodd, *Security Analysis*, 592.

Debt to equity below 50%

By definition, net-net stocks require a strong balance sheet due to their excess of current assets over total liabilities. In theory, this excess liquidity renders the firm safe as an investment.

But real-world asset values can differ remarkably from their stated balance-sheet figures. If receivables prove uncollectable, or inventory unsaleable, the firm may not have enough cash to fund near-term debt obligations or cover interest payments.

Net-net firms are also clear takeover targets, and takeovers are often funded with debt. But if a target company already has a large debt burden, a potential acquirer may not be able to use the debt to fund the purchase. This ultimately reduces the likelihood of a takeover.

To add to the mess, since interest rates were at near-historic lows in 2019, many firms carried debt they could not afford under normal economic conditions. This suggests the presence of many publicly traded zombie firms: undead firms that will bite the dust as interest rates rise. What could be worse than owning a money-losing firm with eroding sales and a large debt load during a period of rising interest rates?

No NYSE

NYSE net-nets have been associated with some of the lowest returns on offer in the net-net universe. Identifying the best net-nets, then, requires us to pass on any company that has a NYSE listing. American net-net investors may be dismayed by this rule. Given the poor performance that NYSE net-nets have shown, though, we've elected to designate this a core, rather than a ranking, criterion.

Quantitative ranking criteria

While all firms must meet every check in the core criteria, ranking criteria is optional. The first set of ranking criteria, quantitative ranking criteria, focuses on factors that provide a statistical boost in returns. The more of these criteria a stock meets, the better it is as a statistical bet. Investors who aim to select the best performing net-nets on a statistical basis should focus on firms that meet as many of these criteria as possible.

Share buy-backs

One of the best ways for net-net investors to boost returns is by selecting firms that are buying back shares. Share buy-backs are beneficial for two reasons. First, buy-backs communicate management's belief that the firm is financially healthy and its problem temporary. Management teams that fear for the survival of their company will not waste cash on buy-backs if they feel that the firm may require significant funds to stay in business. They're also less likely to buy back shares if they assume that the firm's problems will be drawn out. If management spends cash on buy-backs when the business faces a drawn-out business problem, less cash will be on hand to maintain operations. Money spent on buy-backs therefore represents money that management feel they can spend without jeopardising the survival of the firm.

Buy-backs are also beneficial because they increase per-share value by increasing the ownership percentage that each share represents. When shares are undervalued, management may use company funds to repurchase shares in order to reward remaining shareholders. When management buy back shares while they trade below NCAV, they significantly boost shareholder value.

We're specifically looking for companies that spend a material amount on share repurchases, since the more money spent on buy-backs, the more the remaining shareholders benefit.

No dividends

As highlighted in the discussion of net-net stock studies, dividends have a powerfully negative effect on net-net stock returns. Net-nets that pay a dividend provide much lower average yearly returns than their non-dividend-paying peers. It only makes sense, then, to avoid dividend payers if we're aiming to buy the highest returning net-net stocks possible.

If dividends pull down returns so much, why not move this requirement to core criteria?

We prefer to keep this criterion optional simply because some investors prefer to receive dividends to fund everyday expenses. Income investors should be aware of the trade-off they make in order to receive dividends.

Insider buys

Insider buying is a powerful indicator. The term *insider* usually refers to a member of a firm's upper management team or board of directors. Insiders often have the best understanding about their firm and are in the best position to render judgement on the firm's prospects.

Insiders almost always buy shares to profit through capital gains. When insiders buy, they communicate a strong conviction that the company's stock is a solid investment. Given their detailed understanding of the firm's operations, financial health, and prospects, insider buying is a much stronger vote of confidence than anything Wall Street can produce.

The more cash spent on share purchases, and the more insiders who are buying, the better the company looks as an investment.

Market capitalisation below $50 Million

In the core criteria, we demand a market capitalisation below $100 million, claiming that larger net-net firms are poor investment candidates. When setting the limit, we need to strike a balance between statistical returns and stock availability. To help identify the best picks, however, our ranking criterion demands a much tougher standard: a market cap below $50 million.

Smaller firms perform much better as a group, so focusing on them makes sense. Imposing a $50 million cut-off ensures that the stocks we select are tiny and are therefore grouped among some of the highest-returning net-nets available.

Debt to equity below 20%

Debt is a problem for troubled firms in a rising interest rate environment, as discussed in core criteria. Not only does debt reduce a company's attractiveness as an acquisition target but failure to meet debt requirements could push the firm into bankruptcy protection. And as interest rates rise, so do interest payments, making the firm's debt load more of a burden.

Tweedy, Browne's study revealed the performance boost that a debt-free balance sheet provides. Net-nets with debt to equity ratios below 20% see a significant increase, on average. Focusing on the best net-nets from a statistical point of view means avoiding firms with a meaningful amount of debt.

Trading at less than 50% of NCAV

Net-net studies over the last 40 years highlight a relationship between a portfolio's discount to NCAV and average returns. The deeper the discount, the larger the return.

As discussed, the relationship is not as strong as true-blue value investors would like it to be, which is why we demanded a smaller hurdle in core criteria. Still, focusing on the best performing net-nets means investing in firms that have deeper discounts, ideally as deep as possible. We demand a much stricter standard in ranking criteria than we did in core criteria. Rather than simply trading below NCAV, we want to see a discount of 50% or greater.

Qualitative ranking criteria

Investors who want to focus on strong quantitative criteria now have the tools needed to make smart investment decisions. By focusing on a group of net-nets that meet both the core and quantitative ranking criteria, investors can put together a strong portfolio which should provide great market-beating returns over the long run.

But not all investors are satisfied with maintaining a quantitative stance. Without looking deeper into a firm's situation, some investors feel a lack of safety and control. This makes it tougher to start quantitative investing in the first place or stick to it over the long term. Math, in terms of historic performance and statistical expectations, does little to comfort an investor when a strategy fails to perform over a period of time. To address these problems, almost all investors employ qualitative checks.

But adopting a qualitative assessment doesn't just make investing easier from an emotional point of view; qualitative investing can boost returns when done well. This means identifying solid qualitative criteria, and maintaining strict standards when assessing a firm.

The qualitative ranking criteria pulls together some of the factors I consider particularly fruitful when applying qualitative checks. While there is a nearly infinite number of factors that an investor could use when assessing a firm's qualitative situation, I've focused on the few that seem to have the biggest impact on my own investing. Rather than develop this set of criteria from scratch, I lifted all of it from the writings of outstanding investors such as Buffett, Graham, Seth Klarman, and Peter Lynch. It makes sense to adopt the criteria espoused by gifted investors when those criteria are relevant to net-nets.

Catalyst

When selecting net-nets, one of my favourite criteria is a solid catalyst. The term *catalyst* refers to a probable event on the horizon that would likely lift a company's stock price.

Situations in which management shop around for a buyer for the company, a grossly unfavourable contract will soon end, or a commodity price rises rapidly are all catalysts and would likely have a positive impact on a firm's stock price. When a net-net firm is put up for sale, transactions typically take place at or near NCAV, which has a direct impact on the stock price. The elimination of an unfair contract can have a positive impact on the firm's bottom line, which can boost the stock price. Similarly, if a firm's business benefits from a rise (or a fall) in a specific commodity price, a large move in that commodity's price will impact the firm's profitability, moving the stock price.

Catalysts are only probable events, never certain. There is always doubt as to what the future holds, so it's never wise to expect a future event with 100% certainty. Instead, we're simply looking for events that are likely to happen and would probably have a big impact on the firm's stock price. The more certain the event is and the larger the impact it would have on the firm's stock price, however, the better.

High-quality growth

While growth is a catalyst, it's so important that it deserves to be separated as a specific criterion. As Buffett pointed out, growth is a source of value. Investors lucky enough to find a sub-liquidation value firm that's growing its earnings, revenue, equity, or NCAV may have stumbled onto a truly exceptional buy.

Growth in NCAV increases a net-net investor's profit potential and margin of safety. Even if growth slows or stops after an investor purchases the stock, the investor will still benefit from any increased NCAV gained after purchase.

High-quality earnings growth is more lucrative than a mere bump up in price to reflect full NCAV. Continued profit growth can cause investors to shift from seeing the firm as a mere net-net to seeing it as a growth company. Investors smart enough to buy early and hang on as the scenario unfolds stumble onto a Shelby Davis double play. As earnings growth continues, investors revalue the stock to reflect a market multiple of earnings and increase the multiple they're willing to pay. This results in fantastically large stock price appreciation.

But smart investors also demand an equally rapid increase in free cash flow to help management fund operations, and they avoid firms with weak customer credit standards. Sometimes growth in revenue and shrinking losses highlight an exceptional buy. As revenue increases, the firm finds it easier to cover fixed costs, which eventually leads to rapidly growing profits.

Firms that shift from net-net to growth stock are as rare as they are profitable. More often than not a firm will seem attractive from a growth perspective only to see that growth fizzle out. Especially attractive to small investors are cyclical stocks that seem to have rapidly growing earnings and a low PE ratio. But rather than benefiting from this positive trend, investors can be left with heavy losses as the cycle begins its downturn.

Low PE

Joel Greenblatt highlighted the benefits of low PE ratios applied to net-net investing in his 1980s study. My own back tests, however, failed to replicate Greenblatt's findings.

To complicate matters, a low PE ratio does not necessarily signify a cheap market value. Earnings can be inflated for a number of reasons. One-time gains on asset sales, for example, can artificially inflate earnings and make an otherwise expensive firm appear cheap.

But investors who can get past the noise to identify firms with high-quality earnings, and a low PE can really benefit. If growth picks up, or ongoing profits seem likely, investors may revalue the net-net on an earnings basis, leading to a significant boost in stock price.

Significant past earnings

In mid-career, Graham favoured net-net firms that had significant past earnings. The more the company made, the better. The utility of this check is in assessing whether a profitable company has simply stumbled and may regain its footing. In other cases, the firm's industry may turn the corner, allowing it to earn large profits yet again.

When assessing net-nets based on this criterion, investors should look for firms that were significantly profitable in the recent past, ideally no more than ten years prior. The larger these profits were, relative to the company's current size, the better. Investors should also prefer firms that have retained their ability to produce this level of profit. Companies that sold the divisions responsible for that profit, or profited on the back of a fad, such as a hit toy (Cabbage Patch dolls, Beanie Babies, Pogs, etc.), should be immediately suspect.

While investors cannot profit from past earnings, the past record may provide a hint at what's in store for the business. More on this later.

Past price above NCAV

Value investors are rightfully sceptical of the impact past prices have on their ability to profit in the future. The main tenet of value investing, after all, is that stock prices tend to come back to fair value eventually. Past stock price behaviour seems to have little to do with value investing.

Rather than try to predict the future from past price behaviour, my criterion mainly aims to sidestep a common net-net pitfall. Not all managers act as trustworthy stewards of shareholder value. Firms with lacklustre or disinterested management typically trade at depressed prices as investors expect the situation to drag on indefinitely. While a newly minted net-net may slip into this pattern, a chronically depressed stock is strong evidence that management either do not care or do not have the skill needed to right the situation.

But the historic record can also help pinpoint stocks with large, fast swings in price. Some issues contain more speculative enthusiasm (investor sentiment that shifts rapidly) than others. This rapid shift in enthusiasm can help investors unload shares bought well below fair value as the stock price surges.

A speculative shift isn't the only reason for rapid price advancements, however. Investors can also benefit from a speculative capital structure or tiny public float. Companies that have, for example, a large issue of preferred shares relative to their common stock may see extreme and rapid movements in their common stock price. Similarly, a small number of investors rushing to buy stock in a company that is mostly held by insiders or institutions can rapidly boost the stock price, allowing a deep value investor to exit with a large profit.

Insider ownership

Insider ownership refers to share ownership by management or directors. Rather than assess a holding size relative to the size of the company or number of shares outstanding, look for an ownership amount that would be meaningful on a personal level.

Much is made of insiders having majority control of a company. While this certainly plays a role in the success of an investment, less has been said about the personal stake that management have in the company's future. When assessing insider ownership, I look for a dollar amount that would provide insiders with a meaningful personal stake in the success or failure of the business. If business failure would have a powerfully negative impact on the insider's net worth, that insider will work harder to avoid disaster. Likewise, if an increase in market value for the firm has a large impact on the insider's personal fortune, that insider will be more likely to take the steps needed to improve the performance of the company.

But while a material personal stake acts like a motivating factor, insiders with majority ownership may take advantage of their position to benefit family members or treat the company as their own personal piggy bank. Majority control also prevents activist investors from pressuring managers to make needed changes and steer the company in a more promising direction.

Insider ownership is likely more effective when insiders own large personal stakes but do not have a majority control of the company.

Reasonable insider pay

Management and directors of net-net firms often don't deserve even average salaries, typically having led the firm into catastrophe in the first place. But the focus here is on identifying insiders who draw unusually large salaries.

Sometimes management and directors will have a firm grip on the company, resulting in uncomfortably large salaries. This is a clear case of insiders taking advantage of their position to profit. The practice amounts to hoovering up shareholder value and shows a clear disregard for shareholders' welfare. In these situations, management may not be interested in improving the business so long as they can maintain their large salaries.

Contrast this to the board of Si2i, Ltd. operating in Singapore. When shareholders voiced dissatisfaction with their company's languishing stock price, directors vowed to receive a salary of $1 per year until the firm regained profitability. Actions like these communicate a clear signal: insiders have genuine concern for shareholder welfare, have taken responsibility for company performance, and will work feverishly to right the business.

Minority shareholders essentially elect to partner with insiders, retaining ownership but allowing these professional managers to run the company. Typical retail investors have little to no say in how a company is managed, but can spot shady practices before buying shares. If top management are busy raiding the store, they're not likely to care about shareholder value.

A jumping-off point

A scorecard or checklist is only as good as the knowledge behind it, which is why I incorporated in the selection process academic research, plus investment advice from some of value investing's greatest minds. The criteria in the Net Net Hunter Scorecard and their importance have changed over time as we continue to learn and grow. It's only fair to assume that the scorecard will continue to evolve as our knowledge expands.

Take this scorecard as a jumping-off point for your own development as a net-net investor. Smart investors never cease to study their craft, learn and grow. You'll inevitably discover points of difference on how to select net-nets and these differences may add significant value.

11

Step-by-Step Stock Selection

MANY INVESTORS TODAY get stock tips or investment ideas from random sources: business television, the newspaper, their cousin Vinny, and so on. Solid deep value investing, on the other hand, requires a more systematic approach. While it's certainly possible that an investor can pick up a great deep value stock after spotting it on a blog, the best buys are often kept from public view, so smart investors can buy more at more deeply depressed prices.

In the 1950s and 1960s, a young Buffett flipped through thousands of pages of Moody's manuals in order to find true off-the-map gems. Towards the end of one of those guides, he found a solid insurance company trading at a PE of less than 1×. Much later in life he would recount to a room full of Berkshire Hathaway shareholders, "Nobody will tell you about them. They won't be on CNBC and they won't be in brokerage reports. You have to go find them yourself." Developing a systematic approach to stock selection allows investors to find the best candidates possible, even if those finds are well off the map. In the process they may stumble upon a truly exceptional buy.

Systematic net-net stock analysis

This is as true for net-net stock investing as it is for any other deep value approach. By systematising the initial research process, investors can find better buys and can do so faster. A systematic approach, such as utilising a checklist, also allows the investor to reduce error, thereby saving time, money, and earning higher returns.

The entire process starts with a large pool of stock candidates. In early 2019, there were a number of free investing websites that offered screening features. For small cash-strapped investors, this is a decent place to start. By downloading a large list of low price-to-book value (low PB) stocks, tiny investors have the raw material needed to shape their portfolio.

The amount of work it takes to filter through a large list of stocks like this can be daunting, however. While free websites typically offer low-PB screens, they don't usually offer net-net stock filters, so much of the work has to be done by hand. The entire process resembles panning for gold nuggets. Net-net stocks are scarce, making up maybe 15% of the low-PB population. Even if investors concentrate on low-PB stocks, they still have to whittle this list down significantly to arrive at a decently sized shortlist of net-nets for further research.

Just how much time is involved in building the initial shortlist?

Investors aiming for a 30-stock portfolio may need to spend five solid hours sifting through 600 low-PB stocks before arriving at a list of 30 net-nets for further research. This is why it's advisable to pay a small fee to join a net-net stock community such as Net Net Hunter, where much of the heavy lifting in terms of primary and secondary screening is done for you. Alternatively, paid investment screeners may provide some help, and more expensive services such as the Bloomberg terminal or Reuters' Eikon provide advanced screening functionality.

With your initial list of low-PB stocks in hand, the first objective is to cut this list back as quickly as possible by removing the least promising candidates from contention. This process of elimination focuses on a few key criteria that are easily accessible on free investment websites. You start with the core criteria, since all net-net buys have to meet these objectives, and proceed from most to least accessible to conduct the work as quickly and painlessly as possible. Only then do you move on to additional metrics that will help you arrive at your final group of research candidates.

Objective 1: eliminate stocks that fail basic buy ability and quality filters

As previously discussed, quality here refers to the quality of the investment from a statistical point of view, not quality of the business. Net-net stocks are almost always attached to poorly managed businesses or companies going through major challenges. The initial task is to eliminate net-nets that either can't be bought or are associated with poor statistical performance.

Start by navigating to the summary page on the free website you're using in order to run through the first group of filters for each stock on your list.

FILTER 1: LOW AVERAGE DAILY VOLUME

Typically found on the summary page, look for the terms *volume, average daily volume,* or *average daily dollar volume.*

To calculate average daily dollar volume, multiply the average number of shares traded daily by the stock price. If the stock passes the test, keep it. If it fails, strike it off of your list of possible stocks.

FILTER 2: MARKET CAPITALISATION OVER $100 MILLION OR UNDER $1 MILLION

On the same page, you'll see a summary statistic titled 'Market Capitalisation'. This is sometimes abbreviated as 'Market Cap.' or 'Mkt Cap.' If this figure is above $100 million, returns will likely be lower than average for net-nets generally, so strike the company off of your list.

Similarly, we're interested in firms with a minimum level of management competence, which means we want to maintain a minimum firm size of $1 million; if smaller, strike the firm off of your list.

FILTER 3: PROHIBITED INDUSTRIES

Generally, websites provide a description of the company's operations on the summary page, which makes this metric the third easiest to assess when whittling down the pool of candidates. Business descriptions reveal whether a firm is engaged in real estate development, finance, or in a heavily regulated business activity. Closed-ended funds are also typically listed in the business description. Purge all of these businesses from your list. *Also:- Resource exploration / Early stg bio. / pharma.*

FILTER 4: NO NYSE

According to a number of net-net studies we looked at previously, net-net firms listed on the NYSE provide lower returns than almost any other subset of net-nets. For that reason, including these firms will drag down your portfolio returns, on average.

On the firm's summary page, look to see where the stock symbol is listed. The free service will usually list either the market code NYSE, or 'New York'. This is a fairly simple check to make, but just as in the case of dividend stocks, we don't categorically exclude a net-net firm on the NYSE, since the firm may meet a large number of other ranking criteria.

FILTER 5: MAJOR CHINESE BUSINESS OPERATIONS

Nothing is worse than buying into a fantastic, growing company that's trading below liquidation value, only to lose your principal due to fraud. This is why we avoid firms with significant operations in China. While great opportunities in China do exist, the small investor at home in his den is likely to lack the expertise needed to avoid landmines.

The business summary usually includes a reference to operations in Mainland China. Other hints are the company's business address, and the make-up of its management team and board of directors. While the location of business operations and the company's headquarters are frequently a dead giveaway as to whether the company has significant operations in China or not, the make-up of the company's board and top managers is not enough to strike the company from your list.

Western countries such as Canada, the USA, and Australia are immigrant nations (countries almost completely comprised of immigrants or their ancestors). Many made the voyage from Asia, including China, and brought a ferocious work ethic and intelligence that added immensely to our civilisation. The problem net-net investors face is not due to ethnic Chinese, no matter where they are located, but rather, due to a business culture in China where unscrupulous companies prey on ignorant investors. More on this problem later.

For now, remove the company if you highly suspect operations are located in Mainland China. If the board or management team is comprised of a larger than average number of ethnic Chinese, flag the company for further review. Investors will have to comb through the company's financial reports to determine where the business is operating.

Objective 2: filter out candidates that do not meet minimum quantitative standards

By eliminating the stocks that were the easiest to reject, we've now cut the list down to a more manageable size. Our second pass through this list focuses on confirming net-net status and ensuring a minimum level of quality.

FILTER 6: POSITIVE NCAV

On the firm's balance sheet, near the top of the page, quickly access the firm's total current assets. Next, near the bottom third of the page, locate the firm's total liabilities. Subtract the firm's current assets from its total liabilities. Most companies record a negative value here; they do not have enough current assets to cover total liabilities. If so, strike the firm off of your list.

If the firm has enough current assets to cover total liabilities, scan the shareholder's equity section to see if the firm lists a value for preferred shares. If present, reduce the current asset value yet again by the face value of the company's preferred shares. If the resulting figure is positive, you may have found a net-net. If it's negative, strike the firm off your list.

Note: You will have to perform deeper analysis on the company's preferred shares, if present, to determine the exact liquidating value of the issue. This check can come later during the full analysis but is not needed to put together a list of research candidates.

FILTER 7: MARKET CAPITALISATION LESS THAN PRELIMINARY NCAV

What we've now arrived at is the company's preliminary NCAV. A further check, including assessing the firm's preferred shares, will have to be made after we arrive at our list of buy candidates.

It's not enough to find a firm with positive preliminary NCAV, however. We're aiming to buy stocks selling below NCAV. To do so, refer back to the firm's market capitalisation. If the market cap is smaller than the firm's preliminary NCAV, keep the firm. If not, strike it off your list.

FILTER 8: DEBT TO EQUITY RATIO BELOW 50%

On the firm's balance sheet, check the liabilities section for the term *total debt*. This figure denotes the total value of both the company's short-term and long-term interest-bearing debt. We find that many net-nets are actually debt free, so they don't list total debt on their balance sheet. If debt is listed, divide total debt by the firm's total shareholder equity to find the debt-to-equity ratio. If the ratio is above 50%, reject the stock. If it's below 50%, keep the firm for further analysis.

FILTER 9: CURRENT RATIO ASSESSMENT

Sticking with the most recent quarterly (or year end) balance sheet, turn your attention to the firm's asset section. At the top, the statement lists the firm's current assets. Look for the total value for current assets at the bottom of that section.

Next, near the middle of the balance sheet, you'll find the firm's current liabilities. Find the total value for current liabilities at the bottom of that section.

Now, divide total current assets by total current liabilities. If the result is greater than 1.5, the firm has a large enough current ratio to pass inspection.

FILTER 10: NOT SELLING SHARES

Flip to the company's most recent cash flow statement. Unlike our balance sheet assessment, we want to look at each period over the past 12 months. If you're assessing a company at the end of its fiscal year, the company's year-end statement may be the most recent statement listed. In this case, just reference values for this reporting period. If you're assessing the company before the end of its fiscal year, you should look at every quarterly cash-flow statement for the firm to ensure the company has not sold shares over the previous 12 months.

In the section titled 'Cash Flows from Financing Activities', look for a positive value referring to stocks issued or purchased. If the company states a positive value, the company received cash from the sale of shares. Strike the company off your list if it sold shares.

FILTER 11: REASONABLE BURN RATE

Burn rate is simply the rate of negative change (i.e., shrink or loss) between periods. Net-net investors should specifically assess how much the firm's NCAV has shrunk between quarters and yearly results.

To assess the burn rate, simply compare the most recent quarter's NCAV with the NCAV you calculate for the second most recent quarter and the same quarter in the previous year. Subtract the most recent quarter's NCAV from the second most recent quarter's NCAV, and then divide the change in NCAV by the second most recent quarter's NCAV. This will yield a negative percentage in most cases. Repeat this process for the trailing 12 months.

Since the burn rate measures the rate at which the firm's NCAV is shrinking, we want to keep this percentage loss as small as possible. Ideally, the firm will have grown its NCAV and have done so steadily over a number of years. Firms with NCAV shrinking at –25% or worse, either quarter over quarter, or year over year, should be rejected because they suggest that the firm's main source of value, its liquidation value, is unstable.

Objective 3: identify the most promising candidates from a statistical perspective

At this point you've completed the basic filtering to arrive at a shortlist of stocks that meet a minimum level of quality. To get the most out of a net-net stock strategy, an investor has to filter further to arrive at the best possible candidates. Our ranking criteria perform the heavy lifting to identify them.

This section walks you through using the stricter ranking criteria to filter your shortlist. While we only shortlisted stocks that met *all* of the *core* criteria, net-nets rarely if ever meet all of the *ranking* criteria. Instead, we want to identify a smaller subset that meets some of the ranking criteria. Usually, the more of these ranking criteria a stock meets, the better that stock is as an investment.

FILTER 12: SHARE BUY-BACKS

Navigate back to the financial statements for the first company on your shortlist. On the cash flow statement, check to see if the company has recorded a cash outflow related to the purchase or sale of shares. A cash outflow shows that the company spent money buying shares, but we can't yet determine the nature of the transaction. For that, we'll need to read through the notes to the financial statements later. For now, we can simply note that the company has spent money buying shares and move on to check the remaining firms.

FILTER 13: NO DIVIDEND

As we've seen, dividends significantly reduce the average net-net stock return. Since the scorecard was created in order to identify the highest-returning group of net-net stocks, eliminating net-nets that are paying a dividend is a must.

You can check to see whether a company is paying a dividend by looking at the firm's summary page on the free stock-research site you're using. Nearly every summary page has a section showing the dividend the firm is paying. Investors can also cross-reference the firm's cash flow statement. In the financing section of the cash flow statement, look for the line item labelled 'Cash Dividends Paid'. If this line item shows an outflow of cash, the firm is paying a dividend. This is a strike against the firm, but not enough for the firm to be excluded from contention.

FILTER 14: INSIDER BUYS

Insider buying is a great sign that the stock is undervalued and the company is likely to see better times ahead. In fact, it almost always pays to invest alongside management. Again, we're specifically looking for purchases from upper management, and the more stock purchased, the better.

The best place to look for insider buys is on the Security and Exchange Commission (SEC) website. Nearly all publicly listed firms trading in the USA have to publish financial statements, which are listed on the SEC website. For insider buys, the form we want to look at is Form 4.

While it looks intimidating at first, Form 4 is fairly straightforward to master. Along the top row of the form, you have the name of the person filing the form, the company and stock symbol in question, with the date of the filing just underneath, and the filer's role at the company at the top of the right side of the form. Refer to

Table I, 'Non-Derivative Securities Acquired, Disposed of, or Beneficially Owned', which identifies exactly what the title indicates it should. If you spot the letter *P* isolated in the middle column of that table, the filer has purchased securities.

Remember that for this criterion we're specifically looking for situations where insiders have placed their money on the line, along with other common shareholders. Neither stock option grants nor restrictive shares count because they are essentially non-monetary compensation and do not represent a purposeful cash outlay made by the individual.

FILTER 15: MARKET CAPITALISATION BELOW $50 MILLION

We previously filtered out firms with market capitalisations above $100 million. Firm size, at least in terms of market capitalisation, is negatively correlated with return. The relationship is quite strong, which led us to eliminate firms larger than $100 million.

Using this criterion, you can identify firms that are much smaller than the maximum allowable market cap to boost overall performance.

As you did before, recalculate the firm's market capitalisation on the firm's summary page. If the firm's market cap falls below $50 million, make a note of it and move on to the next firm.

FILTER 16: DEBT TO EQUITY BELOW 25%

As a stricter version of the core criteria, we aim to focus on firms that have next to no debt. While net-nets typically have strong balance sheets, they're still troubled companies so it makes sense to reduce factors that could cause the firm to slip into bankruptcy. Problems during the liquidation of current assets and an impending debt issuance may be enough to cost investors their principal investment.

As you did previously, assess the firm's total debt relative to its shareholder equity. This time, make a note if the firm's debt to equity ratio falls below 25% and move on to the next company.

FILTER 17: TRADING AT LESS THAN 50% OF NCAV

By definition, net-net stock investing is the purchase of companies trading in the market for a price less than their NCAV. While any discount to NCAV is a positive, deeper discounts are at least loosely associated with higher returns. This relationship is a no-brainer in the value investing community and has proven valuable when shopping for net-nets as well. It pays to pay less for whatever you buy.

In this case, we want the price to be less than half of the firm's NCAV. As we did previously, compare the firm's market capitalisation to its NCAV. Mark it a significant positive if the firm records a P/NCAV of less than 50%.

A warning about standardised data

At this point, we've completed our initial filtering to find a shortlist of net-nets to research. While we've spent a good amount of time eliminating firms from contention and concentrating on a smaller group of companies, investors have a lot more work to do before they can construct their portfolio.

Up until now, you've sifted through your list using free stock sites. Leveraging these free sites makes the filtering process much faster than if you had to dig through a company's actual published financial statements (e.g., the 10Q or 10K statements) on the SEC website. But there's a catch: standardised data always contains errors.

Free investment sites obtain standardised financial data generated by big data brokers such as Reuters or Bloomberg. These companies compile data from tens of thousands of companies with the goal of presenting that data accurately and in a standardised way so that third-parties can present it to end users. Unfortunately, there's a trade-off between standardising data and presenting it accurately. This results in discrepancies between free (or even paid) consumer finance websites, institutional research platforms, and actual financial statements as presented by public companies. Human error or technical software quirks can even cause mistakes in the end product, and these errors can lead investors to make erroneous decisions.

To make matters worse for net-net investors, the standardised financial data of tiny companies seems to contain more errors than does the data for larger firms. The greater number of investors accessing the standardised financials for large companies could mean that large data brokers are placing extra focus on getting the data right for these firms. Increased errors in the data for tiny companies could also be due to unorthodox financial data presentation by tiny firms. In contrast, large firms may present their financials in a more homogenous way. Whatever the reason, it's critically important that net-net investors double-check the data before buying.

The final step when arriving at a hot list of buy candidates is reading the actual financial statements of each company to ensure that the investment picture is the same as that presented by standardised data. This process is fairly straightforward and a lot quicker than initial screening. Almost all companies have corporate websites, and almost every corporate website has an investor relations (IR) section. This is the first stop when double-checking the numbers.

In accessing the company's IR section to look for SEC filings, the process is the same for investing outside the USA. Investors should at minimum read through the most recent annual financial report, and all quarterly or half-year reports issued by the company. IR sections often include a separate management report, which conveys what was happening in the prior periods, with more colour and less legalese than found in legal filings. Lucky investors may also find supporting documents such as the Form 4 mentioned earlier. Sometimes a firm will even publish additional material that provides significant value for understanding the qualitative situation, a topic we'll turn to soon.

If a company in question does not have a corporate website, or if the IR section is thin on information, legal filings can usually be found on the website of a country's security regulator. Make good use of actual published material.

Reading through the actual financial reports will also help investors tie up some loose ends from the initial filtering process. Reports often discuss operating locations, giving investors a good idea of whether the firm has significant operations in China or not. They may include further details on preferred shares. And by scanning to see the number of stock options granted during the period, investors can make a quick reasonable judgement about whether money spent on buying back shares was an attempt by management to increase shareholder value or simply an effort to mop up the company's option expense.

When it comes to preferred shares, proper treatment will require reading through the security's prospectus, sometimes located on the company's IR page but almost always available through the regulator. Investors have to use critical thinking to gauge the economic cost a would-be liquidator would face in taking over the company and covering all liabilities. There are simply too many possibilities for a sufficient treatment of this step in this book, but investors may want to defer to a shorthand rule: if an acquirer could acquire all of the preferred shares on the open market along with the common stock, the total market value of the issue would be the cost the acquirer would have to bear when attempting to liquidate the firm.

Objective 4: assess the firm's qualitative situation to uncover hidden gems

In the 1960s, Warren Buffett wrote:

> "Interestingly enough, although I consider myself to be primarily in the quantitative school ... the really sensational ideas I have had over the years have been heavily weighted toward the qualitative side where I have had a 'high-probability insight'. This is what causes the cash register to really sing. However, it is an infrequent occurrence,

as insights usually are, and, of course, no insight is required on the quantitative side – the figures should hit you over the head with a baseball bat. The really big money tends to be made by investors who are right on qualitative decisions, but, at least in my opinion, the more sure money tends to be made on the obvious quantitative decisions."[205]

It should come as no surprise, then, that while net-net investors can make a good living by sticking to the quantitative factors provided in these pages, smart – and more importantly, experienced – investors can make better returns by identifying highly lucrative qualitative investment situations.

The catch is that, unlike quantitative assessment, qualitative factors are evanescent. Writing qualitative criteria into a checklist requires the author to be somewhat vague on what to look for, since qualitative situations vary considerably in quality and scope. There are simply more situations an investor could face than could ever be specified in a single book. Proper assessment often requires significant business and investment experience. Inexperienced investors will find it easy to make mistakes when assessing a firm on qualitative grounds.

How much experience is enough to conduct sound qualitative assessment?

Almost by definition, if you have to ask, you lack the necessary experience.

Still, small investors can make significant progress in their ability to understand and spot promising qualitative investment situations. If you're intent on picking the best stocks possible, qualitative assessment can be mastered like any other skill: one inch at a time. By sticking to the quantitative factors you feel you know best, solidifying that knowledge, and then slowly expanding your circle of competence, you can achieve a powerful understanding of what makes one qualitative situation far more attractive than another.

My advice for those wanting to deepen their understanding of qualitative assessment is to read as much great writing from the masters as possible. Peter Lynch's books are a fantastic place to start and are some of the most accessible pieces of writing on the subject. Another great source of learning is Buffett's 1950s articles written for *The Commercial and Financial Chronicle*, found on the Net Net Hunter website.

---

205 Miller, *Warren Buffett's Ground Rules*, 84.

A final caution on picking net-net stocks using this systematic approach

My aim with this chapter is to show would-be net-net stock investors how to institute a rational, systematic approach to identifying promising buys. Properly applied, this method has the power to uncover stocks that fly under the radar of the investing public, allowing investors to capitalise on extreme market inefficiency. It's the approach Buffett used during the 1950s and 1960s.

If this approach seems daunting, my advice (to paraphrase Buffett) is to simply sit down and do it, or pay for access to a website that will do it for you. Investors should not expect to profit from a highly profitable strategy if they're not prepared to put in the necessary work.

Above all else, though, avoid the trap of investing in too few net-nets. While it's tempting to quit once you stumble onto a handful of net-nets, running a highly concentrated portfolio of net-nets could be a recipe for disaster. While the checklist presented here is a good way to focus on the best net-net opportunities available, net-net investing still amounts to buying problem firms. Given the extreme divergence in return between companies, and between year-to-year portfolio returns, reasonable diversification is a must. Buying only a handful of stocks, or employing the strategy for a handful of years, may result in significant losses. Again, it's critically important to demand diversification both in the number of firms in your portfolio and in terms of the number of years that you're using the strategy. In this investor's view, quantitative investors should opt for a portfolio of no fewer than 20, but ideally 30, net-nets and employ the strategy over at least a ten-year period.

PART 4

TACTICS: NET–NET INVESTING BEST PRACTICES

12

My Attitude Towards Money–Losing Net–Net Stocks

A LOT OF INVESTORS instinctively shy away from money-losing companies. Money-losing net-nets are no different. It's almost as if avoiding red on income statements is an evolutionary reflex.

Money-losing net-nets are simply stocks of companies that are losing money and trading below NCAV. A lot of articles warn investors to stay away from net-nets that are bleeding red. Many of these writers enthusiastically discuss the net-net strategy's ability to achieve alpha but warn investors that blindly investing in money-losing net-net stocks can lead to serious losses. Ben Graham himself advised investors to stick to profitable companies and dividends when buying net-nets. Profitable firms are, after all, usually higher-quality businesses.

It's no surprise that many net-nets face large ongoing losses, since, typically, large business problems push them below NCAV in the first place. Sadly, instead of taking a rational approach to stock or strategy selection, many investors who see ongoing losses simply reject the strategy outright. Some small investors even mistakenly assume that companies that never turn a profit are essentially worthless. Businesses are set up to earn a profit for their owners and organisations that can't do this aren't worth anything, or so the argument goes. This assumption highlights a fundamental misunderstanding about investing.

Should investors stay away from money-losing net-nets?

There are few universal principles in investing, so the best approach to money-losing net-nets is not clear-cut.

Think twice before rejecting money-losing net-nets

Long-term investment returns depend on the practical application of sound principles. These principles need to be developed through the critical assessment of the available facts and advice from gifted professionals. Both should be taken into account, but neither should be accepted without further scrutiny. Developing a proper synthesis of the two is the most logical way to approach active money management. This strategy has helped me enormously over the past ten years, first in adopting Graham's net-net strategy and then in honing my net-net stock strategy.

On the whole, money-losing net-nets provide solid returns in academic back tests. As discussed in chapter 6, Oppenheimer looked at the performance of net-net stocks from 1970 to 1983, a period that represented significant fluctuations in the stock market. The results, of course, were great. Near the end of the paper, however, Oppenheimer showed that profitable net-net stocks returned 2.88% on average per month when not paying a dividend, while unprofitable net-nets returned 2.61%.[206] While producing a slightly lower return, money-losing net-nets in the 1970s and 1980s were still extremely lucrative.

Investors should not form their investment policy from a single academic study; it takes a body of knowledge to produce solid conclusions. Oxman et al.'s 2010 study does sweeten the deal, however. The team extended Oppenheimer's test from 1983 to 2008 and found that money-losing net-nets actually performed better, achieving an average monthly return of 3.38% in contrast to the 2.42% of their profitable peers.[207]

In both studies, however, money-losing net-nets did show higher systematic risk, which may suggest sticking to a broadly diversified portfolio when buying them. This additional risk may also be the reason that Graham initially advised investors to pick only profitable companies.

The investing game's core principle

Why do so many people avoid money-losing net-nets when they perform so well?

Part of the reason hints at a major misconception about investing itself. Many modern value investors assume that better businesses make for better investments. While great businesses can be a good place to find great investments, sound investing still comes down to buying assets[208] for less than they're worth. As Charlie

---

206 Oppenheimer, 'Ben Graham's NCAVs'.
207 Oxman et al., 'Deep Value Investing'.
208 The term 'assets' here refers to any sort of asset, from hard assets, to intangibles, common stock, or even entire companies.

Munger said, "The investment game always involves considering both quality and price, and the trick is to get more quality than you pay for in price. It's just that simple."[209] Misunderstanding this critical concept can lead to years of mediocre performance or even permanent losses.

Take Coca-Cola for example, widely considered one of the best businesses in history. With record earnings and a very large competitive advantage, Coke was a profoundly successful company in the late 1990s. Investors loved the stock so much that they bid up its price to $85 by the end of 1997. At that price, Coca-Cola was trading at a PE of roughly 52x.[210] Unfortunately, investors who mistook a great company for a great investment saw their investment principle drop –53% by January 2003. It would take 18 years for the stock to recover its July 1998 high. Clearly, a great company and a great investment are not the same thing.

While no asset is worth an infinite price, almost every asset is a steal at some price – even money-losing businesses. Where is the quality in money-losing net-net firms? Quality comes in the form of realisable net asset value, and the option to participate in a rejuvenated company if management can sort out the firm's problems. Net-net investors are fundamentally asset investors, and assets can have significant value whether the business is profitable or not. Plants, real estate, receivables, and inventories can all be sold off to third parties that may be able to make better use of them, bringing in cash for investors of the challenged firm. Focusing on this residual value is like scooping up cigar butts from the side of the road: the incredibly cheap price makes that last puff highly lucrative.

But not all money-losing net-nets are doomed to liquidation, and investors don't have to go through one to profit. Some businesses are acquired, or raise cash through asset sales to buy profitable turnkey businesses from third parties. Companies rarely continue to lose money until no assets are left. Much of the time, management is able to regain profitability. This is by far the best outcome for net-net investors, especially if management can achieve a rapid turnaround.

A young Buffett would have agreed. Ironically, the man who said that turnarounds seldom turn was himself a cigar butt investor involved in a number of successful turnarounds. As discussed earlier, one of his best-known early investments was Dempster Mills. Dempster wasn't profitable, but Buffett bought it anyway. While he had previously nibbled at the stock, in 1961 he went full in, obtaining majority control at a price a bit above $30 per share. After infusing the company with new

---

209 Lowe, *Damn Right!*, 78.

210 Coca-Cola's earnings and stock price, prior to the 2012 split, are shown in a Macrotrends' chart of the company's stock price and splits history at www.macrotrends.net/stocks/charts/KO/coca-cola/stock-splits.

management, the firm regained profitability, and its market price ballooned to nearly $65 per share.

How to approach money-losing net-nets

Despite the great returns associated with buying a basket of money-losing net-net firms, failing to diversify is fraught with risk. Sometimes it takes management much longer than expected to turn the business around, if they can at all. Ongoing losses erode liquidation value, which, if it drops enormously, can completely erode investors' margin of safety and impair their principal investment. In addition, since the company's performance isn't improving enough to propel the stock price upwards, investors have to rely more heavily on other events, such as a positive media announcement, a buyout, or a financially successful liquidation, to generate a profit.

Diversification is a must. Money-losing net-nets perform very well in the studies discussed above, but these are average returns, not the returns of any single stock. While neither Oppenheimer's nor Carlisle's team discuss the win rate of money-losing net-nets, it's likely to be comparatively low, and a few exceptional gainers are likely to produce the group's market-beating performance. It's therefore very important to fit enough of these stocks into your portfolio to leverage the statistical return profile of the group in general.

Where diversification is not possible or wanted, investors should use the Net Net Hunter Scorecard's ranking criteria to ensure the best chance of a good outcome. Factors such as share buy-backs, heavy insider buying, and investment catalysts may prove invaluable. By identifying net-nets with additional characteristics associated with outperformance or a brighter future, investors should be able to decrease the number of losers in their portfolio.

Should investors avoid money-losing net-nets?

Both academic studies and a little thought suggest that investors can make a lot of money by investing in money-losing net-nets if they approach these stocks intelligently. I have achieved great returns from a small group that possesses additional criteria found in the Net Net Hunter Scorecard. It's unwise to invest in a small group of money-losing net-net companies unless they perform exceptionally well with regard to ranking criteria. On the other hand, fitting a bunch of these stocks into your portfolio and sticking with the strategy over a decade or more is likely to lead to life-changing profits.

13

Past Earnings and Existing Operations

THERE'S A FAMOUS principle in the world of investing: you can't invest by looking in the rear-view mirror. Why incorporate a past profitability requirement as part of the Net Net Hunter Scorecard?

Firms that trade as net-nets often have very poor near-term performance. Almost all net-net firms have a recent record of extreme revenue erosion and are losing money. Despite this track record, net-nets usually work out very well as a group. But there's one situation that I consider particularly appealing: a company hums along smoothly before stumbling into a large, but fixable, business problem that management works feverishly to solve. In such a situation, if the business problems are truly solvable, the stock is likely to get back on track and regain its former level of profitability. The stock price would surge as investors bid it up from a mere fraction of liquidation value to a price based on a multiple of earnings.

Admittedly, looking at the past record as an indication of future profitability is a little like driving a car by looking in the rear-view mirror. An investor is always left with a clear picture of what has been, but not what is yet to come.

The inability to know what the future holds is the chief problem of investing because an investor's ability to profit depends on future developments. Every investment situation includes some element of chance, risk, or luck before the outcome is solidified into the historical record.

Despite the obvious problems with predicting the future based on the past, investors can use the past as a guide if they also incorporate solid critical thinking. As part of the process, investors have to ensure that mitigating factors have not stepped in to derail the business. An investor must be sure to assess management decisions after the firm achieved large profits, after industry changes, and after changes within the firm itself, to be sure it is able to achieve large profits in the future. A problem in any of these areas could render the firm's past performance null and void as a guide to the future. As Graham wrote:

> "The analyst must be on the lookout for any such indications to the contrary. Here we must distinguish between vision or intuition on the one hand, and ordinary sound reasoning on the other. The ability to see what is coming is of inestimable value, but it cannot be expected to be part of the analyst's stock in trade. (If he had it, he could dispense with analysis.) He can be asked to show only that moderate degree of foresight which springs from logic and from experience intelligently pondered."[211]

Before assuming that a great past record means great performance ahead, an investor must intelligently ponder whether the same conditions exist today, or will exist in the future. Some situations are clearer than others, and lend themselves to an enthusiastic purchase. Other opportunities are much tougher to decipher, since industries and consumer demand are constantly shifting. An intelligent assessment of future prospects based on the past record can take as little as plain-vanilla common sense but often require significant business experience.

Graham redux: look at the past as a guide to the future

As we saw previously, Graham sought out companies trading below NCAV that also had shown a record of strong past earnings. Graham was looking for firms that had prospered in the past but had recently sunk to depressing lows due to mismanagement, industry problems, or large business problems. His hope was that at least some of these firms would see their fortunes reverse and begin to produce decent profits again. According to Graham, "In the absence of indications to the contrary we accept the past record as a basis for judging the future."[212] While any company may turn its business around and earn solid profits again, Graham thought that firms with significant past earnings were more likely to see large profits going forward.

Part of the reason lies in industrial structures. While some firms are able to produce steady earnings, many others operate in industries that cycle between prosperity and desperation. The auto industry is a classic example. With strong barriers to entry, investors often mistake auto manufacturers as stable, blue chip companies. When new-car demand grows, firms like GM, Ford, and Volkswagen make better use of fixed assets, leading to increasing earnings, rising stock prices, and growing dividends. But when this demand ultimately falters, sales fall, leading to sharply declining profits and angry shareholders.

Most firms without a strong competitive advantage (moat), face waves of competition, causing them to cycle between profits and losses. When demand outstrips supply, profits rise. But as new firms enter the industry, chasing large profits, supply balloons and margins fall. Weaker participants may end up losing money or even going bankrupt. As participants exit the industry in search of greener pastures, average industry profits rise and the cycle starts over again.

When he looked for large past profits, Graham would buy a greater number of businesses that were hunkering down during troubled times and could rise again to prosper when the industry turned. If past profits are large enough, and the industry upturn strong enough, a company's stock can rise to many multiples of its net-net low.

Existing operations, a critically important factor

When it comes to regaining past profitability, firms with ongoing business operations have a clear advantage over firms that have ceased operations in order to survive an industry downturn. While significant opportunity may still exist in a business that has ceased operations, it is much easier for firms with ongoing business operations to scale their operations, growing sales and ultimately regaining significant profitability.

A retailer, for example, can't simply shut its stores for a year to wait for industry conditions to improve without experiencing a tremendous deterioration in its earning capacity. As stores shut, inventory is liquidated, retail staff laid off, and even lower-level management let go. Landlords turn vacated locations over to new tenants, destroying the company's footprint. If a skeleton team were to be retained to re-enter the market when conditions improved, rebuilding the firm's former store base and support staff would prove onerous. When a retailer shuts its doors, it's usually for good; past profitability, no matter how large, does not suggest future prosperity.

Retailers able to retain their store base during a major downturn are much more likely to regain their former profitability when industry conditions improve. In these cases, an investor could look at the company's historic earnings per square foot for a rough guide to profitability under normal industry conditions. Barring major industry changes (such as the rise of Internet retail) and changes to the company's competitive position, the past becomes a fairly reasonable guide to what the future could have in store.

Industrial companies have an easier time scaling down operations and then jumpstarting sales when conditions improve. This is especially true of manufacturers that are well capitalised and own their fixed assets as opposed to leasing factories or machinery. So long as the firm retains its manufacturing base and essential staff, and no other mitigating factor has come into play, it's likely that a manufacturer could ramp up operations as industry conditions improve.

In the end, a business can only be scaled down so far before it becomes tremendously difficult to regain its former footing. In a situation where only the CEO and his accountant are left in the building, the pair are essentially tasked with rebuilding the entire organisational chart before they can regain the company's former level of profitability. This is much more challenging than simply hiring sales staff. While this is an extreme example, it does highlight just how important ongoing operations are.

Betting on decent firms facing a large business problem

Investors don't have to focus on cyclical companies in order to take advantage of strong past profits. The aim of investing in companies with a great past record is to profit when earnings rebound. Investors can achieve this by skipping the cyclical plays and investing in otherwise decent businesses that are facing large but solvable business problems. Investors may even see their stocks rise sooner as they don't have to wait for industry conditions to turn before profiting.

In 1963, American Express found itself in the middle of a major crisis. It had lent money to Allied Crude Vegetable in New Jersey, headed by Anthony 'Tino' De Angelis. Tino discovered that he could obtain loans secured by the company's salad oil inventory and soon began defrauding lenders by simply faking the amount of oil he had in inventory. Ships supposedly full of salad oil would arrive at the docks for unloading, where inspectors assessed the amounts on board to keep track of the inventory for lenders. But Tino, hungry for cash, began filling the tanks with water, with just a few feet of oil sitting at the top to fool inspectors. At other times, he would simply shift oil from one tank to another based on where the inspectors were heading. When soybean prices dropped, lenders attempted to recall their loans only to find that inventory was short by 39%. Lenders lost a significant amount of money, and American Express itself was out $58 million.[213]

But American Express also had the financial strength to survive the crisis. Buffett, well aware of the franchise possessed by the company, pre-scandal, spent time consulting with merchants to assess the damage done to the company's earning

---

213 The Salad Oil Scandal of 1963 caused over $150 million in losses to major banks and international trading companies.

power and brand. Satisfied with his findings, Buffett bought the stock and earned a massive profit as the price later recovered and the firm grew.

American Express was not, then, a net-net, but the famous event highlights how a major business crisis can significantly depress a company's stock. Investors who are prepared to do their homework and look at the company within the context of eternity, to paraphrase Spinoza, can better place the crisis within the larger context of ongoing business operations. Even if the crisis forces the company to endure temporary losses, so long as the company's ability to earn remains intact, investors can profit when the situation blows over.

If this sounds difficult, don't fret. An investor's ability to identify great qualitative opportunities develops over time. The more an investor studies business, business history, and the past investments of great investors, the better he can tell a promising opportunity from a less appealing buy.

14

How Burn Rate Increases Risk and Reduces Profit Potential

WHEN INVESTORS THINK about the risks inherent in net-net investing, they usually cite bankruptcy as top of the list. This is understandable, since distressed firms have often seen their revenues drop precipitously and are often producing steep losses.

Ironically, few net-nets go bankrupt. As discussed earlier, only roughly 5% of net-net firms suffer declines of −90% or more, compared to 2% for stocks in general. A much more common threat comes in the form of a company's excessive burn rate.

Burn rate represents one of the largest unknowns when it comes to net-net investing. Quantitative figures suggest, but by no means prove, that shrinking valuations are strongly correlated with excess returns. Practical reasoning, plus investment commentary from the great practitioners, on the other hand, strongly favour stability or at least improving values.

Where you side in this conflict will ultimately come down to your preference for either a quantitative mechanical approach or a qualitative stock picking approach to net-nets.

Burn rate: what is it?

Burn rate refers to the rate at which a company's NCAV is shrinking from one period to the next.

I use burn rate to refer to the rate of loss specifically, since a company with a shrinking NCAV is said to be burning through its liquidation value. Firms that increase their NCAV per share are not burning through their liquidation value, so this metric can be simply stated as an increase in NCAV.

Burn rate is measured from one period to the next. In practice, net-net investors should compare the most recent quarter's NCAV with the NCAV in the equivalent quarter 12 months prior. This provides a solid assessment of how the firm's liquidation value has changed over the course of the year.

For a more near-term look at how NCAV has changed, net-net investors should also compare the most recent quarterly figures with those of the next most recent report. By looking back over the most recent quarter, investors can more easily spot new business developments or can dig a bit deeper into the firm's record to get a sense of possible seasonality. But a true understanding of how seasonal business performance affects a firm's liquidation value requires plotting out the firm's quarterly NCAV over a few years to observe a general pattern.

Burn rate example

Burn rate is a simple concept that comes into focus during practical application. Let's assume that Bert's Plumbing and Party Supplies just finished its most recent fiscal year, ending 31 December 2019. At year end, the company's NCAV amounted to $9 million.

To assess the firm's year-over-year burn rate, we'd dig up the firm's fiscal 2018 annual report to calculate the firm's burn rate at year end 2018.[214] In this case, Bert's NCAV amounted to $10 million.

To calculate the firm's burn rate, we simply work through the following formula:

Current period's NCAV
−Previous period's NCAV
Difference
(Difference/Previous period's NCAV) × 100 = Percentage rate of change

If the company's NCAV is shrinking, the percentage rate of change will be negative. In Bert's case, the calculations work out like this:

---

214 Note that while we're referencing 31 December 2018–2019, we're specifically referring to the firm's fiscal year end, not calendar year end 2018–2019. Often a company's fiscal year end will correspond with the end of the calendar year, but firms can (and do) frequently set their fiscal year ends at different dates throughout the year.

$9,000,000
-$10,000,000
-$1,000,000
(-$1,000,000 / $10,000,000) × 100 = -10%

In this scenario, Bert's Plumbing and Party Supplies has a year-over-year burn rate of –10%. If the numbers were reversed, with this year's NCAV of $10,000,000 and last year's NCAV of $9,000,000, the company would have increased its NCAV by 11%.

Almost every net-net company burns through its NCAV. Depending on the rate of shrinkage, a firm can be considered toxic waste, stable, or a serious buy. Let's walk through those scenarios now.

Why do net-net firms burn through liquidation value?

A firm will see lower NCAV over time for a number of reasons. First, the firm may be consuming cash. Businesses need cash to survive, and over time need to purchase things such as inventory, machinery, and equipment to maintain operations. If a firm is not producing cash through operations, it will need to use cash obtained in previous periods, or debt financing, or the sale of assets to fund operations. All of these can reduce the firm's NCAV.

Sometimes a company will use a significant amount of its cash on hand to fund the purchase of a brand, equipment, or entire company. In these situations, the acquired asset is placed among long-term assets, and cash is reduced. This ultimately shrinks the firm's NCAV.

Impairment is another factor. As a part of normal business operations, management may realise that the firm's assets are not worth what they're listed at on the balance sheet. Accounting rules state that management must reduce the carrying value of those assets on the balance sheet. Any reduction of the firm's current assets will reduce the company's NCAV.

For example, management at an entertainment retailer may realise that customers are not taking to the retailer's current line of MP3 players. After closely assessing the situation, they may find that the MP3 players are not worth their carrying value on the firm's balance sheet. If their carrying value is $1 million, management might realise that the inventory is only worth $600,000 and will need to mark down the inventory, taking a $400,000 loss in the process. In this scenario, the company's NCAV would be reduced by $400,000 as well, since inventory makes up NCAV.

Inventory is not the only current asset that may be impaired on the firm's balance sheet. If a customer can't pay bills, receivables may have to be reduced by the expected loss. If a short-term investment experiences a significant drop in value, management may have to reduce the investment's carrying value on the balance sheet as well.

While we've been focusing on the assets side of the balance sheet, liabilities can also play a large role in reducing a firm's NCAV. For example, a company may require cash to fund the purchase of fixed assets. Once the transactions are completed, the firm's long-term liabilities will have increased in relation to its current assets, reducing NCAV.

As you can see, a number of different events can cause the burn rate to spike in any one period, deteriorating NCAV. As you can probably tell, some of these events are worse than others and many develop over the normal course of business operations. Therefore, a higher burn rate is not always a negative from a business point of view, but it does have meaningful implications for net-net investors.

Burn rate: the good and the bad

Is –10% a good burn rate? Should you abandon a company that is burning through its liquidation value? Where is the cut-off?

The answers to these questions really depend on your approach to net-net investing. It seems hard to believe that anybody would favour firms that are burning through their liquidation value, but this is essentially what academic studies suggest as best practice. As we saw in our overview of the net-net literature, the stock of money-losing net-net companies actually produces better risk-adjusted returns than shares of profitable net-net firms. Most unprofitable companies burn through working capital. While this principle often varies from one company to the next, it usually holds true for 1000 companies viewed as a group. Therefore, they're also more likely to burn through NCAV. Remember that NCAV is essentially working capital less long-term liabilities.

For this reason, quantitative mechanical investors may prefer to opt for money-losing net-nets that are burning through liquidation value. By focusing on money-losing firms that are also on average burning through net current assets, the argument goes, an investor will ultimately come ahead on average over a large number of stocks.

While common sense suggests that this approach is nonsense, common sense and investing are often in conflict. Common sense dictates that investors buy profitable and fast-growing firms that are popular on both Wall Street and Main Street. It also tells investors to avoid troubled companies, or even ones that seem to be going through a mild rough patch. Net-net investing, as a discipline, flies in the face of common-sense investing.

On the flip side, value investors are primarily concerned with sticking to solid investment tenets. According to Graham, an investment had to meet the criteria of safety of principle and a good chance of a solid return. Everything else was suggested to be speculation.[215] Seen in that context, qualitative investors with a more focused portfolio would be taking an additional risk by only picking net-net stocks that are burning through NCAV. It's likely that more profitable net-net companies make better investments than do money-losing firms trading below NCAV. In fact, the superior performance of money-losing companies trading as net-nets may be due to the smaller number of outliers with vastly superior returns.

From a qualitative investing point of view, investors may be able to avoid more risk by sticking to net-nets with either stable or increasing NCAV.

Since I shifted more towards qualitative selection criteria, I've grown to favour companies that have at least stable NCAV. Firms with stable NCAV or increasing NCAV seem to have superior investment characteristics when running a more concentrated portfolio. In the rest of this chapter, I'll walk you through burn rate from a more qualitative investing point of view.

Risks of a high burn rate

Burn rate is not always a negative, especially in cases where management make good use of capital to purchase distressed assets to boost profitability. Where burn rates spell trouble is when management need to mark down asset values due to slow-moving inventory, or investment losses, or when business operations consume more cash than they produce.

Net-net investors have to keep a watchful eye on the firm's burn rate, or they may face an impairment of their principal investment. As investors, we focus on buying distressed companies below a hyper-conservative assessment of their liquidation value, roughly assessed as a firm's NCAV. The firm's NCAV, therefore, is the initial value against which we judge whether a company is a bargain or not. Often, the only thing a company will have going for it will be its bargain price relative to NCAV. If that value erodes, so does our margin of safety and profit potential. At some point, NCAV may erode below purchase price, and may impair principal investment. If the firm does not recover, it may have to liquidate, or sell out to a third party at a price below acquisition cost.

Another major risk has to do with liquidity. As mentioned above, companies need cash to fund operations. If the business keeps burning through its working capital, then it may need to sell out to a third party in a panic to avoid bankruptcy. Where a third-party acquisition is not forthcoming, management may need to

215 Graham, *The Intelligent Investor*, 18.

file for Chapter 11 bankruptcy protection. (While British Investors often use the term *administration*, American and Canadian investors often refer to the event as filing for bankruptcy protection.) In these cases, stockholders may lose their entire principal investment. At other times, management may be forced to issue new shares to keep the company's lights on, or sell off assets which may impact the firm's medium- to long-term prospects.

Investors set on adopting qualitative analysis really need to peer into the actual business events to get a good sense of why NCAV has been impaired. A blanket approach is probably not the best approach when it comes to investing in promising net-nets based on qualitative factors. Still, a –25% reduction in NCAV, quarter over quarter, or year over year, should be seen as a big red flag.

Stability: biding time for a big event

While shrinking NCAV raises complications for net-net stock investors, it's always good to see a NCAV that's at least stable.

Net-net stocks typically increase in value rapidly, but it's often difficult to tell when those enormous price advances will occur. When they do come, they're often the result of business developments such as a sudden return to profitability, a takeover offer, an announcement that management will return capital to shareholders, great news coming out about the company which suggests much-improved future operations, or investment-focused news highlighting the firm as an investment.

These events can take place shortly after purchase, but more frequently, months or years later. As Graham cautioned in his writings, often the time it takes for a net-net investment to become profitable may seem considerable. A stable NCAV, one which is not advancing or deteriorating by a meaningful amount, allows a net-net investor to wait patiently for a development to transpire. The more robust the firm's NCAV, the longer investors can wait without their principal investment being put at risk. This is a far superior position to be in, when compared to investing in a firm that is persistently shrinking in value.

Best practice: buying firms steadily increasing their liquidation value

While a stable NCAV can make for a great investment, investors can really benefit from investing in firms that are increasing their liquidation value. Ultimately, an increasing NCAV means a widening margin of safety and a growing profit potential.

While most net-net companies experience a stable or shrinking NCAV, some see an increasing NCAV and a rare few see ongoing growth. These rare net-nets are essentially hidden-growth companies. Buying into one means buying into a company for less than it can be liquidated for and seeing that liquidation value increase over time.

The advantage of this should be obvious. Increasing NCAV ultimately increases your profit potential as the stock has further to rise before trading back up to NCAV. Where investors buying into net-net firms with stable NCAVs have the luxury of being able to wait for some event to move the stock price, their compound annual returns decline the longer it takes that event to materialise. By contrast, investors who buy into firms with growing NCAV can maintain their eventual compound annual growth rate or even see it increase. Let's see this in action.

Table 9: Comparing NCAVs of two companies

Company A	2010	2011	2012	2013	2014	2015
NCAV	100	100	100	100	100	100
Potential CAGR	25%	11.8%	7.72%	5.74%	5.56%	3.79%

Company B	2010	2011	2012	2013	2014	2015
NCAV	100	125	150	175	200	225
Potential CAGR	25%	25%	23.31%	21.61%	20.11%	18.81%

In table 9 we have two companies purchased for a price to NCAV of 80%. Company A has a stable NCAV. Company B has an increasing NCAV. While the initial purchases were made at identical discounts, Company B offers a greater chance of larger profits. Over time, the firm's NCAV grows, maintaining much of the investment's profit potential.

In this example, Company B is adding 25 to its NCAV each year. This is typical of firms that produce a stable income or free cash flow over time. But firms that can compound their NCAV, as in the case of growing firms, can maintain profit potential to much greater degree.

The final word on burn rate

Net-net stocks are similar in nature to call options because both can provide sudden tremendous upside if the investment works out. But while call options have a definite expiry date, net-net companies that consume cash through operations tend to wither away, eventually impairing an investor's principal investment and profit potential.

In this light, net-nets with a stable NCAV can be seen as perpetual call options. Buying into a troubled firm that's at least able to limp along without eroding value provides an investor with much more time to wait for the firm to regain its stride. So long as the business remains in purgatory, there's always the chance that the company will see a sudden improvement in its fortunes. With a soft catalyst, an activist accumulating stock, or management busy at work trying to improve performance, the chance of a good eventual outcome is fairly high.

On the other hand, firms with a much higher burn rate due to cash consumption provide investors with a much shorter window of opportunity in which to profit. They therefore pose a greater risk for investors, who may need to diversify more widely to compensate.

While net-net investors running a mechanical quantitative portfolio will want to diversify heavily anyway, those employing qualitative analysis should understand why a firm's NCAV is dropping in order to make a smarter investment decision.

Over time, Net Net Hunter members have grown to prefer net-nets that increase their NCAV from period to period. Doing so may indicate an outstanding opportunity – just the type we prefer to buy.

15

Market Cap – Don't Assassinate Your Small Investor Advantage

SMALL RETAIL INVESTORS have a real advantage over professionals. Unfortunately, they often forfeit this advantage to battle in an investment arena where the odds are heavily stacked against them.

Small investors often choose an impossible task

Earlier in this book, I discussed the institutional constraints that professional money managers face. Given their large portfolio size, professional money managers have to stick to investing in larger companies. This acts as a competitive disadvantage, since sophisticated investors are forced to compete against each other for a smaller pool of investable stocks.

For whatever reason, small investors tend to get swept up in the hunt for great large-cap firms. This is tragic, since it means having to compete against a mountain of professionals who are well equipped with prestigious degrees; $30,000 Bloomberg terminals; or the home phone numbers of CEOs and suppliers available to provide key company insights. In short, the small investor faces stiff competition that's nearly impossible to match.

A strong emotional temperament and a preference for Graham and Dodd do not provide small investors with an advantage over the pros, either. Many Wall Street professionals have cultivated a strong temperament, so that icy-cool demeanour is now merely the cost of entry. The same goes for *Graham and Dodd*. With so many professionals having read all the old classics, *Graham and Dodd* has become required reading rather than a secret recipe for success.

The key advantage small investors overlook

But small investors have one massive advantage that professionals cannot match: small investment portfolios. By virtue of their small size, most private investors have the ability to invest in some of the world's smallest publicly traded firms. As previously mentioned, professional investors simply can't buy these firms, which drastically reduces the competition for the remaining investors.

Since Wall Street's tremendous brain power, sophisticated tools, and deep connections only provide value when applied to buyable firms, this area of the market is also much less efficient. Greater competition for bargains among large-cap firms means that the pool of larger firms is likely to be more picked over, with fewer bargains on offer or at lower quality for the given valuation.

By contrast, as market caps continue to drop, firms become too small to constitute a full portfolio position. That makes following these firms a waste of time for the professional money manager. With fewer eyes on each company, stock prices dip lower relative to value, and sometimes good-quality companies trade at unjustified discounts. As firm size shrinks to micro-cap or nano-cap territory, it becomes far easier to find quality companies trading at deep discounts to intrinsic value. All of this means that the opportunities among smaller firms are, on the whole, far superior to those of larger firms.

Results shown in academic and industry studies support this hypothesis. Tiny companies, as a group, outperform larger companies over longer spans of time. Tweedy, Browne reported a wide range of investment studies in a 2009 white paper.[216] A common theme among these studies is the outperformance of small stocks over a range of valuation techniques.

For example, in one study spanning 27 years, Tweedy, Browne shows the effect that company size has on stocks grouped in terms of price to book valuation.[217]

---

216 Tweedy, Browne, *What Has Worked in Investing*, 8.
217 Ibid.

Table 10: July 1963–December 1990 annual investment returns for low versus high price/book value stocks according to market capitalization within each price/book value category for New York Stock Exchange, American Stock Exchange, American Stock Exchange and NASDAQ listed stocks

| | Ratio of price/book value decile | | | | | | | | | |
| | (Highest price/book value) | | | | | (Lowest price/book value) | | | | |
Market capitalization decile	1	2	3	4	5	6	7	8	9	10
1 (Smallest market capitalization)	8.4%	13.7%	14.4%	17.2%	18.7%	18.1%	20.4%	20.5%	21.8%	23.0%
2	5.2	12.6	11.5	14.3	16.0	14.3	19.0	15.4	17.2	21.5
3	6.7	10.6	14.8	11.4	16.3	15.6	15.6	16.8	18.5	19.2
4	4.7	8.6	12.7	16.3	13.6	14.5	16.1	19.1	18.1	17.6
5	10.6	7.8	13.0	17.6	13.6	17.2	17.3	15.1	18.2	17.9
6	8.4	11.8	13.7	14.8	11.3	15.2	14.3	14.3	14.9	18.0
7	11.4	12.0	11.9	10.0	11.9	13.6	11.9	13.9	13.2	17.6
8	7.9	13.6	10.9	11.4	11.9	12.1	13.8	12.6	15.5	18.6
9	5.3	10.7	11.0	12.0	12.6	11.2	9.8	13.3	12.5	14.6
10 (Largest market capitalization)	11.2	10.6	10.1	8.5	9.5	10.0	9.7	11.5	11.6	14.2
All companies in each price/book value decile	7.7	11.8	12.7	14.0	14.9	15.1	16.7	16.8	18.0	19.6

Source: Tweedy, Browne: *What Has Worked in Investing*, rev. ed, 2009.

As you can see, portfolios of smaller companies with low PB ratios clearly outperform portfolios of larger firms trading at low PB ratios. At each rung, as the average market cap shrinks, returns grow. This alone should be enough to make classic Graham investors rethink the size of the firms they're looking at.

Likewise, David Dreman studied value stocks ranked based on PE ratio and market capitalisation from 1970 to 1996.[218] While low PE ratios are strongly associated with outperformance, so is company size. Controlling for valuation, the smaller the company, the better the return.

218 Dreman, *Contrarian Investment Strategies*, 329.

Table 11: Small cap or small low P/E? 1970–1996

Market capitalization (1 Jan 1995)	Low P/E	2	3	4	High P/E	Market
$100–500m	18.6%	18.0%	15.7%	14.6%	12.5%	16.0%
$500m–$1bn	18.8	17.7	14.1	11	10.4	14.6
$1–2bn	15.9	15.1	13.7	12.4	10.3	13.7
$2–5bn	15.3	14.1	11.6	11.8	10.2	12.8
>$5bn	14.2	13.7	11.1	11.2	8.7	11.9

Source: Dreman, *Contrarian Investment Strategies*.

Dreman follows with a similar study, this time assessing the performance of PB ratios when firms are segmented by market capitalisation.[219] Aside from firms with the highest PB ratios, the stocks of smaller companies outperform.

Table 12: Small car or small low price/book? 1970–1996

Market capitalization (1 Jan 1995)	Low P/BV	2	3	4	High P/BV	Market
$100–500m	18.1%	17.1%	15.1%	14.0%	8.8%	14.8%
$500m–$1bn	18.2	15.9	14.0	11.9	8.7	14.0
$1–2bn	15.2	15.5	12.1	13.1	10.7	13.5
$2–5bn	16.2	13.9	11.4	11.7	9.7	12.9
>$5bn	15.0	12.5	12.6	9.9	10.0	12.2

Source: Dreman, *Contrarian Investment Strategies*.

Further evidence comes in the form of equally weighted portfolios often outperforming market weighted portfolios. Market weighting is a portfolio construction strategy where more money is invested in larger firms. Equal weighting, by contrast, is a portfolio construction practice where the same amount of money is invested in each stock regardless of market capitalisation. The fact that equally weighted portfolios consistently outperform market weighted portfolios means that smaller firms provide better returns.

The above studies focus on two classic value strategies: low PE and low PB value investing. These are just two examples of classic value strategies that perform much better when investors concentrate on smaller firms.

But focusing on small firms provides a much more powerful advantage: it unlocks a value investor's ability to use far more lucrative value strategies, chiefly net-net stocks. As previously discussed, net-nets usually only surface among the micro-cap and nano-cap segments of the market. During periods of pricier global

219 Ibid.

markets, net-nets are relegated to some of the smallest publicly traded companies in existence. But by focusing on this area of the market, value investors can take advantage of the exceptional track record of net-nets.

The lesson is clear: value investors can improve their returns tremendously by simply focusing on smaller companies, which both improves the performance of classic value strategies in general and unlocks more lucrative strategies, such as Graham's net-nets.

Smaller net-nets outperform

It's no secret that in controlling for price to value, small firms provide higher returns, as a group. But few investors realise that this same trend holds true for net-net stocks. The smaller the firms trading below NCAV, the better the average performance.

We've already discussed the effect of size on portfolio returns earlier in this book. Vanstraceele and Allaeys's 2010 study of European net-nets found a material negative relationship between firm size and returns. Market-adjusted returns among the smallest net-nets came in at 16.57%, versus just 1.58% for the largest group. Ying Xiao and Glen Arnold's more recent study of net-nets in the UK found similar results. The smallest decile of net-nets far outpaced the largest, averaging 30.6% per year versus 17.17%.

Investors who focus on small companies clearly have an enormous advantage when value investing. Small firms provide much larger market-adjusted returns than do their obese peers. Net-nets are no different. When buying net-nets, it clearly pays to invest in tiny companies, the smaller the better.

16

How I Sidestep the Problems of Low Liquidity and Large Bid–Ask Spreads

VALUE INVESTORS TODAY assume that Graham's net-net strategy is fundamentally flawed because net-net firms are extremely small and therefore very illiquid with huge bid-ask spreads. In 2019, markets sat at their all-time highs in terms of price and overall valuation. As Graham commented decades earlier, net-nets tend to dry up as markets rise, so it's not surprising that net-nets today are anything but large and illiquid. Instead, companies trading below NCAV tend to have tiny market capitalisations, with very little stock traded day to day.

As a result, investors dismiss net-net investing, claiming that no reasonably sized investor could possibly use the strategy. Take this comment on my 2013 analysis of Sangoma Technologies, for example: "Great article – but with a volume of 19,819 shares/day at price of 0.20 CAD/share, that's extremely low liquidity levels and if you want to invest any significant amount of money it will take forever to get in and out of the position."

Sangoma Technologies was indeed thinly traded at the time. With a market capitalisation of less than C$5.77 million, it was among the smallest publicly traded companies in the Western world. That tiny size didn't help investors who spotted the bargain and faced an average daily dollar volume of only $3,964. Compared to mega-cap names such as Apple, which traded stock worth $9.5 billion per day at the end of 2018, Sangoma's volume was tiny!

But did this thin volume exclude Sangoma from contention? And more to the point, what are small investors to make of the objections that net-net investing is not viable due to tiny market caps, thin volumes, and large bid-ask spreads?

Large and medium-sized private investors forced to watch from the sidelines

Sangoma was clearly off the radar of most professional money managers. Earlier, I discussed just how much money fund managers have to invest and what that means for position sizing. Even if major investors were to stumble onto Sangoma, they could only buy an irrelevantly small position, excluding Sangoma as a purchase candidate. Net-net investing is almost always reserved for private investors managing much smaller portfolios, not pros.

Large private investors would have been kept out of the stock as well. Private investors managing anywhere from $50 million to $100 million, small by institutional standards, just couldn't buy enough of Sangoma to move the needle. Assuming an investor with a $50 million portfolio was able to buy half of the company's average daily volume, it would take 1,260 days (including weekends and holidays) to build a 5% position; and an investor putting $25 million to work would still need 630 days to fill a 5% portfolio. Faced with such constraints, focusing on another strategy becomes the most rational course of action.

If net-net investing is more or less out of the question for larger private investors, what about those managing a smaller $5 million to $10 million portfolio?

With smaller portfolios, investors have a much easier time buying thinly traded stocks. Managing a $5 million portfolio, an investor would need to spend 126 days out of the year to buy enough Sangoma stock to fill 5% of his portfolio. At a market cap of $5.77 million and average daily dollar volume of $3,964, Sangoma Technologies was just on the cusp of viability for private investors managing smaller portfolios.

But Sangoma was really in the sweet spot for those managing tiny portfolios under $1 million dollars. With just $1 million under management, it would take small private investors only a month to stick 5% of their assets into the stock; and just a little over 12 days for investors managing only $500,000. Ultimately, the smaller the portfolio, the easier it was to take advantage of the outstanding opportunity Sangoma offered investors.

Net-nets out of reach for $1 million portfolios?

The above discussion really highlights the constraints faced by knowledgeable investors trying to manage larger personal portfolios. Only a small amount of money could be put to work buying Sangoma shares. While it is still possible to find a good number of firms with market capitalisations far in excess of $5.77 million, the typical company trading below NCAV is tiny. Investors managing tiny sums of money have a lot more opportunities open to them and can earn the highest possible returns using the strategy.

Those managing $5 million or $10 million can still take advantage of Graham's net-nets, but they do need to adapt. Since average daily dollar volumes generally increase with firm size, the obvious solution is to look for larger businesses. Instead of cheap nano-cap companies such as Sangoma Technologies, larger private investors would have to step up to the micro-cap space, companies with market capitalisations between $50 and $300 million. Managers selecting stocks for a $25 million portfolio could fill a 5% portfolio position in just over three months if they stuck to $100 million companies with $40,000 in average daily dollar volume. However, as we saw earlier, because company size is negatively correlated with portfolio returns, even these investors would want to buy the smallest companies possible.

Market level determines who can play

Just how prevalent these larger net-net firms are is a matter of market valuation. Entering 2019, American investors faced a ten-year-long bull market and some of the highest stock market valuations in history. This has a large impact on both the typical firm size trading below NCAV and the number of net-net stocks available. Today, those trying to employ Graham's net-net stock strategy have a much smaller number of opportunities available in the USA. Market caps are typically around $1 million to $50 million. Larger investors have to think about investing internationally in countries such as Japan where market values are much lower and therefore offer more opportunities.

This is excellent news. Even today, investors managing $5 million to $10 million should be able to fill their portfolio with net-net stocks if they are willing to be flexible. And since markets have historically traded at much lower valuations, more opportunity should be available when market valuations fall back to earth.

Take small bites to fill a position

The above discussion highlights another difference between net-net investing and investing in large companies like Starbucks. Given the thin liquidity, investors have to tiptoe into and out of positions rather than trying to buy their entire stake all at once. This is a key factor for any net-net investor managing more than $200,000. Rather than placing an order for an entire position at one time, net-net investors have to set a number of small orders to acquire a position. The more money being invested, the more small trades an investor has to make.

While a nuisance, this is exactly how larger professional money managers buy securities for their portfolios. Given their large size, attempting to buy an entire position all at once pushes the stock price up, resulting in a higher cost basis. Investors buying net-nets likely face even greater liquidity issues, causing prices to spike when orders are placed without due care.

In other cases, tiny traders can string buyers along, placing single share trades to move the price, causing other investors to chase the stock into more expensive territory. Placing smaller orders for 25% or 50% of the average daily dollar volume can help derail these problems.

Large bid-ask spreads: how to transverse the chasm

So much for average daily dollar volume, but what about large bid-ask spreads? Don't these provide a major roadblock for investors?

There's a scene in *The Wolf of Wall Street* movie where Jordan Belfort first stumbles upon penny stocks:

> "Jesus Christ, the spread on these is huge!"

> "Yeah, and that's the point ... Jordan, what do you get on that blue chip stock?"

> "I make 1% ..."

> "Pink sheets, it's 50 ..."

> "It's 50%? Fifty percent commission?!"

> "Yup ..."

> "For what?"

> "It's our mark-up for our services ..."

> "So, if I sell a stock at $10,000, my commission is $5,000 bucks?!"

When most small investors think of tiny companies with stocks trading for less than a dollar, they naturally think of conversations like this one.

What exactly are they talking about?

Small investors often assume that the quoted market price is the price that they can buy and sell shares for. Unfortunately, stock trades are more complicated than that. All stocks have three basic prices:

- Bid price: The amount of money that a dealer or buyer offers to buy a stock for.
- Ask price: The amount of money a dealer or seller is asking for the stock.
- Market price: The price that the trade is executed for.

Orders can be executed as either market orders or limit orders. Market-buy orders instruct the broker to execute the order at the best possible price, while limit-buy orders instruct the broker not to buy above a specified price. When the bid price corresponds to an asking price, the trade is made and the execution price becomes the new market price.

The extent to which the asking price exceeds the bid price is known as the bid-ask spread. At least some of that value is captured by brokers as a fee for buying or selling a block of shares, as shown in the above discussion from *The Wolf of Wall Street*. Typically, the fee is small for large liquid companies such as eBay where it's easy to find a buyer or seller for the stock. When buying or selling mega-cap companies, it often makes sense to place a market order, since the trade is virtually guaranteed to go through. Any additional cost encountered due to the bid-ask spread is not likely to affect the return much. *? Bid Price - Yes !*

It's an entirely different scenario for tiny firms with illiquid shares. Jordan Belfort's penny stock had a bid-ask spread of 50%. If unlucky investors had unknowingly placed a market order to buy the shares, they could have paid 50% more than intended. With a market price of $1, assuming the current asking price was $1.50, investors would have unwittingly asked for their trade to be executed at $1.50 and paid 50% more for their shares than intended.

Net-net stocks are almost always highly illiquid and therefore subject to unusually large bid-ask spreads. Inexperienced investors used to buying large cap companies often make the mistake of placing market orders when making their first purchase. Dumbstruck by their immediate sizeable loss, they conclude that the strategy is unusable and swear off nano-caps in favour of large mediocre blue chips. Without circumventing large bid-ask spreads, Graham's net-net stock strategy is practically useless.

Luckily, intelligent investors can simply set limit orders to completely sidestep the issue, rendering large bid-ask spreads a minor footnote to a brilliant strategy. By setting a limit order to buy a stock, experienced net-net investors dictate the price they buy or sell their holdings for, retaining great profit potential. When investors set a limit buy order for $1, for example, in the absence of competing bids, sellers have to sell their shares for $1 in order to unload their block. Buyers placing a limit sell order for $1.50, on the other hand, would simply refuse any offer below $1.50, forcing buyers to pay up for their shares.

Net-nets: easier to sell than to buy

Buying net-net stocks is a lot less problematic than many people realise. Neither small firm size nor large bid-ask spreads are a significant roadblock for the average retail investor. By simply keeping an eye on firm size and liquidity, and setting limit orders when buying shares, it's possible to fill a typical portfolio with well-selected net-net stocks.

This is only half of the equation, however. To reap the financial rewards associated with net-nets, investors eventually have to sell their holdings.

Given how slowly net-net investors have to move into their positions, what happens when it comes time to sell?

The good case: a stock that's gone up

Net-nets are usually much easier to sell then they are to buy. Part of this is associated with net-net returns. As a net-net stock rises in value, investor interest is perked and more buyers flock to the stock to scoop up shares. Their buy orders boost volume, allowing investors who bought much earlier to exit positions much more easily.

This phenomenon is somewhat helpful for smaller investors, who have typically built up their holding with only one or two buys and have no problem exiting with a single sell order when investor sentiment takes off. But increasing volume is excellent news for larger net-net investors who tiptoed into their position. Volume can expand significantly, allowing larger investors to exit in just a few trades. Depending on the stock in question, larger net-net investors may even be able to dump their position on the market in just one or two orders.

The bad case: a stock that's disappointed

But not all net-net stocks rise in value. Sometimes, even a well chosen net-net stock will fail to rise in price or will decline meaningfully, due to some unforeseen event. If the investment prospects have changed, it may be wise to exit the position.

As we saw above, small investors can step into their positions fairly easily, while those with larger portfolios need to focus on more liquid firms and make more trades to fill a position. The exact same situation is true with regard to selling a disappointing net-net stock. While investors managing tiny portfolios can usually jump out of a holding with just a couple of trades, even without a spike in investor interest, larger investors who insisted on buying smaller illiquid stocks will probably need to place a large number of small trades over time to exit a position. Trying to exit the position in fewer trades, out of frustration, is likely to move the market price lower.

A unique case: the volume trap

Unfortunately, disappointing net-nets aren't the only challenging scenario an investor has to face when selling. On occasion, trading volume will almost totally dry up, trapping an investor in the position for an uncertain length of time.

Interestingly, this doesn't just happen to net-net stocks that have disappointed, or traded lower. Sometimes an unexciting net-net stock will have risen in price before investors abandon the company for something more exciting. Scholium Group on the London AIM is a good example. While thinly traded, the company's stock had enough volume for me to form a position throughout 2017. After doubling that year, volume almost totally dropped off, locking even small investors into their holding with little chance of exiting.

While a frustrating aspect of net-net investing, this phenomenon detracts little from the strategy's excellent returns. Volume traps are comparatively rare, occurring perhaps only 5% of the time. If net-net investors take care to buy improving companies, they can simply wait for the market to revalue the company. As time marches on, their investment's underlying value will increase, providing for a larger upside.

On the other hand, if intrinsic value remains stagnant or withers away over time, other positions in the portfolio reduce its impact on overall results. As other buys work out as investments, the portfolio increases in size so these disappointing positions come to have a smaller and smaller impact on the portfolio.

Final thoughts on addressing illiquidity

Volume is an important factor when it comes to solid net-net stock investing, as I learned the hard way with Scholium Group. While it certainly plays a large role in an investor's ability to buy net-net stocks, volume changes over the holding period also have to be considered and addressed. This is especially true for investors managing larger portfolios.

Low liquidity today does not relegate Graham's net-net strategy to the dustbin of history, however. By focusing on net-nets with a reasonable amount of trading volume, and then adopting a few simple strategies for entering and exiting positions, net-net investing is still viable today. As market values drop, investors will see larger, more liquid firms trading below net current asset, which will make net-net stock investing much more viable for those managing larger portfolios.

Investors with larger portfolios have to pay special attention to issues of volume and plan accordingly. Sticking to firms that have a larger average daily dollar volume and a history of liquidity will go a long way towards achieving easier entrances and exits. Rather than aiming for excessive volume, investors should look for a minimum average daily dollar volume suited to their position size. Where to draw the line is necessarily an arbitrary judgement and depends a good deal on opportunity cost and the time an investor can dedicate to placing orders.

Another way to address low liquidity is to focus on companies where qualitative research suggests that the future is likely to be much brighter. Companies that can regain profitability, grow earnings, and spark optimism tend to have stocks that become more liquid over time. If larger investors study their companies carefully before buying, they have the opportunity to pick more promising investments and exit them without issue, even if buying smaller, less liquid firms.

Finally, investors who face increasing liquidity constraints would do well to heed the advice of Seth Klarman: "You have to feed the birdies while they're hungry."[220] Stocks that rise in price often experience a strong increase in volume, providing an excellent opportunity for investors to exit their positions. Unless the business is expected to continue to improve, investors should not assume sudden increases in volume will continue indefinitely. Waiting may mean facing much thinner volume and investors may find themselves locked into a position when they try to exit.

220 Klarman, *Margin of Safety*, 219

17

Share Buy-Backs – Befriend the Cannibals

AFTER YEARS OF studying the investment habits of great investors, it's clear that there are a few simple and reliable ways to identify the best investment candidates. These techniques involve assessing simple characteristics inherent in investment situations themselves. When you stack a few of these characteristics together, the odds of profit are overwhelmingly in your favour.

Share buy-backs: a primer

I first read about share buy-backs when ploughing through one of Peter Lynch's classic books. Since then, share buy-backs have always been one of the top things I look for when evaluating net-net stocks.

Companies typically first sell shares, literally ownership stakes in the firm, to raise funds for expansion or debt relief, or to allow founders to realise capital gains. Once a company makes its public offering, the investing public has the ability to trade shares in the company as they see fit.

But the firm itself can also buy back the shares it issued to the public. In doing so, it can significantly increase or decrease the underlying value of the company for the remaining shareholders. Firms that repurchase their own shares when they trade below intrinsic value disproportionately increase per-share value for the remaining shareholders. The extra value they capture per dollar spent accrues to the remaining shareholders, boosting the per-share value of their stake. When firms buy back shares above fair value, exactly the opposite happens.

Say, for example, that Burt's Plumbing and Party Supplies has a fair value of $1 per share, in this case comprised of net tangible assets. If Burt's CEO decides to spend $400 of the firm's own money to buy back the company's shares at $1 per share, he exchanges $1 in value (cash) for $1.25 in fair value and the remaining shareholders come out ahead.

Table 13: Burt's Plumbing and Party Supplies before buy-back

Cash	$500
Inventory	$550
Fixed assets	$300
Liabilities	$100
Net tangible asset value	$1250
Shares outstanding	1000
Intrinsic value per share	$1.25
Price per share	$1
Amount spent on buy-backs	$400

Table 14: Burt's Plumbing and Party Supplies after buy-back

Cash	$100
Inventory	$550
Fixed assets	$300
Liabilities	$100
Net tangible asset value	$850
Shares outstanding	600
Intrinsic value per share	$1.42

As you can see, Burt's Plumbing and Party Supplies was able to increase the per-share value of the firm's remaining shares by making the repurchase below fair value. The firm's cash account was reduced by $400 to account for the money spent on the buy-back. Burt's shares outstanding also dropped from 1000 to 600, representing the shares repurchased by management. In this scenario, the company swapped $1 in value for $1.25, collecting the excess $0.25 per share for the remaining shareholders.

If the firm had bought back shares for more than they were worth, however, the per-share value would have eroded.

Table 15: Burt's Plumbing and Party Supplies before buy-back

Cash	$500
Inventory	$550
Fixed assets	$300
Liabilities	$100
Net tangible asset value	$1250
Shares outstanding	1000
Intrinsic value per share	$1.25
Price per share	$1.50
Amount spent on buy-backs	$400

Table 16: Burt's Plumbing and Party Supplies after buy-back

Cash	$100
Inventory	$550
Fixed assets	$300
Liabilities	$100
Net tangible asset value	$850
Shares outstanding	733
Intrinsic value per share	$1.16

In this second situation, Burt's management buys back shares above intrinsic value, assessed here as net tangible asset value. Burt's cash account was reduced by $400, representing the amount management spent on the buy-back. The firm's outstanding shares were also reduced, but this time by just 277. Because Burt's management swapped $1.50 in cash for $1.25 in intrinsic value, the firm's per-share intrinsic value was reduced to $1.16. Buying back shares above fair value decreases the per-share value for the remaining shareholders.

Whether a company repurchases shares above or below intrinsic value has an enormous impact on the remaining shareholders. In a 1985 article in *Fortune* magazine, Buffett was quoted as saying:

> "All managements say they're acting in the shareholders' interests. What you'd like to do as an investor is hook them up to a machine and run a polygraph to see whether it's true. Short of a polygraph the best sign of a shareholder-oriented management – assuming its stock is undervalued – is repurchases. A polygraph proxy, that's what it is."[221]

---

221 Loomis, 'Beating the market by buying back stock', *Fortune* (21 November 2012).

Management who habitually repurchase shares above fair value, for example to boost the value of their stock options, destroy a large amount of shareholder value. Management who make a habit of repurchasing shares below fair value, on the other hand, grow shareholder value over time.

Share buy-backs in the context of net-net investing

Share buy-backs have an obvious impact on net-net investors. By buying shares below a conservative assessment of liquidation value, management grow intrinsic value per share for the remaining shareholders. The excess liquidation value obtained through the share repurchases accrues to the remaining shareholders.

But there's another important aspect to share repurchases within the context of net-net investing. When management buy back shares below fair value, they signal to investors that the firm's problems are less serious than the market assumes them to be.

Few if any management teams concerned with the survival of the enterprise they're running will waste precious cash on share repurchases. If the firm's business problems are serious, and future sales and profit are in question, management will try to conserve as much cash as possible to cover expenses and ensure business survival.

On the other hand, when management shed cash through repurchases, they signal to the market the belief that the company does not need all of its cash to survive the crisis. This strongly suggests management's belief that the crisis is less serious than the market believes, or that the crisis may be shorter-lived than the market believes. If this is the case, the company may soon be on firm footing again, a lucrative situation that smart net-net investors try to identify. Ultimately, when the company does better, the stock will follow.

Buy-backs below liquidation value also signal to investors management's shareholder-friendly leaning. Sometimes, management will buy back shares completely unprodded to provide value to long-term investors. Since buy-backs below fair value increase the firm's per-share value for the remaining shareholders, management may select buy-backs rather than dividends to reward long-term shareholders.

While typically unprovoked, buybacks sometimes do come as an attempt to fend off activist investors who are accumulating stock to take control of the firm. In these situations, reducing the company's float by buying back shares reduces an activist's ability to grow his percentage share of the company. If the activist holds 15% of the firm's outstanding shares and a management-friendly shareholder owns 25%, for example, reducing the shares available for purchase essentially locks ownership percentages in place. If the shares simply aren't available for purchase, an activist has no way to take control of the company.

This is another positive development for net-net investors. Activist investors are usually instrumental in forcing management to adopt a better business strategy or to adopt more shareholder-friendly policies. When this happens, investors may see better business results or significant share price appreciation. Even if an activist is blocked and can't take control of the firm, the added pressure on management due to the mere presence of the activist may cause them to either adopt better policies or take measures that are more in favour of shareholders, both of which are positive developments for minority shareholders.

Any of these situations increases the odds that a net-net stock will significantly rise in price. Investors who stick to net-nets whose management repurchase shares will see much better portfolio performance over time. Net Net Hunter studied the effects of share buy-backs on portfolio returns from 1999 to 2017 and found a 40% jump in compound annual returns. This amounted to an additional 8% in CAGR, boosting performance from 20.5% to roughly 28.5%. These portfolios also showed a greater number of winning stocks that increased in price at 54% versus 50% for net-nets in general.

These results were consistent with earlier studies of non-net-net stocks. In one study discussed in *Fortune* magazine, researchers identified firms in Value Line, between 1974 and 1983, that had voluntarily repurchased at least 4% of their own stock in a given year.[222] The outcome was stunning. Firms buying back stock enjoyed a compound average return of 22.6% versus the S&P 500's 14.1%.

Buffett buys Brooklyn, Rockwood & Co.

In the mid-1950s, Buffett bought a little chocolate manufacturer that would turn out to be one of his most lucrative early investments.[223] While it's uncertain whether Rockwood was a net-net, this curious story showcases just how powerful share buy-backs can be for net-net investors.

Brooklyn, Rockwood & Co. was a scantily profitable chocolate chip and cocoa butter manufacturer when cocoa beans suddenly spiked from 5 cents to over 50 cents per pound. The enormous spike in cocoa prices meant a corresponding jump in Rockwood's inventory value. Management knew they were sitting on an enormous opportunity that would soon slip away if they didn't act. The price spike was an anomaly and could collapse just as fast as it had developed.

222 Ibid.
223 Schroeder, *The Snowball*, 193.

The problem was how to best realise the potential windfall. The company lacked pricing power and couldn't pass on cocoa prices to its customers. Selling the beans also seemed out of the question due to the 50% tax bill the company would face.

Graham-Newman acquaintance Jay Pritzker had a plan, so began acquiring shares. Pritzker believed that he could use a provision in the 1954 tax code that allowed for the tax free sale of inventory if a company was to liquidate a business segment. This would allow the company to dodge the enormous tax bill associated with selling the beans. But, instead of selling inventory for cash, he would offer shareholders a warehouse certificate for $36 worth of cocoa beans in exchange for their stock.[224] The company's stock was trading for $34.50, so Pritzker was offering just enough value to make the exchange interesting for shareholders.

Exchanging cocoa beans for stock isn't common practice on Wall Street but Rockwood's transaction works out to a share buy-back. In essence, a share buy-back amounts to management trading some of the firm's assets for the firm's own outstanding shares. Typically, management offer cash for stock and make the trade through a stockbroker as any other investor would. But sometimes management get creative. Rather than buying back shares for cash and reducing the company's cash account, as in our examples above, Pritzker had Rockwood offer cocoa beans to investors, which reduced the firm's inventory rather than its cash account.

At Graham-Newman Corp., Graham spotted the small gap between Rockwood's share price and the value in cocoa beans so decided to take advantage of it through an arbitrage play.[225] He instructed Buffett (who was a young employee of Graham-Newman at the time) to buy Rockwood shares for $34.50 on the stock market and sell them to Rockwood for the warehouse certificates. Then he sold the certificates at market value to realise a $1.50 profit per share, which was tiny, but the investment's short duration made it highly lucrative.

Buffett spent a considerable amount of time in the New York subway system, ferrying shares and warehouse certificates back and forth to complete the trade. While he understood what Graham was doing, he worked out a better way to profit. Rather than taking part in the arbitrage, Buffett simply bought 222 Rockwood shares and hung on to them.

He had given considerable thought to Pritzker's plan, and realised that shareholders who accepted Pritzker's offer were collecting far fewer cocoa beans per share than the amount of cocoa bean ownership each share represented. On top of that, the remaining investors retained all of the company's other assets and its ongoing business. Since the underlying net asset value of each share was considerably

224 Ibid.
225 Ibid.

higher than the price Pritzker was offering for the stock, the remaining investors would assume this excess value, and their investment in the company would grow significantly. Since Pritzker was the company's major shareholder, he would reap an enormous profit. And Buffett decided to invest alongside him.

Alice Schroeder reports that the stock shot up from a low of $15 to a high of $85 immediately after the buy-back was completed. Buffett's early buy had yielded approximately $13,000 in capital gains, an enormous sum in the 1950s.[226]

Active buy-backs a boon for net-net investors

When buying stock in any sort of distressed firm, investors have to guard against loss and look for signs of a better tomorrow. It's clear that share buy-backs help satisfy both. Insiders are in the best position to assess their firm's business problems and whether they put the survival of the company in question. Few if any management teams will spend money on share buy-backs if they feel the money is needed to survive the crisis.

Ultimately, share buy-backs well below intrinsic value provide enormous benefits for remaining shareholders, as excess value captured accrues to the value of their ownership interest. This could be one of the reasons why share prices often rise when buy-backs are conducted. It's also why I prefer to concentrate on these firms as much as possible.

226 Ibid.

18

Chinese Reverse Mergers – Financial Poison

THERE'S A PERCEPTION in the West that Chinese goods are shoddy, and sometimes dangerous. Poisoned baby formula and lead toys easily come to mind. For better or worse, a small number of cases have tainted the image of Chinese goods in the eyes of Western consumers.

While not as widely known, foreign investors have had their own run-in with questionable Chinese merchandise: worthless shares attached to Chinese reverse merger companies. In the summer of 2010, investors started reporting issues with the quality of Chinese reporting, specifically Chinese companies trading on American exchanges. In fact, many of the financial statements investors used to make decisions seemed to be nothing more than blatant lies. All of this points to a troubling fact: many Chinese firms have taken advantage of international investors and the good reputation of first-world markets to dupe people out of billions of dollars.

Buffett and Munger extol the virtues of Chinese business leaders and speak highly of Chinese stocks in general. Without question, many Chinese business leaders are talented and have an upstanding moral character. There are a lot of solid companies in China that show tremendous promise. But the problem lies with Chinese firms traded on foreign exchanges, not with Chinese businesses in general.

The Chinese reverse merger scam

In a *Businessweek* article, Dune Lawrence cites sources who report major fraudulent activity by Chinese firms trading on the American markets.[227]

227 Lawrence, 'Worthless Stocks from China', Bloomberg (13 January 2011).

The scam goes like this: a small Chinese company will shop for a publicly listed shell company in the USA, inflate its numbers, and then combine with the American firm through a reverse merger. Management then waits to build up legitimacy in the American market before issuing additional shares to the public. The public, reassured by the firm's track record, the good name of the American capital markets, the SEC, and various American auditors, buy into the firm's promising growth story. They scoop up stock backed by this fabricated record and assets that have been vastly overstated. Once the fraud is discovered, the stock collapses, and investors lose their principal investment.

The SEC and investors generally, according to *Businessweek*, have little recourse since the majority of the company's assets and operations are in China, governed by Chinese law. The Chinese authorities, on the other hand, don't seem willing to prosecute since these firms generally comply with Chinese law.

Investors, such as Muddy Waters Research, Chapski & Chapski, and Audit Integrity, have found that the story given to the State Administration for Industry & Commerce (SAIC), China's version of the SEC, is far different from the story sold to investors on first-world markets. According to the *Businessweek* article, in one case, the assets of China Marine Food Group were marked up over 3000% in just one year. In another case, customer numbers and sales figures that passed audit and were made available to investors on American markets were completely made up. And while some auditors seem to be grossly negligent or even complicit in this problem, other auditors who take responsibility for auditing these companies' statements opt to exit the situation.

The Sino Forest fiasco

Sino-Forest is an excellent example. The company operated tree plantations in China, and sold wood fibre for various uses in the Chinese domestic market. Shares were issued on the Toronto Stock Exchange in 1994 and the firm operated without issue for 27 years.

Sino had presented international investors with a picture of a thriving enterprise throughout the early 2000s and used this record to raise $2.9 billion in funds on the Canadian markets.[228] From 2004 to 2010, management recorded asset growth from $0.756 billion US to $5.7 billion US.[229] With liabilities of just $2.4 billion US, the company's net assets stood at $3.3 billion US, according to management. The company was seemingly profitable, with a net income of nearly C$400 million.[230]

---

228 Thomson Reuters, '$2.6 billion award in Sino-Forest fraud case', *Financial Post* (15 March 2018).
229 Sino Forest 2006 Annual Report.
230 'Sino-Forest Corporation', Wikipedia.

In 2011, Muddy Waters published a report calling the firm a Ponzi scheme, complete with fraud, theft, and undisclosed related party transactions. Royal Canadian Mounted Police and Ontario Securities Commission investigations followed, and the company soon filed for bankruptcy protection.

Confirmation came in a civil case judgement in 2018 that handed plaintiffs an award of $2.6 billion US.[231] According to the judgement given by Ontario Superior Court Justice Michael Penny, Sino-Forest Corp co-founder and CEO Allen Chan had abused his unique position. Rather than investing in legitimate business initiatives, he funnelled hundreds of millions of dollars into fictitious operations with inflated values and then used related party transactions to stuff cash into operations he secretly owned.

Big Four auditor Ernst & Young, tasked with auditing and approving Sino's financial statements, failed to champion investor interest. In 2012, one year after the scandal broke, they agreed to settle a class action lawsuit filed by shareholders, paying $117 million. They later settled with regulators as well, shelling out another $8 million.

Net-net investors at increased risk

Sino-Forest was a multi-billion dollar fraud, far from the sort of firms that dip below NCAV. Yet there are many more examples of this sort of fraud on Western financial markets. Worse, given their solid balance sheets and beaten-down prices, many surface as statistical net-nets.

Unwitting investors new to net-net investing often stumble onto these firms, scan their seemingly outstanding track records, and make the mistake of purchasing shares. A quick glance at their financial reports makes it clear why. These companies are often dirt cheap, with a strong record of growth and conservative balance sheets, and seem free from significant business problems. In fact, they appear to be ideal net-net investments.

While their financial performance looks beautiful, there's often an ugly story lurking behind the numbers. Many of these firms will have had accusations of fraud hurled against them, and some will be undergoing investigations. This presents an interesting dilemma for would-be net-net investors: buy the stock betting on management's upstanding moral character, or avoid the shares only to miss out on what may be an outstanding investment.

---

231 Thomson Reuters, '$2.6 billion award in Sino-Forest fraud case'.

Best practice for net-net investors

The short-selling firm Muddy Waters was named after an ancient Chinese proverb that translates as 'Many fish can be caught in muddy waters.' This seems to characterise the opaque nature of Chinese firms trading on foreign markets. Fraudulent Chinese companies have surfaced on a broad range of foreign exchanges, from the USA and Canada to South Korea.[232]

Despite all the managerial brilliance that legendary investor Munger says is being unleashed in the country, it's clear that outsiders are at a distinct disadvantage due to their ignorance about Chinese culture and language. When operating in foreign countries with a sharp difference in culture and language, foreigners are usually the least likely to understand what is happening and the last to find out.

Avoiding frauds is a basic requirement when it comes to successful investing. Unfortunately, spotting fraudulent firms is a special skill that few investors possess. While there are undoubtedly many fine firms operating in China, and listed on both Chinese and international markets, small investors simply don't have the ability to screen out the questionable businesses. Given the widespread fraud by Chinese businesses listed on international markets, investors are advised to stay clear of firms with significant operations in China. There are simply too many other great options for investment. As Buffett points out, once dumb money recognises its limitations, it ceases to be dumb money.

---

232 Yoon, 'Chinese Firms Listed on KRX Receive Disclaimer', BusinessKorea (22 April 2019).

PART 5

NET–NET CASE STUDIES

19

How Insider Ownership Led Trans World Entertainment to Massive Returns

DEEP VALUE INVESTORS have to get into the habit of looking past preconceptions to uncover hidden gems. Often, investors have preconceptions about a company or industry and therefore pass on buying a seemingly cheap stock that will ultimately produce beautiful capital gains.

When insiders own a large piece of the company, they'll often work very hard to try to right the business. A large ownership stake means that management and directors have a lot of money at stake. If the business does well, they'll do well financially. On the other hand, if the company continues to erode in intrinsic value, their fortunes will erode as well. This incentive often places management interest in line with shareholder interest, leading to an increased focus on shareholder value. No investment illustrates this better than my 2011 purchase of Trans World Entertainment.

Company background

Trans World was a US CD, DVD, video game and novelty toy business originally founded in 1972 by Robert Higgins. The company had been successful throughout the 1990s and early 2000s, growing from 712 stores in 1994 to 881 stores ten years later. Growth had come through a number of acquisitions, which helped the firm expand its retail footprint to 47 US states.

While the firm had successfully navigated technological changes before, as records turned to 8tracks, tapes, and then CDs, the Internet was proving a more formidable challenge. In the year 2000, one year after the music-sharing site Napster launched, the company recorded $61 million in profit, on $1.36 billion in sales. Four years later, its profit had shrunk to just $21 million on $1.33 billion in sales and Trans World had experienced a sizeable loss the year prior.

The old model of balancing inventory between old and new tech was clearly broken, as thousands and then millions of people began downloading content through sharing sites. By 2008, it was clear that the firm's main business was in serious danger. Not only were people buying fewer CDs, but remaining CD and DVD buyers were increasingly turning to a snappy little start-up named Amazon which carried a large assortment of content which it sold at rock-bottom prices.

By 2010, it was obvious to most investors that the era of bricks-and-mortar CD and DVD shops was nearing a close. In 2010, the rental juggernaut Blockbuster filed for Chapter 11 bankruptcy protection, hit hard by the same forces that were impacting Trans World: online sales and digital downloads.

Trans World's stock cratered from $15 per share in 2007 to just over $1 per share entering 2010, a decline of over 93%. Investors had rushed for the exits and those remaining had lost the majority of their invested principle. Investors who had held on since 1998 when the stock was trading at $28.51 suffered a much longer and much more painful decline.

Investment characteristics

When I spotted the company in 2011, the stock had already doubled from its extremely depressed 2009 low of $0.61. The enormous stock price decline sparked my interest, so I began digging into the firm's story.

On the surface, the firm seemed to meet all of my Net Net Hunter Scorecard's core criteria. The company was buyable – volume wasn't an issue – and traded on the NASDAQ, *not* the NYSE. It was also trading below NCAV, meeting net-net status. At $65 million, the firm was tiny but not so tiny that basic managerial quality was an issue. It was operating in retail and was based in the USA, not China. Burn rate was also adequate: the firm was losing just 14% in NCAV year over year.

The firm also had a fairly solid balance sheet, with little debt and a current ratio of 2x. The one dark spot seemed to be share sales, since the company's diluted share count had increased over the previous two years. Digging deeper, I found that the company wasn't actually selling shares, just issuing shares to management as part of a compensation package. This was reassuring, since management weren't disregarding shareholder value or raising cash to survive further headwinds. I did find another $9 million in off-balance-sheet pension liabilities, though, so I made sure to subtract it when arriving at the firm's final NCAV.

While the firm met all of the core criteria, I didn't yet count it as a buy. Assessing ranking criteria is a key part of the process when it comes to uncovering exceptional bargains. As it turned out, the firm scored well in terms of ranking criteria:

- Debt was below 20% of equity, helping to solidify the balance sheet.
- Trans World was not paying a dividend, placing it among the highest returning net-nets from a statistical point of view.
- While the firm didn't quite meet the 50% price-to-NCAV hurdle, it came close at a 46% discount after factoring in off-balance-sheet items.
- Insiders, still led by Robert Higgins as CEO, owned 41% of the company, so there was a strong incentive to improve performance.

In 2011, that stake was worth around $20 million – a significant amount to stake on the survival of the company. If the company had folded, Higgins would have lost a good chunk of his personal fortune. If he were able to turn the business around, on the other hand, he would see his fortune multiply.

Other factors hinted at the fact that management worked feverishly to turn the business around. Trans World had climbed out of a disastrous 2009, losing $2.20 per share against a stock price of just $0.61!

But over the following three years, management implemented a right-sizing strategy, closing unprofitable locations in order to curtail losses. Most retailers have a mix of profitable and money-losing stores. If management feel that a location isn't likely to regain profitability, it often makes sense to close the store. In almost all cases, closing money-losing locations leads to an overall higher level of profitability. If Trans World could close its money-losing locations, the company would be left with profitable shops only and a much healthier operation. Management could also consolidate their time, focusing attention on other parts of the business that were likely to lead to long-term success.

Not all managers are willing to take this step, however. Some enjoy reigning over a larger kingdom, even if it means subsidising money-losing stores. It takes an ownership mindset to make the changes needed to ensure the long-term health and success of a business. Given management's recent activity, it was clear they took the firm's predicament very seriously.

This wasn't management's only focus, however. They were also refocusing the firm on lifestyle products such as collectables and toys. Given their previous focus on CDs and DVDs, the shift was at least not a terrible idea. Fewer people were buying music or movies, and remaining buyers were becoming more discriminating shoppers. Management needed to shift its product mix to maintain sales and boost margins.

Post-purchase events

It was fairly clear where things were heading. For the previous two or three years the company's financial results had improved substantially.

I decided to put a large chunk of money down on the company at a price just above $1.82 per share in January 2011. That proved to be a poor entry point, as the stock immediately sank to the low $1.50s.[233] The initial paper loss was painful, but what mattered was that I had bought into a solid net-net.

Trans World kept closing stores throughout 2011 and 2012. Sales declined in sympathy, from $988 million in fiscal 2009 to just $543 million in fiscal 2012. But rather than showing larger losses, the firm's bottom line continued to climb. In fiscal 2012, the company posted a small $0.07 per-share profit, the first positive result in three years. To top it off, store closures had slowed dramatically, down to just 33 stores from the prior year's 71.

This was an extremely positive sign. Looking back over four years, it was clear that management's store closure strategy was working. They had eliminated a large number of money-losing locations and focused more heavily on profitable products. This had led to lower sales but higher margins, resulting in profitability.

At the end of 2012, Trans World announced a special dividend of $0.47 per share. It was a clear sign that the situation had changed dramatically compared to four years earlier. In January 2013, Trans World posted their second annual profit, now $1.07, which sent the stock price up to $5.22 per share. Investors brave enough to pick up shares for 60 or 70 cents during the dark days of 2009 and hold until the firm regained significant profitability would have seen a return of over 700% in just four years.

Conclusions to draw from Trans World Entertainment

My investment didn't fare nearly as well, but it was still an excellent two-year return. I had decided to exit my position at $4, after the special dividend, for a 146% return. If I had held on a little longer, I might have been able to squeeze out a better performance, but I felt that the stock price fully reflected value, so I sold my position. My solid return is proof that you don't have to time purchases and sales carefully to do very well investing in net-nets.

---

233 Like Mohnish Pabrai, I've found that many of the stocks I purchase sink after my initial buy. It's said that value investors tend to buy early (since the stock continues to drop after purchase) and sell late (since the stock continues to advance after the sale). Luckily, this does not derail the great performance that net-net investors achieve.

Not all net-nets work out as profitably as Trans World Entertainment. They're often troubled companies facing serious business challenges. But a terrible company and a terrible investment are not the same thing. Trans World's great investment performance from 2009 to 2013 is an example of how management, working for the good of the business and shareholders, can turn around a dire situation.

Trans World Entertainment is quite a different company at the time of writing. After hitting their $5.22 high, retail operations turned south and the stock tumbled. Robert Higgins passed away in 2017, leaving a leadership vacuum in his wake. With its 2016 purchase of etailz, Trans World is busy trying to transform itself into an online retail services company. Unfortunately, the transition is proving very difficult and the future not nearly as clear as it appeared in 2013.

20

GTSI Corp.'s Soft Catalyst Earned Me 85% in Five Months

I N 2011, GTSI Corporation (GTSI) had a big problem. The firm had just been slapped with a large penalty by the US Small Business Administration (SBA). As a result, the firm had lost 50% of its revenue and most of its sales staff. Investors were calling the firm's future into question – there was serious doubt as to whether the firm could weather the storm.

Founded in 1983 in Herndon, Virginia, GTSI sold software, hardware, and related services to government agencies. It had been quite successful and had grown fat on these contracts throughout the 1990s and early 2000s. By the mid-2000s, GTSI was rapidly outgrowing the small business status it retained on many of its contracts.

The SBA had been involved in the procurement of government contracts, implementing a program under the Firstsource program that reserved these contracts for small businesses. The aim was to promote small American firms in order to grow small businesses nationwide. Larger firms were excluded from contention.

But GTSI was anything but small. By 2006, it had grown to 411 sales staff, and $850 million in revenue.[234] If GTSI were to continue to grow, it would be at serious risk of losing many of its government contracts, and management were well aware of the problem.

234 GTSI, SEC Form 10K (31 December 2006).

The GTSI scandal

To sidestep this disaster, management partnered with three smaller firms that would continue to have access to government contracts through the SBA, long after GTSI had grown too large.[235]

One of those firms was EyakTek, an Alaska-based company initially founded by Eyak Corporation (Eyak) and GTSI in 2002. As a native Alaskan company, EyakTek had special contracting privileges, namely the right to receive contracts of any size without competition.[236] Eyak retained a 51% interest in the company, while GTSI retained minority investor's status at a 37% interest.[237] As a minority shareholder, GTSI could simply claim that its ownership of the firm represented an investment interest and that Eyak was involved in managing the firm. This may have helped GTSI sidestep SBA rules.

In 2006, GTSI and Eyak formed another firm, EG Solutions, which later won part of a $3 billion contract through the SBA's Firstsource program to supply equipment and services to the US Department of Homeland Security.[238] The third company was MultimaxArray, a small firm also involved in the program that GTSI was thought to be subcontracting for.

But GTSI did not seem intent on simply standing back as a passive investor, or playing a small role as a subcontractor. Later allegations suggest that management planned to retain much of the activity and revenue that GTSI had enjoyed during its younger years.[239] GTSI, allegedly, used its smaller affiliates as a public face through which it could obtain contracts, engaging in much of the work and retaining much of the income. In one case, *The Washington Post* alleged that GTSI had sought to do all of the work on a contract awarded to one of its affiliates, offering the smaller firm a 0.5% royalty for procuring the contract.[240] GTSI management are even alleged to have gone so far as to use the corporate email addresses of the smaller firm when interacting with government employees, in order to appear as employees of the smaller firm.[241] If not committing outright fraud, GTSI seemed to be walking dangerously close to the line.

The scheme unfolded without a hitch, until *The Washington Post* published an investigative story uncovering corruption in the world of government contracts.

235 O'Harrow Jr., 'SBA suspends major contractor GTSI', *The Washington Post* (1 October 2010).
236 Ibid.
237 Ibid.
238 Ibid.
239 Ibid.
240 Ibid.
241 Ibid.

GTSI's involvement was reported, which sparked an investigation by the SBA. Shortly after, GTSI management received an unsettling email:

From: Smith, Michael B.

Sent: Tuesday, July 22, 2008

To: Bob Deegan

Subject: FW: Adobe Software

Mr. Deegan – My name is Michael Smith, and I am the Program Manager and COTR for FirstSource. It has been brought to our attention that GTSI may be submitting quotes, and otherwise conducting FirstSource business on behalf of Multimax Array. I want to assure you that if this is the case, this is an unacceptable business practice, and must cease immediately.

Thank you,

Michael B. Smith, Director

Enterprise Solutions Office

Source: Firstsource Program Manager Michael Smith's letter to GTSI management, 22 July 2008.[242]

Nearly two years later, the SBA had enough evidence on the company to warrant action. On 1 October 2010, the agency banned GTSI from receiving new government contracts, operations worth hundreds of millions of dollars in revenue.[243] By then the firm was listed as the forty-ninth largest of 100 companies on *Washington Technology*'s list of the top 100 government contractors.[244]

The news was catastrophic, since GTSI had relied on government contracts for up to 90% of its business over the previous few years. The penalty threatened the livelihood of GTSI's 615 employees and, many thought, the very survival of the company.[245] The SBA penalty was the most severe the SBA had ever levied and aimed to make an example out of the firm to deter future cheating within the industry.[246]

242 'Unacceptable business practice', *The Washington Post*.
243 O'Harrow Jr., 'SBA suspends major contractor GTSI'.
244 Ibid.
245 Ibid.
246 Ibid.

Within two years, the company was in dire straits. Revenue had fallen from $762 million in 2009, to just $357 million by 2011.[247] In the chaos, investors sold the firm's stock down from $8 to just $3.54. At that price, the entire company was selling for just $34 million dollars.

GTSI investment merits

In early 2011, it was clear that GTSI's business was in serious distress, but how was the company's stock as an investment?

To the typical investor, the answer was clear. GTSI was a dog, a real loser, and was best avoided. Given the revenue decline and the fact that a lot of the firm's business was wrapped up in contracts designated for small business, the company's future seemed bleak. Adding to the concern, the stock had been hammered and remained extremely volatile throughout 2011.

While investors rushed for the exits, GTSI was following a long pattern that characterised one of the most lucrative investment strategies available. GTSI had a full $7.74 per share in NCAV, so shares were trading at an enormous 54% discount to conservative liquidation value. The company at least warranted a closer look.

From a deeper dig into the 2011 year-end financials, it was clear that the firm was not at risk of bankruptcy. Not only did it have a sizeable NCAV; it also had a solid 1.75× current ratio, and no outstanding debt.[248] To top it off, GTSI wasn't burning through much cash: losing just $3.2 million from operations despite its problems.[249] Given the firm's $182 million in current assets, this was a tiny figure. Even more assuring was the firm's NCAV burn rate. While book value had edged down slightly, GTSI's NCAV had actually increased 67% year over year.[250] On quantitative grounds, the firm looked like a solid net-net.

The notes to GTSI's financial statements revealed something even more enticing. While investors focused on the SBA penalty, GTSI had actually settled with regulators just a week after the penalty was imposed. In exchange for the freedom to bid on government contracts, the company agreed to refrain from any operations relating to contracts designated for small business, to retain a government-approved auditor, and to let go of some of its top managers, including its CEO, Scott Friedlander.

Since a lot of GTSI's business was comprised of government contracts designated for small business, investors were also wary of a sizeable drop in revenue. But

247 GTSI, SEC Form 10-K (31 December 2011).
248 Ibid.
249 Ibid.
250 Ibid.

free to bid on other government contracts, GTSI could now shift its focus and rebuild its business. This amounted to a soft catalyst. Unlike hard catalysts (definite future events almost certain to improve the stock price), soft catalysts are much less certain. If GTSI's efforts were even marginally successful, the company would likely achieve significant profits which would lift the stock.

The company still retained the talent needed to obtain and execute government contracts, and wasted no time expanding its capability. By mid-2011, it had already purchased InSysCo for $15 million, which expanded GTSI's software and database development capabilities.[251] Management were already underway rebranding and refocusing the company in order to chart a more profitable future.

By year end, the company's stock had settled in a tight range between $4.25 and $5.25 per share. Investors seemed less panicked about perceived impending implosion but were still doubtful as to GTSI's ability to regain its footing. At $4.25, the firm still traded 45% below its $7.74 NCAV per share.

This market value completely ignored the industry expertise, connections, and organisational infrastructure GTSI possessed. These intangible assets had significant value, since they represented the cost of entry into the industry. Firms wanting to enter the industry would have to spend time and effort, never mind money, setting up these intangible assets. Given the strong possibility of a turnaround, GTSI, at minimum, deserved a valuation equal to the firm's liquidation value, likely more.

Unicom Systems agreed. In May 2012, Unicom made a bid for GTSI stock, offering $7.75 per share.[252] This offer was just shy of GTSI's pre-crisis $8 market value and nearly on par with the stock's ten-year average price. Unicom had clearly spotted the significant value investors had overlooked. Investors who bought GTSI stock at the $3.54 low in 2010 would have come out with a 120% return in three years, just shy of a 30% CAGR. Those who bought after the stock stabilised at around $5 came out with a 55% return in about a year's time. I managed to pick up shares in the low fours near the end of 2011 for an 85% return in just eight months – or 128% annualised.

251 Censer, 'In rebuilding effort, GTSI buys services business', *The Washington Post* (21 August 2011).
252 Echols, 'GTSI to be acquired', *Washington Business Journal* (7 May 2012).

21

How Debt Killed Albemarle & Bond Holdings

IT SEEMS ODD to avoid debt-ridden companies when net-net investing. Since net-nets have more in current assets than total liabilities (including off-balance-sheet liabilities) you'd think that avoiding debt would be unnecessary.

But as the case of Albemarle & Bond highlights, debt can still add a significant amount of risk. This is especially true when investing in distressed companies. For investors intent on safeguarding their principle, in accordance with Buffett's Rule #1: Don't Lose Money, it's still very important to avoid debt.

Albemarle & Bond Holdings' meteoric rise

Albemarle & Bond Holdings (A&B) was a pawnbroker founded with a single shop in 1983. Unlike the pawnbrokers frequently found in small towns and less-well-to-do urban areas, A&B was a high-street British pawnshop that catered to wealthy clients. It mainly dealt in gold jewellery, buying and selling fine used pieces, operating retail locations, and offering loans against gold pieces at higher interest rates. Rather than being deadbeat dads selling their TVs to buy beer, A&B's clientele were business owners and investors whose unique employment circumstances made it difficult for them to obtain loans.

The company was privately held for years and considered a fine firm by customers and competitors alike.[253] But A&B eventually went public, listing in London, and its priorities changed. Instead of being content with solid operations that

---

253 Robinson, 'Upmarket pawnbrokers boom', *Financial Times* (18 October 2013).

balanced profit with long-term survival, the pressures of public ownership meant an increasing focus on growth.[254]

And grow it did. After 19 consecutive years of growth, the company had a base of 140 shops around the country, a 14% increase from the year prior. It had grown into the second largest pawnbroker in the country, and was even granted membership of the British Retail Consortium in 2010.[255]

A&B's meteoric rise was mostly due to the decade-long rally in gold prices. Gold rose steadily from its 2001 inflation-adjusted low of $376 to an incredible $1271 per ounce by the start of 2010. This 238% expansion blew past the Dow Jones Industrial Index's 8% nominal rise over the same period. As gold prices rose, a greater number of Britain's asset-rich but cash-poor elite realised they could leverage their gold to obtain cash loans.[256] Scrap gold rose nearly 8x, from 10.7 tonnes in 2006 to 76 tonnes by 2011.[257] This swell of gold onto the market increased traffic into A&B's shops, and helped grow the firm's pledge book. With more gold circulating, A&B could offer a greater number of loans to reap larger profits.

Swept up in the gold boom, in 2011 A&B's management declared that "the age of the pawnbroker" had arrived.[258] Indeed it had. Two years later, gold hit $1965 per ounce and Rolexes had increased 72% in just four years.[259] The number of British pawnbrokers grew from just 650 shops in 2007 to 2250 by the end of 2013.[260]

A&B itself expanded heavily, opening pop-up gold shops in order to rapidly increase the firm's footprint to take advantage of the new era.[261]

A&B's folly

But A&B's new age proved to be a short one. Experienced investors realised that A&B management were walking into a trap. Gold is a commodity and, like all commodities, gold prices cycle between boom and bust. In 2001, prices had been clearly depressed at $376 per ounce but had shot up rapidly over ten years to reach a fevered pitch by the end of the decade.

A&B's declaration that the world had entered "the age of the pawnbroker" came at the high-water mark of an amazing run for the industry. Rather than expanding

---

254 Ibid.
255 Albemarle and Bond, 'Pawnbroking gains recognition', www.investegate.co.uk.
256 Gammell, 'Pawning my Aston Martin', *The Telegraph* (30 May 2012).
257 Robinson, 'Upmarket pawnbrokers boom'.
258 Rankin, 'Pawnbroker Albemarle & Bond put up for sale', *Guardian* (2 December 2013).
259 Robinson, 'Upmarket pawnbrokers boom'.
260 Ibid.
261 Robinson, 'Albemarle & Bond's fundraising efforts', *Financial Times* (2 October 2013).

their store base as the market entered a frenzy, A&B management should have begun hoarding cash, paying down debt, and finding ways to reduce fixed costs when the market turned against them. Shrinking the firm's loans outstanding or demanding greater collateral would also have been solid steps to prepare for a downturn.

The gold price bucked violently through the second half of 2011 and most of 2012. A&B's revenue kept climbing, but keen observers noted a problem. Management were still aggressively expanding their store base, with expansion costs and costs related to central infrastructure up 27% for the year.[262] By June 2012, A&B began to see significantly lower growth in gold purchases, from a 50% year-over-year growth in the first half of fiscal 2012 to mid-single digits by year end. While management still expected an increase in full-year profits by the end of September, they would now come in well below market expectations.[263]

Six months later, the situation had gone from bad to worse. Despite management's initial optimism, profits were down –33% due to a reduction in gold buying.[264] Even more troubling, the company was facing an acute cash shortage. All of this led CEO Barry Stevenson to bail on investors, commenting that the company needed "new leadership."[265] This was a bad omen for the company.

By June, the same pop-up stores the firm had opened to cash in on the gold selling craze were losing money. Because the company was now getting very short on cash, it approached its largest shareholder, EZCORP, with a rights offering in an attempt to raise capital.[266] When EZCORP refused, the stock dropped –76%.

An attractive net-net?

It may seem cheeky at this point to ask if A&B shares were a strong buy or not. But almost all net-net stock investments start with tragedy. A&B's story certainly fits the mould. Its shares had fallen from a high of 401p in 2011 to just 19p by the second half of 2013, a drop of –95%. At that price, the company was clearly depressed and trading for a total of just £10 million in the market. But was it a net-net? And if so, was it worth buying?

In early October, interested investors would have to rely on the firm's June year-end financial statements. Scanning A&B's June balance sheet reveals the results shown in table 17.

262 BFN News, 'Albemarle hikes dividend', investegate.co.uk (21 February 2012).
263 BFN News, 'Albemarle & Bond sees slowdown', investegate.co.uk (15 June 2012).
264 BFN News, 'Albemarle pre-tax profits fall 33%', investegate.co.uk (12 February 2013).
265 Cooper, 'Albemarle and Bond loses lustre', *The Telegraph* (22 April 2013).
266 Kaminska, 'Pawned Out', *Financial Times* (2 October 2013).

Table 17: Albemarle & Bond Holdings June Balance Sheet

Current assets	GBP
Cash	10M
Receivables	64M
Inventories	20.5M
Total current assets	94.3M

Long term assets	
PP&E	14.3M
Intangibles	7.2M
Goodwill	24.9M
Total long term assets	46.4M

Total assets	140.7M

Current liabilities	
Accrued liabilities	5.8M
Current tax liabilities	0.3M
Trade payables	2.7M
Bank loans	53.5M
Total current liabilities	62.3M

Long term liabilities	
Derivatives	0.5M
Deferred taxation	0.7M
Total long term liabilities	1.2M

Total liabilities	63.5M

Shareholder equity	77M

On the surface, the company looked like a real bargain. With £77 million in equity, the company was trading at just 13% of book value. It also had a NCAV of £30.8 million. At a market cap of £10 million, the firm was trading at just 32.5% of NCAV, an enormous discount.

Long-time net-net investors would have noticed a chink in A&B's armour, however. Despite A&B's strong balance sheet, the firm had £53.5 million in short-term debt. That made for a total debt-to-equity ratio of 69.5%. This raised two serious questions: 1) Would A&B be able to cover its debt repayment? and 2) was the firm subject to series debt covenants that might put the firm's future in jeopardy?

While cash-strapped firms can typically factor receivables or offload inventories to cover obligations, they require these assets to be liquid. Without a stable and fairly active market for assets, firms may find them tough to sell or may have to mark their selling price down significantly. Specific stipulations firms agreed to in order to access debt financing may also complicate matters including being forced to make an immediate repayment or face a much higher interest rate.

Smart net-net hunters would have ruled out A&B shares as an investment given its enormous debt-to-equity ratio. More inexperienced investors may have still picked up A&B shares, however, assuming that the firm had enough liquid assets to repay its debt.

A&B unravels

A&B's failed rights offering was a disaster for the company because it strongly suggested that A&B's current assets were not liquid enough to cover its debt obligations. Rather than factoring receivables or attempting to sell inventory, it went to its largest shareholder in an attempt to raise money. This would have diluted shareholders, and was seemingly an act of desperation by management.

Unfortunately for investors, A&B was also subject to debt covenants which required it to maintain a certain amount of cash on hand. Weakening business results put the company at risk of breaching this agreement. An investment from EZCORP would have given the firm some breathing room, possibly giving it time to scale down operations and cut its way to stable profits.

When EZCORP's financing fell through, A&B began melting down gold jewellery to raise emergency cash.[267] Since gold jewellery typically sells for a higher price than the gold it's made of, the only advantage to melting down jewellery to raise additional cash is to leverage the much more liquid market for gold bars. With the price of gold falling, the firm might have seen a significant decline in the value of its inventory if it attempted to liquidate it through regular retail sales. Prices had already fallen significantly and the bubble in gold suggested that the firm's gold inventory valuation might have been overstated.[268] Instead of simply reducing inventory through retail sales, A&B was essentially trading the excess value of its jewellery for access to the much more liquid gold market. This is strong evidence that the markets for both its receivables and jewellery would not support

---

267 Rankin, 'Pawnbroker Albemarle & Bond put up for sale', *Guardian* (2 December 2013).
268 Kaminska, 'Pawned Out'.

larger asset sales, a common occurrence in rapidly declining markets. Just like the customers it served, the firm became asset rich, cash poor.

Management also negotiated a covenant extension with lenders. In many cases, a breach of lending covenants leads to lenders requesting the immediate repayment of loans, or imposing significantly higher interest rates. As part of the agreement, however, A&B's lenders reduced the firm's borrowing facility from £65 million to just £53.5 million. This gave the firm just £2.5 million in emergency funds to work with.[269] With so little cash to work with, the firm lacked much operational manoeuvrability, making a comeback tough.

Just days later, it put itself up for sale, seeking bids from what management predicted would be fairly disinterested buyers. Despite the firm's more than 140 stores, it had little appeal in what had become a troubled industry. The announcement came the morning after five of the firm's directors tendered their resignation.[270] With an inside view of the firm's situation, their departures signalled a bleak outcome for A&B shareholders.

The firm was silent for much of the rest of 2013. While it noted that it had a number of parties interested in it, it only named one: Jon Moulton's Better Capital. Shareholders would have their hopes dashed on Christmas Eve, when A&B announced that Moulton had pulled out of negotiations. No other party was close to making an offer, and shares dropped from 8 to 4.4p, leaving the firm with a £4.4 million market value.[271]

The firm finally pulled the plug on finding a buyer in late January, 2014. Despite leaving bidding open for a couple of months, an absence of decent offers suggested that the firm was worth much less than management's selling price. At this stage, merely handing the business over to an acquirer at the firm's then-depressed market cap would have been a solid opportunity for investors to exit the position and retain a sliver of their invested capital. Unfortunately for the remaining shareholders, a sale now seemed only remotely possible.

Just one month later, A&B decided to halt trading in the company's stock, effectively locking existing ownership in place. Management cited the remote chance of shares trading higher again as a reason, and also its lender's lack of cooperation:

> "Over the weekend, the board was informed by the company's lenders
> that they will not be able to support the management turnaround

269 Robinson, 'New chief starts early', *Financial Times* (7 October 2013).
270 Rankin, 'Pawnbroker Albemarle & Bond put up for sale'.
271 Neate, 'Possible Albemarle & Bond buyer walks away', *Guardian* (24 December 2013).

plan for the business. The board is continuing to work with the company's lenders on possible alternative options for stakeholders."[272]

The firm's lenders had lost faith in management, and simply did not believe that more value could be extracted through a sale of the company. In a statement to the London Stock Exchange, management admitted there was little chance of any value being attributed to the firm's shares. One option, they admitted, was selling the firm for less than the value of the debt alone.[273] A day later, the company announced it was appointing administrators to begin the bankruptcy proceedings. Shareholders had lost their entire principal investment.

What to take away from A&B's disaster

A&B was a disastrous investment for almost everyone who bought after the company announced the new golden age of pawn broking. Still, investors can gleam some important lessons from this episode.

While rookie net-net investors may assume that all net-nets are safe since they own more in current assets than they owe in total liabilities, avoiding debt-ridden companies remains the best practice. A firm's ability to meet its obligations requires balance sheet liquidity, and current asset accounts may be substantially less liquid than presumed. This poses a problem for struggling firms with large debt loads. If a firm can't use its liquid assets to cover its debt obligations, bankruptcy is still a real possibility.

Investors also have to pay attention to the nature of a firm's assets. While diversified mechanical investors may come out alright simply playing the odds by investing in a large number of net-nets, more concentrated investors need to assess accounts carefully. In A&B's case, the inventory account was comprised of gold jewellery that was rapidly declining in value and proving tough to sell. Since most of the firm's NCAV sprung from its inventory and receivables, illiquidity in either of these accounts would spell major problems for the firm.

In fact, while there seems to be no difference between NNWC and NCAV in terms of statistical returns, more concentrated investors with a stronger focus on a firm's qualitative situation may want to prioritise more liquid balance sheets. A&B would not have been in as much difficulty if it had most of its NCAV in cash. Applying a NNWC approach, or at least demanding a significant amount of cash relative to total liabilities, would grant an investor a larger margin of safety when dealing with debt.

---

272 Rankin, 'Pawnbroker Albemarle & Bond put up for sale'.
273 Ibid.

Investors who decide to employ an NNWC approach to net-net selection, however, should remember that deriving an NNWC valuation requires more than a simple formula. Crafting a net-net working capital figure requires applying business insight and judgement in order to assess asset values during a fire sale. Buffett, for example, always assessed NNWC valuation based on what he thought a quick sale of the firm's liquid assets could bring.

Finally, all investors should recognise how dangerous debt is when investing in distressed firms. It reduces operating flexibility, can eliminate a firm as a takeover candidate, and may actually force a firm into bankruptcy. Avoiding debt-ridden firms should help net-net investors minimise risk further, making it more likely that their portfolio will satisfy Graham's investment requirement: safety of principle and a good chance of a good profit.

22

The (Almost) Perfect Net–Net Stock

Based in Markham, Ontario, Sangoma Technologies was a tiny tech company in the Internet telephony space. David Mandelstam brought the firm to life in 1984, and in 2000, it was listed on the Toronto Venture Exchange.

Sangoma's long slide

Sangoma made a nice business for itself developing, manufacturing, and selling software and hardware that enabled servers to communicate with telephone networks and high-speed wide-area networks in the mid-to-late 2000s.[274] The company navigated the Great Financial Crisis with ease, suffering only a small dip in sales and profits. Two years out, it had completely regained its top-line revenue.

Profitability, however, was another matter. In the early 2000s, Sangoma took advantage of the Asterisk PC-based telephony platform, and manoeuvred its way to near the top of the industry. By 2010, Sangoma was the second largest Asterisk card provider in the USA.[275] While this position initially proved extremely lucrative, Sangoma's industry was changing. The arrival of VOIP programs made voice connection easier for end users, and the technology's adoption forced Sangoma to develop new offerings to maintain revenue. Unfortunately, the new product mix resulted in lower margins: while the company remained profitable through the Great Financial Crisis and the ensuing years, Sangoma was not as profitable as it once was.

---

274 Sangoma, 2011 Q1 MDA, sangoma.com.
275 Ibid.

Complicating matters were the periodic hits Sangoma was taking from asset write-downs. Anticipating the technological shift, management began acquiring complementary products, sometimes through the purchase of small technology companies. The idea was to diversify Sangoma's offerings and find new profit streams for the company. Some of this was done the old-fashioned way, through research and development. But buying small tech firms allowed Sangoma to accelerate the process by acquiring interesting pieces of technology that it could then distribute through its existing channels. Sometimes these smaller firms had advanced R&D projects that were near completion, or customer relationships that Sangoma could leverage by selling additional products. Overall, the strategy was sound, but not all the acquisitions would bear fruit. A few of them had failed to perform as expected, leading the company to write down goodwill. By the end of 2011, accelerated amortisation and goodwill impairments amounted to a whopping C$3.67 million, pushing the company into losses for the year.[276]

By the end of fiscal 2012, Sangoma had regained bottom-line profitability but ended the year with a whimper.[277] The firm had grown its revenue by 16% for the year, but operating profits were down year over year, from C$1.23 million to C$1.05 million. Management's increasing focus on building a product portfolio that would yield significant sales and profitability going forward meant increasing investment in product development and expanding the firm's sales channels.[278] All of this took cash, money that Sangoma was expensing on its income statement. In 2012, the company's growth initiatives increased operating expenses from C$7.61 million in 2011 to C$8.41 million by fiscal year-end 2012. This was enough to push the firm into losses for the fourth quarter.

Despite the mixed performance, shares remained stable for the month post-announcement, hovering around the C$0.45 mark. A couple of weeks later, however, management released a proposed poison-pill plan, and shares began to slide.[279] The plan called for a rights offering in the event that a third party acquired more than 20% of the firm's outstanding shares. The pre-emptive move was officially aimed at ensuring the equal treatment of all shareholders and allowing management the chance to evaluate a hypothetical tender offer. But investors seemed to think otherwise. Implementing a rights plan also meant that a third party couldn't take control of the firm and force changes. Any proposed acquisition of the company also had to go through management, rather than letting shareholders – the firm's rightful owners – decide their company's fate. Following this news, the company's shares dropped 22% over a two-month period.

---

276 SEDAR, 'Management Discussion and Analysis'.
277 SEDAR, 'Sangoma Technologies 2012 MD&A'.
278 Ibid.
279 SEDAR, 'Shareholder Rights Plan Agreement'.

To make matters worse, the company's performance continued to slip, entering the new year. In the first three quarters of fiscal 2014, the company suffered continuing net losses and a small drop in revenue.[280] This was too much for investors, who pushed the stock price down to C$0.25 per share.

Sangoma's investment merits

Despite the firm's recent losses, its shifting business environment, and management's poison-pill plan, it was clear that investors were making a major error. A brief look at the facts reveal that Sangoma was a solid buy, the sort of firm investors should have been stuffing into their portfolios.

In early 2013, investors would have had to rely on the firm's 30 June 2012 year-end financials, which came out on 10 October 2012. While a bit dated, the firm's operations were fairly stable so the statements proved a useful tool to assess the quality of the investment.

Even a quick glance revealed that the firm was clearly no bankruptcy candidate. Sangoma had ample cash and next to no debt. Debt amounted to just $17,000, a tiny sum. The firm also had a large 6.18× current ratio, and much of its current assets were of high quality. A significant amount of Sangoma's NCAV was comprised of cash, receivables, and a much smaller amount in inventory and other assets. In fact, the company even had net cash (cash less all liabilities). If they ran into problems, management had the ability to cover all of the firm's outstanding obligations with cash before liquidating the firm and passing the remaining assets to shareholders.

In terms of valuation, the firm's C$13.6 million in current assets dwarfed its total liabilities, for a NCAV of C$11.1 million. With 29.75 million shares outstanding, that NCAV amounted to C$0.373 per share. As shares edged downward to C$0.25 in April 2013, they slipped below an adequate one-third margin of safety. Investors could count on this valuation as well; the firm had maintained a steady NCAV over the previous three years despite its problems.

---

280 SEDAR, 'Condensed Consolidated Interim Financial Statements of Sangoma Technologies Corporation'.

Table 18: Sangoma Technologies 30 June 2012 Balance Sheet

Item	Millions, CAD
Current assets	
Cash	$5
Receivables	$4.45
Inventories	$3
Taxes receivable	$0.5
Sales taxes receivable	$0.2
Other investments	$0.1
Other current assets	$0.4
Total current assets	$13.6
Long term assets	
Property, plant, and equipment	$0.4
Development costs	$2.3
Intangible assets	$2.6
Goodwill	$3.5
Total long term assets	$8.8
Total assets	$22.4
Current Liabilities	
Accounts payable	$2.1
Deferred revenue	$0.1
Total current liabilities	$2.2
Long term liabilities	
Deferred income tax liability	$0.3
Total long term liabilities	$0.3
Total liabilities	$2.5
Shareholder equity	$19.9

While the stock's investment merits looked promising, there was still the issue of volume. Shares were thinly traded, and at a price of C$0.20 per share, only C$4,000 worth of stock was being traded each day.

Most retail investors – if they know anything about trading volume – consider this a barrier to successful investment. With just C$4,000 traded daily, there's no way an investor can obtain a decently sized position. Or so the thinking goes. But professional investors face considerable volume constraints as well and, as a result, have developed an obvious workaround: buying a position bit by bit over a span of time. While C$4,000 of average daily dollar volume was much smaller than the volume for other net-net stocks, an investor could obtain a decently sized block by diligently setting smaller limit orders to take advantage of the selling. Setting small orders is key. Larger orders would signal the presence of a more sophisticated investor, causing sellers to demand more for the stock.

The company seemed nearly as promising in terms of ranking criteria. A sharp eye would have immediately noticed the firm's shrinking share count. A quick look at the company's cash-flow statement revealed that management were busy spending the firm's cash on share repurchases. This was a promising sign, since it strongly suggested that management didn't consider the company's situation dire. Instead of retaining cash to survive a deep crisis, management were busy scooping up shares at depressed prices, increasing the per-share value for the remaining shareholders.

One of those shareholders was the company's chairman, David Mandelstam, who held a meaty 18% of the firm's outstanding shares, valued at C$1.34 million.[281] While his block was somewhat smaller compared to the previous year, this sizeable holding encouraged Mandelstam to maintain a focus on long-term shareholder value. Given his position as chairman, he commanded a significant amount of leverage over the board and the company's management and could therefore sway policy as he saw fit. With this in mind, it's likely that Mandelstam was also instrumental in implementing the company's buy-back program. The more shares the firm repurchased, the more his stake would be worth and the greater his grip on the company.

Eventually that stake could be worth a lot more, too. At just C$7.4 million in market capitalisation, its dropping share price due to its current troubles made the firm one of the smallest publicly traded companies around. Statistically speaking, this smaller market capitalisation was associated with higher stock returns. Now management just had to get the firm back on track.

But was there any chance of that happening?

One of the more important questions was how operations would unfold going forward. While a company does not have to recover to produce excellent returns, improved financial performance is one of the reasons investors bid the price of the stock back up to fair value.

While the company had regained profitability in 2012, it was not priced low relative to earnings, and it wasn't showing steady growth in terms of earnings, NCAV, or book value. Earnings had been rocky over the previous few years and net asset

---

281 SEDAR, 'Sangoma Technologies Corporation Management Information Circular and Notice'.

values were nearly stable. Nothing suggested that a revaluation based on earnings or ongoing growth would boost the stock price.

The company's past earnings also weren't significantly relevant. While the company had earned large profits as part of its board business, technology was shifting, so Sangoma was unlikely to reap the same profits from that business again in the future. In fact, the firm needed to make a smooth transition in order to retain revenue and profitability. For Sangoma's operating business, everything came down to whether management could develop new revenue streams.

Luckily, management worked hard on the problem by pouring money into research and development and acquiring small tech companies to leverage their existing offerings, or product pipeline. In terms of R&D, while the company had historically kept its new product offerings to a minimum, Sangoma shifted focus, bringing 12 new products to market in 2012.[282] While there was no guarantee that any of these new offerings would achieve significant sales, the more well-thought-out products Sangoma introduced, the more likely it was that the company would stumble upon a huge winner. When this happened, sales, earnings, and ultimately the stock, would see a sizeable jump. This amounted to a catalyst, albeit a soft catalyst because success wasn't certain.

Despite the technological shift, management's new poison pill, and the thin volume on offer, Sangoma was an obvious buy. It checked every one of the Net Net Hunter Scorecard's core criteria, and offered a few solid characteristics that put it among the best net-nets available. The firm was tiny, nearly debt free, and buying back shares, plus it had a large insider ownership and a soft catalyst that offered a solid chance of improved business performance.

A quick turnaround

Sangoma's operations deteriorated throughout 2013, with both revenue and bottom line profits down. To make matters worse, the company decided to restructure its operations to better align its operating expenses with sales. This resulted in a C$0.2 million charge. But as part of its floundering sales, the company was also forced to swallow a C$4.6 million impairment to goodwill and intangibles, which led to a massive loss for the year.[283] Investors had little stomach for these issues and punished the stock.

I stumbled onto the stock in November 2013 and quickly got to work combing through the financial statements. Realising the opportunity at hand, I began placing limit orders and was lucky enough to build at position at C$0.20 per

282 SEDAR, 'Sangoma Technologies Corporation Management Discussion … June 30, 2012'.
283 SEDAR, 'Sangoma Technologies Corporation Management Discussion … June 30, 2013'.

share, just above the stock's ten-year low. By then NCAV had shrunk slightly year over year, but the stock price drop meant a much larger 45% discount to NCAV.

With a position locked in, all I had to do was sit and wait for a product to catch fire in the market. The company had continued its product development through the first three quarters of fiscal 2013 and had brought 20 products to market in the previous two years. It had also identified a number of new high-growth product categories and planned product offerings for them.

The firm's products were starting to gain traction – a full one-third of sales came from new product sales by the end of 2013, but nothing yet had truly taken off. Luckily, the firm had kept working hard to expand its marketing and sales channels. With more products offered through more sales channels, there was a much larger chance that the firm would stumble upon a hit product which would really boost sales.

But net-net investors didn't have to wait for that to happen. By the end of December, indiscriminate selling was coming to an end as the firm's pessimistic shareholder base had mostly filed out. With fewer shares dumped onto the market, interested investors had to increase their bid price to attract sellers. The stock settled into a thin trading range by December, nudged up slightly by Christmas, and then leapt up 40% entering 2014. The stock continued climbing until the beginning of May when it peaked at C$0.38 per share. Investors lucky enough to buy near the firm's ten-year low had nailed a 90% return in just four months.

Sangoma's 584% share price jump

A 90% return in just four months is an extraordinary outcome for any investor. Despite the firm's problems, bargain hunters had found the stock, and pushed its price back above NCAV. This provided a nice opportunity for net-net investors to unload their shares, and recycle their winnings into further depressed stock picks.

But to paraphrase Munger's mantra, the big profits are made by waiting. In early 2014, the investment's upside potential was still intact despite the run-up in price. While the firm was no longer trading below NCAV, it was still bringing many new products to market and expanding its sales channels. If any of these products were to prove a big winner, the firm would still see a large jump in its profitability and stock price.

Investor patience would be tested, however. The stock traded back down to around C$0.25 per share over the following year and a half. During that period, Sangoma made two acquisitions and released a substantial number of new products. Its newest acquisitions significantly reduced NCAV, but management's efforts were slowly being rewarded with higher revenues and a rebound in profitability. Both EBITDA and net profits were improving.

By the end of fiscal 2015, it was clear that Sangoma's business was out of the funk it had found itself in two and a half years earlier. Revenues and profits were up. So was the stock price. Sangoma's shares had risen back to just under its C$0.38 high, reflecting improved sentiment about the company.

In February 2016, the company released its six-month results for fiscal 2016.[284] Finally, management's strategy had really started to pay off. Sales were up a staggering 58% for the first half of the year and Sangoma's EBITDA more than doubled. This was excellent news for investors, who expected more of the same lacklustre performance from the company. Most of the improvement was made through two recent business acquisitions.

Within six months, the stock was trading at C$0.80 per share on newfound optimism. Eight months later, the stock hit C$1.30 per share, for a 584% increase from its ten-year low of C$0.19 at the end of 2013. Investors with enough faith to hold the stock for just over five years were rewarded with a compound annual return of roughly 45%.

Key takeaways from Sangoma Technologies Corporation

Sangoma remains one of the better opportunities Net Net Hunter members have come across in the last six years. Few investors beat the market, let alone achieve a 45% compound annual return on any of their investments. As of 24 June 2019, Sangoma shares were trading for around C$1.66, and the company was continuing to pump out earnings for investors.

A number of factors made Sangoma a solid investment. Insider ownership, share repurchases, and a soft catalyst in terms of new product releases all helped. With these factors in place, and an initial robust NCAV, the stage was set for a good return.

But the most important lesson in this story has to do with timing. While, statistically, a 12-month holding period is associated with the highest portfolio returns, Sangoma's initial large surge in price was more a matter of luck. Despite its advantages as an investment, investors could not have been at all certain about the timing of the price surge.

For qualitative investors, patience is key. It takes time for distressed businesses to turn their operations around. If the prospects of recovery seem good, and the

---

284 SEDAR, 'Sangoma Technologies Corporation Management Discussion ... December 31, 2015'.

business has the potential to earn significant profits in the future, it may pay to hold a company for a much longer period of time.

Over time, improved business performance may cause investors to revalue a company, based on a multiple of earnings rather than net asset values. When this happens, the stock price can return multiples of an investor's initial purchase price. At a PE ratio of 36×, investors now clearly consider Sangoma a growth company better valued on a multiple of future earnings, not mere liquidation value.

23

Forgiveness – How Improving Fundamentals Caused Me to Bend One of My Core Principles

VALUE INVESTORS OFTEN focus on price to value over and above everything else. But while valuation is important, it's just one determining factor when it comes to net-net investing. A focus on deeper discounts over everything else can lead investors to dismiss more promising investments.

While much discussion revolves around stocks and ratios, value investors are, of course, buying partial ownership in businesses. It's business developments going forward that often move the stock. Simply focusing on the quantitative metrics rather than trying to assess the business's prospects or even management can cause net-net investors to miss out on more expensive net-nets that have real potential as businesses, and ultimately investments.

The Net Net Hunter Scorecard aims to provide deep value investors with a list of important factors to look at when assessing a company's qualitative situation, but a deep understanding of how to assess a company's qualitative prospects is built up over time through reading and managing businesses.

As a new net-net investor, I was overly focused on buying the cheapest net-net stocks I could find. Rather than simply looking for a one-third margin of safety, I demanded discounts of 50% or greater before fitting a stock into my portfolio. Over time, though, I realised just how powerful the qualitative aspects were when buying net-nets. These firms, after all, are already trading at hyper-conservative valuations. With prices so low relative to a conservative assessment of intrinsic value, a recovering business can experience a tremendous price increase over time if the business improves.

This lesson was really driven home with one of the most successful net-net stocks I've ever bought, Creightons, PLC. Unfortunately, while I'd like to write a chapter highlighting my ability to foretell the enormous stock advance Creightons experienced over the last six years, I was too set in my ways as an investor and so missed most of the opportunity.

New net-net stock investors should sit up and take notice. Those intent on running a mechanical net-net stock portfolio should earn great returns over time by sticking to their rules-based mechanical approach. But as Buffett pointed out in the 1960s, the best returns are earned when you have a high-quality insight, capitalise on it, and then have the courage to hold the stock as the investment scenario unfolds.

Creightons in brief

Creightons is a tiny toiletry manufacturer based in the UK. Founded in 1975, the company focused on contractual manufacturing and producing products such as shaving creams and hair-care lotions for private label brands. Products were typically made of all natural ingredients, tapping into the ever-growing health-conscious market.[285]

In 2003, the company began looking to expand by developing its own brands and seeking out acquisition opportunities. By 2007, the company had hit its stride. Creightons had launched a major new initiative, The Real Shaving Company, in part capitalising on the extortionate prices of men's shaving supplies. It had also purchased Potter & Moore out of bankruptcy and had nearly completed transitioning Creightons' production to the newer and more efficient Potter & Moore manufacturing facility.[286] This meant more output, at a lower cost.

Financial results had improved dramatically over the period. By calendar year 2007, the company was producing ever-larger profits. Rather than simply being figures at the bottom of the firm's income statement, each British pound of profit amounted to £1.35 in free cash flow.[287]

Creightons: three serious problems

The firm had achieved significant sales and profit increases by its March 2008 year end. Revenue was up 31%, while net profits were up a solid 19% over the previous year.[288] But while results were up, investor sentiment was down. Despite the jump

285 Creightons, 'Group Financial Statements for the year ended 31 March 2009', creightonsplc. com.
286 Ibid.
287 Creightons, 'Annual Report for the year ended 31 March 2007', creightonsplc.com.
288 Ibid.

in performance, investors weren't as optimistic about Creightons' prospects and so began to sell off the stock. The stock slid -43% that year and soon gave up all of its gains over the last few years. The issue wasn't the firm's performance, which had improved significantly. Investors had their eye on the global economy and were worried about what America's Great Financial Crisis might mean for Creightons' business.

As 2008 pressed on, the Great Financial Crisis sent the global economy into a tailspin. Job losses grew, and consumer confidence dropped significantly.[289] As the recession hit, consumers scaled back their spending, opting for value brands rather than smaller luxuries they may have indulged in just 12 months earlier. This hit Creightons' up-market offerings, reducing sales and causing a disproportionately larger drop in profitability.[290]

Unfortunately for Creightons, increasing consumer price consciousness was just one of several challenges management would have to face. Another was the rising cost of business. Brent oil had screamed ahead in price throughout 2007, from a low of $60 per barrel to nearly $150. With the increase in oil prices, the company's raw material cost – a good portion comprised of petroleum products – began to rise as well.[291]

A falling pound sterling added to the pressure on profits. Since Creightons sourced most of its raw material from overseas suppliers, those raw materials were proving more costly for the firm to acquire.[292] Creightons couldn't simply pass those costs on to consumers, either, since it lacked pricing power.[293] Management was therefore left scrambling to find ways to contain cost.

The Great Financial Crisis forced many of Creightons' customers to source inventory directly from overseas suppliers in Asia, undercutting Creightons' sales.[294] This showed up mostly in the firm's seasonal Christmas production contracts – a significant source of revenue the company counted on each year. Rather than turning to UK-based producers such as Creightons, firms bypassed domestic suppliers in an attempt to boost the margin on lower-priced products that consumers had developed a taste for.

All of this meant that investors were increasingly wary of Creightons' business prospects. The firm would have to change strategic direction if it were to survive,

---

289 Trading Economics, 'United Kingdom Consumer Confidence', tradingeconomics.com.
290 Creightons, 'Annual Report for the year ended 31 March 2008', creightonsplc.com.
291 Ibid.
292 Creightons, '2010 Annual Report', creightonsplc.com.
293 Creightons, 'Annual Report for the year ended 31 March 2008'.
294 Ibid.

let alone thrive. By November 2009, Creightons' shares were down 87% from their November 2006 price of 5p.

Significant value on offer in this microscopic net-net firm

That enormous price drop meant that Creightons' share price was trading for 0.63p, less than an American penny. With a share price like that, most investors would immediately dismiss the company, calling the shares a reckless speculation. But was it?

Compare the perception of investing in a stock trading at a penny per share with that of buying a small stake in a small, profitable, long-established business at a steep discount to its underlying value. Most investors would consider the first a risky speculation, and the second a much safer, or even prudent, investment. Penny stocks are often considered risky stakes in fly-by-night ventures with fraud-ridden management and shaky business models. Long-established and profitable small businesses are often thought to offer tangible value and a chance at a good profit. In Creightons' case, it was a long-established business selling for a sharp discount to fair value with shares that just happened to have a microscopic stock price. Founded in 1975, and replete with a strong balance sheet and profitable operations, it certainly didn't fit the mould of a risky fly-by-night speculation.

Combing through the firm's fiscal 2010 (Creightons' fiscal year end was on 31 March, so most of the company's operating performance occurred in the previous calendar year) financial statements highlighted the firm's solid footing. The company had a NCAV of £2.78 million, a book value of £3.65 million, a current ratio of 2.35×, and a tiny debt to equity ratio of just 5.9%.[295] With such a solid balance sheet, Creightons was clearly no bankruptcy candidate.

In fact, despite the economic storm ripping through the world economy, little Creightons was still producing profit. Over the previous 12 months, the firm produced £303,000 in net income – which was more than many large American businesses could say. Much of that, £151,000 to be exact, was in cash – nearly enough to retire all of its debt.[296]

On a per-share basis, Creightons earned 51p in net income. With a share price back up to 2p in April 2010, the firm was trading at a PE ratio of 4×. The question was whether investors could rely on these profits for valuation purposes or not, given the serious challenges the world economy was facing. Since Creightons was manufacturing small, everyday necessities, the firm's business was fairly stable. But given the firm's 2.2% net profit margin, a small drop in revenue could see earnings

295 Creightons, '2010 Annual Report'.
296 Ibid.

completely wiped out. In fact, Creightons' bottom line dropped by –20% year over year due to a –10% reduction in revenue.[297]

But investors wouldn't necessarily have had to rely on the 2010 earnings to value the stock. If Creightons could survive the downturn and the economy were to recover, the firm might be able to regain its former level of profitability. Investors who bought in at the current depressed price would reap a windfall profit when things turned around.

Creightons was also backed by significant NCAV. With 59.7 million shares outstanding, the firm's £2.78 million in NCAV came in at 4.64p for a P/NCAV ratio of just 43%. This 57% discount to Creightons' liquidation value meant that if the firm slipped into losses, and couldn't regain its former level of profit, shares would still be seriously undervalued relative to liquidation value. That liquidation value, if sustained, could provide investors the chance to profit in an otherwise lacklustre company. As luck would have it, the firm's NCAV was also increasing, despite the turmoil. NCAV was up slightly from £2.62 million to £2.64 million for the year.[298]

Creightons' Achilles' heel came in the form of its low trading volume. With an average daily volume of just a few pounds sterling, Creightons was impossible for even retail investors to buy. While the investment prospects seemed lucrative, there was little chance that any investor could take advantage of the situation.

Creightons rebounding from crisis

The management team was up to the task. Spotting the shift in consumer preference, they directed Creightons to develop lower-priced brands that it could offer retail customers in an attempt to capture the trend towards value.

Done well, Creightons had the potential to leverage shifting consumer preferences to retain, or even improve, sales. If Creightons became the UK market leader in a number of niches, it could reap significant profit. The challenge management had to overcome was crafting brands that would resonate with consumers. Luckily, like Sangoma Technologies, it was busy developing a number of new products and not betting on any single attempt.[299]

Lower-priced products could also hurt gross margins, however. Given the ever-increasing cost of raw materials, management needed to take big steps towards reducing costs. As the crisis hit, management found that they could re-engineer

---

297 Ibid.
298 Ibid.
299 Ibid.

products using lower-cost raw inputs.[300] This had the effect of boosting the profit on each item sold, which would help cover the firm's fixed costs and increase net profit.

In addition, management got to work diversifying the company's base of suppliers for a greater number of options when purchasing raw material.[301] A diverse supplier base meant that Creightons could vary its purchases based on pricing. Sometimes this meant purchasing from suppliers located in countries with weaker currencies, reducing the effect of the lower pound sterling. In the end, lower raw material costs meant higher profits on each item sold and higher overall profit for the company.

The year 2010 proved to be the low mark for the company's performance. By the end of the year, the world economy had begun to pull out of its funk as the Great Financial Crisis reached its conclusion. Investors slowly woke up to the fact that the world was not coming to an end and economic life would continue much as it always had. Consumer confidence began to rebound, which helped propel Creightons' sales.

By March 2011, Creightons' revenue was up 4% to £14.13 million, small, though an improvement from the firm's –10% reduction the prior year.[302] Some of this was due to the new brand initiatives management took throughout the downturn. For the year, the sale of new products more than made up for the decrease in contractual Christmas manufacturing.[303] Excluding the firm's Christmas contracts, revenue was up 13% year over year. Creightons seemed to have remade itself as a strong niche player in the retail toiletries market.

Net profit, on the other hand, was down to just £135,000.[304] The major issues were the continued increase in raw material costs, a change in the sales mix, and increased product development costs.[305]

Despite the downturn, Creightons' management had poured money into product development, comprised mostly of developing new brands and re-engineering products.[306]

The firm's brand portfolio was a key consideration for the firm. Rather than laying off staff, Creightons focused on utilising its manpower to develop new products and increase sales efforts to win new business.[307] Just like Ford a couple of years

300 Ibid.
301 Ibid.
302 Creightons, '2011 Annual Report'.
303 Creightons, '2010 Annual Report'.
304 Creightons, '2011 Annual Report'.
305 Ibid.
306 Creightons, '2010 Annual Report'.
307 Ibid.

earlier, relentless focus on developing products consumers wanted and containing costs would provide the firm with a leg-up when the economy rebounded.[308]

Twelve months later, management's relentless focus on building its brand offerings, and increased spending on sales channel development led to a 16% jump in the firm's revenue. Revenue was up 21% excluding the firm's eroding Christmas manufacturing business.[309] Management's efforts were clearly paying off.

More of management's focus was hitting the bottom line, as well. By the end of the following year, product re-engineering and greater revenue pushed over the firm's fixed costs translated into a 65% leap, from £135,000 the year prior to £223,000.[310] The company had clearly turned the tide, and had entered a period of growth.

But surprisingly, while the firm's operating results were up, the stock languished at depressed levels. By the summer of 2012, Creightons stock was sitting at just 2.13p, unchanged from the economic terror of 2009. The crisis was clearly over for the firm, and management had navigated the company through strong headwinds throughout the Great Financial Crisis without suffering a loss, yet investors seemed completely disinterested.

My brief stint with Creightons

I stumbled onto Creightons when it was listed on the Net Net Hunter Shortlist in mid-2013. The firm was one of the few companies that made the cut with the right mix of buy ability, stability, and profit potential. Since it was one of the smallest firms we listed, and was based outside North America, I was immediately curious.

Digging deeper into the company's financial statements revealed a strong and growing firm. The company had £892,000 in debt, against a book value of £4.34 million.

With a debt-to-equity ratio of 20.5%, debt was sufficiently low. The firm also had a current ratio of 2.03x and had earned an average of £315,000 in cash over the previous two years, so it was clearly not a bankruptcy candidate.[311]

A brief scan of the firm's last few yearly income statements showed a growing firm. Management seemed to be doing a good job of addressing the company's problems, and had managed to grow both revenue and net profit. While this could have been due to a rebound in the economy coming out of the Great Financial Crisis, the trend was enticing and there seemed no sign of it letting up.

---

308 Hoffman, *American Icon*, 383; Creightons, '2010 Annual Report'.
309 Creightons, '2011 Annual Report'.
310 Creightons, 'Summary Annual Report and Notice of Meeting 2012'.
311 Creightons, 'Annual Report for the year ended 31 March 2013', creightonsplc.com.

In terms of valuation, the company had 5.83p in NCAV per share against a 4p share price.[312] That made for a price to NCAV of 68.6%, not nearly cheap enough for me. Given that most of my stocks were purchased at a discount of 40% or greater, Creightons' discount of just 31.4% immediately got my back up. It was not even a classic Graham one-third margin of safety. Still curious, I pressed on with the analysis.

The company earned 0.51p on a per-share basis.[313] At its 4p price, the company was trading at 7.84× earnings. This was pretty small, based both on the US market's historic 15.5× PE ratio and relative to the current market level. Considering the fact that the firm was trading for less than NCAV, the company's low PE ratio seemed more enticing. If earnings fell apart, the shares would still be more than backed by the firm's liquidation value.

Returning to the company's record, it had managed to grow revenue at a decent clip, and given the firm's thin net profit margin, net income had surged back post-crisis. While revenue was up 22.6% from March 2011 to £17.33 million, net profits were up 123.7% over the same period. The best news was that management recorded these performance gains during a very difficult time for the industry, and a significant portion of the improved results were from the firm's new products.[314] According to the firm's annual report, management expected to stick to their winning strategy going forward. With these insights, the investment seemed a little easier to swallow.

Digging deeper, I noticed that management owned a lot of the company's equity. CEO and Chairman William McIlroy had the largest ownership stake at 25%, while Managing Director Bernard Johnson owned another 6%.[315] With a market capitalisation of £2.38 million, their stakes amounted to £596,000 and £143,000 each. This was certainly enough to provide them with a solid incentive to manage the company with an eye for shareholder value.

All of this made me rethink my initial reservations. Creightons was clearly worth a small position, at least. If the company continued its performance improvements and grew, the shares could see a nice bump-up in price.

The stock had already seen a bit of a jump, from just over 2p to just over 4p in price. While I missed the bottom, looking back at the company's trading history, it became clear that I would have had a tough time building a position anyway. Now with about £600 of stock traded daily, it would be tough to build a position, but it could be done by placing tiny daily limit orders over a number of months.

312 Ibid.
313 Ibid.
314 Ibid.
315 Ibid.

I decided to start a position, and I eventually built up a small holding by March 2014 at 4.09p.

That month, the company reported 12% revenue growth which yielded a 56% jump in profits.[316] More revenue from new-brand offerings over the prior 12 months had helped cover costs and lead to a disproportionately larger increase in profits. Despite the significant gains, the stock only advanced 25%, reflecting lingering investor disinterest. By the end of the year, the stock had advanced to 6p, amounting to a 50% profit on my 4.09p average cost.

In March 2015, Creightons released its year-end results, revealing a 9% improvement in sales and an 80.7% surge in net profit, half coming from the sale of one of the company's legacy hair brands, Twisted Sista. Management had begun the process of trimming underperforming brands and launching new initiatives they hoped would fare better. The sale of Twisted Sista was a step towards strengthening their brand portfolio, and brought in a significant profit on their initial investment. Excluding the sale, profits were up slightly for the year to £476,000.[317]

Along with the sale of Twisted Sista, management announced that they were selling The Real Shaving Company, another legacy brand, for £1 million. A full £844,000 of that sale price was profit on the company's initial investment – a 540% return, excluding the profits the brand had brought in for Creightons.[318]

These two sales finally prompted investors to sit up and take notice. By the summer of 2015, Creightons' NCAV per share had improved 68% from my initial purchase to 6.9p per share. Profits were up 39%, from 0.5p to 0.71p before exceptional items.[319] The stock price quickly shot up to 8.75p on the earnings announcement. At that price, Creightons was trading at a PE of 12.3x. While still a bargain based on a multiple of earnings, it was not as cheap as it was when I picked it up. Conscious of the fact that the price was well over NCAV per share, I quietly exited my position. In a little over a year, I had nailed a solid 114% return.

Creightons' long run

I mentioned a number of times in this book that net-net investors can achieve a great long-term record by sticking to a mechanical strategy. By employing simple buy and sell rules, and maintaining a diversified portfolio over the course of a decade, investors are likely to achieve superinvestor-like returns. That's the

---

316 Creightons, 'Annual Report 2014', creightonsplc.com.
317 Ibid.
318 Ibid.
319 Ibid.

inevitable result of doggedly sticking to a high-performance strategy such as net-net stocks.

But I also discussed a second approach to net-net investing, one that may produce even better returns. I've dubbed this the qualitative approach to net-net selection, since it focuses to a much greater degree on assessing a company's (or investment's) qualitative characteristics. Typically, this amounts to assessing management's plan and behaviour to determine whether the company is likely to significantly improve business results. At other times, this can mean identifying firms with significant earning power that have stumbled hard as businesses but are getting back on track and are expected to regain much of their former profitability.

When investors find a net-net firm like this, patience is a must. It takes time for businesses to turn around and start producing great results. If investors sell with an eye for a quick gain, they may leave a lot of money on the table and increase their tax bill.

Initially, my sale of Creightons stock seemed like a smart move. I had nailed down a great return in a short amount of time. Having cash in hand, I could then spot a different highly promising net-net to buy and achieve another 100%+ return in a little over a year. By identifying stocks that are likely to rise by an enormous amount ahead of time, I would far outpace net-nets and even Buffett's superinvestors.

The catch, of course, is that identifying promising opportunities with a disproportionate chance of achieving an outstanding profit is not easy. Extraordinary opportunities arise every once in a while, and never on demand. In fact, most of the net-net opportunities on offer simply look cheap relative to NCAV, and present little reason to assume that recovery is inevitable, or even likely. They're statistical bargains, cheap stocks, as identified by their balance sheet figures. And while a few of these stocks usually show extraordinary returns post-purchase, it's usually impossible to identify them ahead of time. Generally, the best that investors can do is simply buy a group of net-nets that possess characteristics associated with higher-than-average returns, and sit on the portfolio for a year or two to see how the crop performs.

But every so often an investor will recognise that a particular stock is likely to lead to significant profits. When the opportunity presents itself, it really pays to load up on shares and hold them until events run their course. Time would slowly reveal this lesson to me as I watched Creightons' share price inch ever higher on its stock chart.

Creightons stock initially sunk below my purchase price, providing a brief feeling of validation. I had managed to exit my position during a brief price spike. At 6.5p per share, the stock was not yet cheap enough to re-buy. But I had certainly picked the top for the stock and was relieved that I had unloaded my holdings for a seemingly excellent price.

That feeling of achievement was short lived, however. Just over nine months later, Creightons announced its 2016 year-end results. The firm had completed the sale of The Real Shaving Company earlier in the year, resulting in a £1.329 million net profit for the year. Excluding the company's extraordinary gain of £768,000 for the asset sale, the company managed to pull in £561,000 in net profit, a 17.9% increase.[320]

Management maintained the same amount of revenue achieved in the prior year, despite selling those two revenue streams, indicating very strong performance from the firm's other brands. To top it off, management also managed to acquire the manufacturing assets and brands of a competitor in bankruptcy. This purchase would provide Creightons with an improved product profile, manufacturing capability, and ongoing customer relationships in the up-market segment of the industry.[321]

Over the next six months, I watched with increasing frustration as the stock inched ever higher. By the end of the year, shares were up to 17.25p, more than double the price that I'd sold mine for a year earlier.

Three months later, the firm announced its fiscal 2017 results. Sales were up a staggering 45.7%, due to expansion into international markets, sales growth in the company's legacy brands, and growth in the firm's contract manufacturing segment. The recently purchased manufacturing capacity and contracts boosted the firm's contract segment by an explosive 210%. Net profits were up 62.9%, on the increased revenue and continued focus on containing costs.[322]

The stock price leapt 95.6% post-announcement, from 19.75p to a high of 38.63p per share. By the end of the year, the stock would hit 44.5p, which was 11 times my initial purchase price and five times the price at which I had exited my position. At that price, the company was trading at 23.7× its previous year's earnings. Assuming investors had purchased shares at 4p and sold somewhere between 38p and 44p per share, they would have reaped an 850 to 1000% return in just three and a half years. The return would have amounted to between 90 and 98% compound annual growth rate.

320 Creightons, 'Annual Report 2016', creightonsplc.com.
321 Ibid.
322 Creightons, 'Annual Report 2017', creightonsplc.com.

Creightons' key lessons for small investors

As Buffett said in his partnership letters in the 1960s, the big money is made when an investor gets a high-quality insight and acts on it. While concentrating capital in a stock that's highly likely to achieve great returns has obvious value, Creightons highlights another important factor: patience.

It takes time for an investment situation to work out. Companies don't turn around in a day, and annual financial reports come out on an annual basis only. If you expect a company's earnings to improve significantly, and you're well justified in your reasoning, it will often pay to hold the stock long enough for the company to realise those profits. Doing so allows you to take advantage of a phenomenon known as the Davis Double Play.

The Davis Double Play is named after an exceptional value investor, Shelby Davis. It occurs when a company with a low PE ratio steadily increases its earnings year after year, resulting in a revaluation on an earnings basis. Over time, investors take notice of the continuing growth, so the stock price increases both due to the increase in earnings and the increase in expectations going forward. The first factor – the increase in earnings – helps the stock price keep up with the company's earnings growth. The second factor – the continued earnings growth – causes investors to revalue the company upwards on a PE basis.

Combining moderate growth with deep value investing can yield terrific returns. In table 19, Deep Value Stock A achieves a 5× return due to the combination of earnings growth and PE expansion.

Table 19: Example returns to a deep value stock based on moderate profit growth and an expanding PE ratio

Deep Value A	2014	2015	2016	2017	2018
EPS	$1	$1.10	$1.21	$1.33	$1.46
PE	5×	5×	8×	12×	18×
Share Price	$5	$5.50	$9.68	$15.96	$26.28

Source: Broken Leg Investing.

As earnings continue to rise, the company's stock price advances disproportionately to the company's earnings growth. In time, a cheap company relative to earnings will see its shares revalued back to a market PE, or higher. The share price increase can be exceptionally large.

The risk is always that earnings will peter out, or evaporate altogether. In that case, buying a firm at a cheap PE valuation could lead to significant losses. But in the case of net-nets, since net-net investors buy a company below a conservative assessment of the firm's liquidation value, it's much less likely that they will permanently lose part of their principal investment.

Creightons is an excellent example of how these investment scenarios can play out. Unfortunately, I did not fully realise the significant opportunity I was stepping into. Hopefully, my experience investing in Creightons will help you avoid the same mistake, yielding a much larger profit over time.

Epilogue: Build Your Character

IT NEVER CEASES to surprise me how overlooked Graham's net-net stock strategy is in this day and age. Despite Graham peppering admiration for the strategy throughout his writings, the profound success some professional investors have had with the strategy, the academic and industry studies that show incredible performance, and the handful of practitioners alive today making good use of the strategy, retail investors seem content to make investing more complicated than it has to be... and earn lower returns as a result.

Part of the problem seems to be temperament rather than any technical issue with the strategy. Some small investors reject the strategy without even reviewing the available evidence for it, preferring to stick to their prejudicial beliefs about how investing is supposed to work. For them, the simple practice of buying tiny distressed firms below a conservative assessment of their liquidation values seems too simple a strategy to produce the stated returns. Others lack the long-term perspective and gag reflex needed to keep buying these terrible tiny companies over the long term, so fail to stick with the strategy long enough to achieve great performance. Often a two- or three-year stretch of poor performance is enough to 'buck them off their horse'. This temperamental weakness provides a strong competitive advantage for those who seek truth through research and critical thinking, then find the stomach, patience, and long-term horizon to employ the strategy successfully.

Having reached the end of this book, you now have a solid understanding of Graham's strategy that is little-used these days. You're also well aware of how it works in real life and of best practices when employing it. Your job now, if you plan to use the strategy, is to refine your own personal approach to net-net investing, learn the ins and outs of business and financial accounting, and to develop your own psychological temperament.

It's hard to overstate just how valuable this personal progress will prove over the course of your life. The difference between sticking to Graham's net-nets over the long term or bouncing between lower performance value strategies can amount to over a million dollars in lost savings for the average investor – more if your investment horizon is longer. Likewise, after having adopted Graham's net-net strategy, improving your understanding of business and investing may yield just a few percentage points advantage per year, but will likely have a powerful impact on your eventual net worth.

Investing is a journey that is tightly wrapped up with personal development. It requires patience, worldly wisdom, and a strong emotional temperament to do well. These are factors all of us could use work on. This book has provided you with one high quality map, originally developed by the Dean of Wall Street, for achieving outstanding long-term returns. Finding the destination is now up to you.

Bibliography

Albemarle and Bond. 'Pawnbroking gains recognition on the UK high street', company announcement, Investegate (8 October 2010).

Arnold, Glen. 'Warren Buffett: Learning through the School of Hard Knocks', *Financial History* (Spring 2018), www.MoAF.org.

Berkshire Hathaway. Annual Meetings, 'Afternoon Session – 1995 Meeting', video, Warren Buffett Archive, CNBC, buffett.cnbc.com/video/1995/05/01/afternoon-session---1995-berkshire-hathaway-annual-meeting.html.

Berkshire Hathaway. Annual Meetings, 'Afternoon Session – 1998 Meeting', video, Warren Buffett Archive, CNBC, buffett.cnbc.com/video/1998/05/04/afternoon-session---1998-berkshire-hathaway-annual-meeting.html.

Berkshire Hathaway. Annual Meetings, 'Afternoon Session – 2001 Meeting, video, Warren Buffett Archive, CNBC, buffett.cnbc.com/video/2001/04/28/afternoon-session---2001-berkshire-hathaway-annual-meeting.html?&start=8719&end=9074.

Berkshire Hathaway. 2014 Annual Report, www.berkshirehathaway.com/2014ar/2014ar.pdf.

BFN News. 'Albemarle hikes dividend as pre-tax profits rise', Investegate (21 February 2012).

BFN News. 'Albemarle & Bond sees slowdown in gold buying', Investegate (15 June 2012).

BFN News. 'Albemarle pre-tax profits fall 33%', Investegate (12 February 2013).

Bleker, Evan. 'Benjamin Graham, Is Japan Where Money Goes to Die?', Net Net Hunter (13 February 2014).

Buffett, Warren. 'The Security I Like Best', *The Commercial and Financial Chronicle* (6 December 1951).

Buffett, Warren. '1957 Letter: Second Annual Letter to Limited Partners' (published January 1958), Buffett Partnership.

Buffett, Warren. '1958 Letter' (published February 1959), Buffett Partnership.

Buffett, Warren. '1961 Letter' (published January 1962), Buffett Partnership.

Buffett, Warren. '1962 Letter' (published January 1963), Buffett Partnership.

Buffett, Warren. '1963 Letter' (published January 1964), Buffett Partnership.

Buffett, Warren. '1965 Letter' (published January 1966), Buffett Partnership.

Buffett, Warren. 'The Superinvestors of Graham-and-Doddsville', *Hermes* (Fall 1984) (article based on speech given at Columbia Business School, 17 May 1984).

Buffett, Warren. 'Berkshire Hathaway 1989 Annual Shareholder Letter', www.berkshirehathaway.com/letters/1989.html.

Buffett, Warren. 'Berkshire Hathaway 2014 Annual Shareholder Letter', accessed 7 January 2020, www.berkshirehathaway.com/letters/2014ltr.pdf.

Buildersee, John, John Cheh, Ajay Zutshi. 'The Performance of Japanese Common Stocks in Relation to Their NCAVs', *Japan and the World Economy* 5 (1993): 197–215.

Carlen, Joe. *The Einstein of Money: The Life and Timeless Financial Wisdom of Benjamin Graham* (Prometheus, 2012).

Carlisle, Tobias. *Deep Value: Why Activist Investors And Other Contrarians Battle For Control of Losing Corporations,* 1st ed. (Wiley, 2014).

Censer, Marjorie. 'In rebuilding effort, GTSI buys services business', *The Washington Post* (21 August 2011). www.washingtonpost.com/business/capitalbusiness/in-rebuilding-effort-gtsi-buys-services-business/2011/08/16/gIQAiQtfUJ_story.html.

Cooper, Rachel. 'Albemarle and Bond loses lustre as FTSE 100 fades', *The Telegraph* (22 April 2013).

Creightons. 'Annual Report and Financial Statements for the year ended 31 March 2007', creightonsplc.com/assets/reports/Creightons_2007_AR.pdf.

Creightons. 'Annual Report and Financial Statements for the year ended 31 March 2008', creightonsplc.com.

Creightons. 'Group Financial Statements for the year ended 31 March 2009', creightonsplc.com.

Creightons. 'Creightons 2010 Annual Report', creightonsplc.com.

Creightons. 'Creightons 2011 Annual Report', creightonsplc.com.

Creightons. 'Summary Annual Report and Notice of Meeting 2012', creightonsplc.com.

Creightons. 'Annual Report for the Year Ended 31 March 2013', creightonsplc.com.

Creightons. 'Annual Report 2014', creightonsplc.com.

Creightons. Annual Report 2016', creightonsplc.com.

Creightons. 'Annual Report 2017', creightonsplc.com.

Cundill, Peter. *The Financial Times Global Guide to Investing: The Secrets of the World's Leading Investment Gurus,* ed. James Morton (Financial Times/Prentice Hall, 1995).

Cundill, Peter. Presentation at The Ben Graham Centre for Value Investing, Richard Ivey School of Business (28 March 2005), video,www.youtube.com/watch?v=UWMrBJxy3us.

Damodaran, Aswath. 'Dealing with Operating Leases in Valuation', New York University Working Paper No. FIN-99-023 (1999).

Damodaran, Aswath. 'Session 19: Asset Based Valuation' New York University, Leonard N. Stern School of Business (25 August 2014), youtu.be/HmDQISjLxig.

Dreman, David. *Contrarian Investment Strategies: The Next Generation* (Simon & Schuster, 1998).

Dudzinski, Jonathan and Robert A. Kunkel. 'Benjamin Graham's NCAV (Net Current Asset Value) Technique in the 21st Century', *Journal of Investing* 23:1 (Spring 2014):17–26.

Echols, Tucker. 'GTSI to be acquired by Unicom Systems for $76M', *The Washington Business Journal* (7 May 2012).

Gammell, Kara. 'Pawning my Aston Martin was the best option', *The Telegraph* (30 May 2012).

Goebel, Joseph M. and Manoj Athavale. 'The Persistence of the NCAV Stock Selection Criterion', *Global Business and Finance Review* 18:1 (Spring 2013): 77–92.

Graham, Benjamin. 'Inflated Treasuries and Deflated Stockholders', *Forbes* (1 June 1932).

Graham, Benjamin and David Dodd, *Security Analysis: Principles and Technique,* 2nd ed. (Whittlesey House, 1940).

Graham, Benjamin. 'The Decade 1965–1974: Its Significance for Financial Analysts', *Elliot Control* (1975), Heilbrunn Center for Graham & Dodd Investing, Columbia University.

Graham, Benjamin. 'Three Simple Methods of Common Stock Selection', Proceedings of the Financial Analysts Research Foundation seminar, Charlottesville, Virginia (1975).

Graham, Benjamin. 'A Conversation with Benjamin Graham', *Financial Analyst Journal* 32: 5 (September–October 1976): 20–23.

Graham, Benjamin. *The Interpretation of Financial Statements* (HarperBusiness, 1998).

Graham, Benjamin. *The Intelligent Investor: The Definitive Book on Value Investing,* rev. ed. (HarperBusiness, 2003).

Greenblatt, Joel M., Richard Pzena, and Bruce L. Newberg. 'How the Small Investor Can Beat the Market by Buying Stocks That Are Selling below Their Liquidation Value', *The Journal of Portfolio Management* 7:4 (Summer 1981): 48–52, doi.org/10.3905/jpm.1981.408811.

Greenwald, Bruce. *Value Investing: From Graham to Buffett and Beyond.* (Wiley, 2004).

GTSI. United States Securities and Exchange Commission (SEC), Form 10-K (31 December 2006).

GTSI. United States Securities and Exchange Commission (SEC), Form 10-K (31 December 2011).

Hanlon, Sean. 'Why The Average Investor's Investment Return Is So Low', *Forbes* (24 April 2014).

Harner, Stephen. 'Whither Japan Stocks: Price-to-Book Ratios Hit 1:1', *Forbes* (20 June 2011).

Hoffman, Bryce G. *American Icon: Alan Mulally and the Fight to Save Ford Motor Company* (New York: Currency, 2013), 383.

Investment Company Institute. '2019 Investment Company Fact Book: US Fund Expenses and Fees'.

Kahn, Irving, and Robert D. Milne. 'Benjamin Graham The Father Of Financial Analysis', Occasional Paper Number 5, The Financial Analysts Research Foundation (1977).

Kaminska, Izabella. 'Pawned Out', *Financial Times* (2 October 2013).

Klarman, Seth. *Margin of Safety: Risk-Averse Value Investing Strategies for the Thoughtful Investor.* (HarperCollins, 1991).

Lawrence, Dune. 'Worthless Stocks from China', *Bloomberg Businessweek* (13 January 2011).

Loomis, Carol J. 'Beating the market by buying back stock', *Fortune* (21 November 2012).

Lowe, Janet. *Damn Right! Behind the Scenes with Berkshire Hathaway Billionaire Charlie Munger.* (Wiley, 2000).

Markowicz, Sean. 'Where Is the Value in Value Investing?', Schroders (December 2018).

Mauboussin, Michael. 'Mauboussin on Strategy: Death, Taxes and Reversion to Mean', Legg Mason Capital Management (14 December 2007).

Miller, Jeremy C. *Warren Buffett's Ground Rules: Words of Wisdom from the Partnership Letters of the World's Greatest Investor* (HarperCollins, 2016).

Montier, James. 'Graham's Net-Nets: Outdated or Outstanding?', The Société Générale Group (30 September 2008).

Montier, James. *The Little Book of Behavioral Investing: How Not to Be Your Own Worst Enemy* (Wiley, 2010).

Moody's Transportation Manual, Moody's Investors Services (1954).

Morton, James. *The Financial Times Global Guide to Investing : The Secrets of the World's Leading Investment Gurus* (Financial Times/Prentice Hall, 1995).

Munger, Charlie. 'All Intelligent Investing Is Value Investing' (2017), youtu.be/Lsaj6fmAtNk.

Neate, Rupert. 'Possible Albemarle & Bond buyer walks away', *The Guardian* (24 December 2013).

O'Harrow Jr., Robert. 'SBA suspends major contractor GTSI from government work', *The Washington Post* (1 October 2010).

Oppenheimer, Henry. 'Ben Graham's NCAVs: A Performance Update', *Financial Analysts Journal* 42:6 (November–December 1986): 40–47.

Oxman, Jeffrey, Sunil K. Mohanty, Tobias Eric Carlisle. 'Deep Value Investing and Unexplained Returns', (16 September 2011), paper presented at the 2012 Annual Meeting, Midwest Finance Association.

Rankin, Jennifer. 'Pawnbroker Albemarle & Bond put up for sale amid mass walkout', *Guardian* (2 December 2013).

Risso-Gill, Christopher. *There's Always Something to Do: The Peter Cundill Investment Approach* (McGill-Queen's University Press, 2011).

Robinson, Duncan. 'Albemarle & Bond's fundraising efforts to stave off debt falter', *Financial Times* (2 October 2013).

Robinson, Duncan. 'New chief starts early at Albemarle & Bond', *Financial Times* (7 October 2013).

Robinson, Duncan. 'Upmarket pawnbrokers boom as asset-rich struggle to raise cash', *Financial Times* (18 October 2013).

Ross School of Business. 'A Conversation with Charlie Munger and Michigan Ross', video, University of Michigan (20 December 2017), youtu.be/S9HgIGzOENA.

Sangoma Technologies. 'Sangoma Technologies 2011 Q1 MDA', (15 November 2010).

Schroeder, Alice. *The Snowball: Warren Buffett and the Business of Life* (Bantam Books, 2008).

SEDAR. 'Management Discussion And Analysis Of Financial Condition And Results Of Operations Fiscal Year Ended June 30, 2011', (Sangoma MD&A, 27 October 2011).

SEDAR. 'Sangoma Technologies 2012 MD&A', (10 October 2012).

SEDAR. 'Shareholder Rights Plan Agreement Dated As Of October 10, 2012 Between Sangoma Technologies Corporation And Equity Financial Trust Company As Rights Agent'.

SEDAR. 'Sangoma Technologies Corporation Management Discussion And Analysis Of Financial Condition And Results Of Operations Fiscal Year Ended June 30, 2012' (10 October 2012).

SEDAR. 'Sangoma Technologies Corporation Management Information Circular and Notice of Annual and Special Meeting of Shareholders' (8 November 2012).

SEDAR. 'Condensed Consolidated Interim Financial Statements of Sangoma Technologies Corporation For the three month and nine month periods ended March 31, 2013 and 2012'.

SEDAR. 'Sangoma Technologies Corporation Management Discussion And Analysis Of Financial Condition And Results Of Operations Fiscal Year Ended June 30, 2013' (25 October 2013).

SEDAR. 'Sangoma Technologies Corporation Management Discussion And Analysis Of Financial Condition And Results Of Operations Second Quarter Fiscal 2016 Ended December 31, 2015' (24 February 2016).

Singh, Jaspal and Kiranpreet Kaur. 'Testing the Performance of Graham's NCAV Strategy in Indian Stock Market', *Asia-Pacific Journal of Management, Research and Innovation* 9:2 (2013): 171–179.

Thomson Reuters, '$2.6 billion award in Sino-Forest fraud case expected to open the litigation floodgates', *Financial Post* (15 March 2018).

Trading Economics. 'United Kingdom Consumer Confidence'.

Tweedy, Browne. 'What Has Worked In Investing: Studies of Investment Approaches and Characteristics Associated with Exceptional Returns', rev. ed. (Tweedy Browne, 2009).

Vanstraceele, Philip and Luc Allaeys. 'Studying Different Systematic Value Investing Strategies on the Eurozone Stock Market' (May 2010) Value-Investing.eu.

'Unacceptable business practice', *The Washington Post*.

Vu, Joseph. 'An Empirical Analysis of Ben Graham's NCAV Rule', *The Financial Review* 23:2 (May 1998): 215–225.

Xiao, Ying and Glen Arnold. 'Testing Ben Graham's NCAV Strategy in London', *The Journal of Investing* (Winter 2008): 11–19.

Young-sil, Yoon. 'Chinese Firms Listed on KRX Receive Disclaimer of Opinion from Korean Auditors Again', *BusinessKorea* (22 April 2019).

Zakaria, Nadisah and Fariza Hashim. 'Emerging Markets: Evaluating Graham's Stock Selection Criteria on Portfolio Return in Saudi Arabia Stock Market', *International Journal of Economics and Financial Issues* 7:2 (2017): 453–459.

Wikipedia. 'Sino-Forest Corporation'.

YouTube video. "Greenblatt Columbia Lecture 2005 11 04 including Brian Gaines from Springhouse Capital." YouTube video, 2:33:42. Posted by Net Net Hunter, 9 March 2020. youtu.be/xQYnK9b4gXw.

Acknowledgements

The plan for this book was a simple upgrade to a manuscript I had written a few years back, but developed into a monster-sized project due to my pathological love affair with perfection. So many have helped with the rough draft over the past two years that I'm bound to leave someone out by mistake. If that's you, my sincerest apologies. It's been a long journey.

I would like to thank the good people over at Harriman House in the UK, especially my editorial team, for their hard work and patience. The book was roughly a year late, but better late than never, I suppose?

I would also like to thank Hya at Net Net Hunter for her help preparing the book for publication. Many thanks to Mike who prepared the citations, and our members who encouraged and supported me to put my knowledge and experience down on paper. A special thanks to Luis, a great up and coming investor, for reading over the first couple chapters and encouraging me to continue.

Like all value practitioners, I owe a debt to Benjamin Graham, who wrote so prolifically and helped so many people to develop as intelligent investors. Few of us would have succeeded without him.

Lastly, thank you Sulhee for your never-ending encouragement, a resource I've needed to draw on more than I care to admit. And to James, thanks for lighting the fire.

Index

Note: Page numbers in **bold** refer to tables

Lightning Source UK Ltd.
Milton Keynes UK
UKHW020657221221
396067UK00004B/187

9 780857 197078